A Devout Exposition of the Holy Mass

A DEVOUT EXPOSITION OF THE HOLY MASS.

A DEVOUT EXPOSITION

OF THE

HOLY MASS,

WITH AN AMPLE DECLARATION OF ALL THE RITES AND CEREMONIES BELONGING TO THE SAME.

COMPOSED BY JOHN HEIGHAM,

THE MORE TO MOVE ALL GODLY PEOPLE TO THE GREATER VENERATION OF SO SUBLIME A SACRAMENT.

The Second Edition, reviewed and augmented by the Author.
1622.

EDITED BY AUSTIN JOSEPH ROWLEY,
Priest.

London:
R. WASHBOURNE, 18 PATERNOSTER ROW.
1876.

APPROBATIONES.

PERLECTO hoc libro cujus titulus est, " A Devout Exposition of the Holy Mass," a Domino Joanne Heigham composito, nihil in eo reperio, quod fidei aut bonis moribus contradicat, quin potius multa notavi quæ ad consolationem et devotionem Catholicorum excitandam conducere possunt.

JOANNES NORTONIUS,
S. Theol. Doctor.

CONTINET hic liber devotam explicationem cæremoniarum et mysteriorum sacrosanctæ Missæ, ad fidelis populi eruditionem, ut Sacrificio piè assistere discant : nec sese intromisit auctor in materias sublimes aut questiones controversas, sed omnino devotionem et affectûs inflammationem spectavit : quod ita fecit, ut nihil dissonum rectæ fidei aut sanis moribus, sed omnia solida et pia et proficua piis mentibus collegerit.   Ita lecto libello testor.

F. LEANDER DE S. MARTINO,
Benedictinus, Sacræ Theologiæ Doctor.

HORUM testimonio subscripsi et eundem librum utiliter excudi posse censui.

GEORGIUS COLUENERIUS,
S. Theol. Doctor, et Professor, et in
Academia Duacena, Librorum Censor.

Duaci, 15 Julii, 1612.

CONTENTS.

CONTENTS.

THE PREFACE TO THE CATHOLIC
READER.

FOUR causes there were, right courteous reader, which first moved me to explicate unto thee, according unto my small capacity, the mysteries and ceremonies of the Holy Mass.

1. The first was, the incomparable dignity and most excellent sublimity of this divine and dreadful Sacrifice; which although it be such that neither the tongue of man nor angel can worthily magnify, as it deserveth, yet the very excellency of the thing itself inviteth every one, with what praises he can, to set forth, extol, and celebrate the same.

2. The second was, the most singular honour, respect, and reverence, which the devout and Catholic people of all places, of all ages, and of all callings, the greatest Doctors themselves, and the most learned divines of all the world, Emperors, Kings, Princes, and Commons, have ever borne and carried to this Sacrifice: whose example it behoveth every good and godly man to follow.

3. The third was, the deep, mortal, and cankered malice of wicked heretics, their most execrable blas-

phemies, together with many most fearful, wild, and damnable facts, done and committed by them, in hatred and contempt of this divine Sacrifice: and what good Christian is there that will not, to the uttermost of his power, defend a treasure so inestimable from the savage assaults of such wicked miscreants?

4. The fourth was, the great and long want of a full and perfect exposition of this so divine a mystery in our English tongue, by reason that none of our nation have purposely written of the same (for aught that ever I saw) these forty years; which four motives seemed unto me matter more than sufficient, to explicate unto thee this unexplicated secret, and to unfold unto thee a mystery of such majesty.

5. Of the supereminent dignity, as also of the great and singular respect, which Catholics do bear to this ineffable mystery, I have amply treated and discoursed unto thee, in the third, fourth, fifth, and sixth chapters of this ensuing treatise. I beseech the infinite mercy and goodness of God, that thou mayst receive abundant consolation and edification for thy pains in perusing of them. But touching the deadly hatred and malice of our adversaries, or of their blasphemies and other abuses of this Blessed Sacrifice, I have nowhere made any mention of them; and would to God there were no cause at all, ever to defile the paper of my Preface with their execrable, enormous, and filthy facts.

6. Now against this most singular Sacrament, pearl of inestimable price, adamant of angels, rose of our religion, only life, only laurel, only triumph, only treasure, only glory, only beauty, and only crown of all Christianity, the heretics of our age, do bear so rabid a rage, so mischievous a mind, and so spiteful a spleen, joined with such audacious attempts, barbarous abuses, and insolent outrages, as never the like were heard of before our days; yea, and in a manner is incredible, could ever enter into the heart of a Christian.

7. For some rushing violently into the Church where the Priest was celebrating this unbloody Sacrifice, stamping under their filthy feet the Sacred Host, and spilling upon the ground the blessed Blood, used the consecrated Chalice as a common utensil, and having compelled the priest to drink it off, next presently hung him up on high, fastened and bound with cords, unto an image of Christ crucified, and then with many shots of guns and pistols pierced quite through both the Priest and the picture as witnesseth Laynay in his "Replique Chret."*

8. Another seeing the Priest at Mass to hold up the Sacred Host, that it might be adored of the people, took up a dog by the legs, and held him over his head, shewing him unto the people in mockage and contempt of the Priest and of his Sacrifice.†

* Lib. 2 cap. 16.   † Fox. Act and Mon. p. 1033.

9. Another, as witnesseth the same Foxe, finding a Priest administering the Blessed Sacrament to the people with great devotion, offended to see them so devoutly and reverently upon their knees, presently pulled out a whyniard or wood-knife which he wore about him, and very grievously wounded the Priest in divers places, both of head, arm, and hand, wherewith he held the holy Chalice, full of consecrated Hosts, which were sprinkled with the blood of the Priest; nor would have left him till he had killed him outright, if he had not been prevented by the people present.

10. But lest thou, gentle reader, mayest think that God, Who is the just avenger of all such villanies, hath permitted these men to escape unpunished, let this example next ensuing satisfy thee, and serve for a warning to all the adversaries and malicious enemies of the Mass. After that the Holy Mass was, by public proclamation of the late Queen,* commanded to surcease in all places of England, by Midsummer day immediately following, four men of Dover, in the county of Kent, besides others which assisted at the same action, went into the Church of the same town and took forth the copes, vestments, and other priestly ornaments belonging thereto, giving forth and boasting abroad that they would go fetch the Pope from Canterbury, and the very next day after Midsummer day, these companions

* Elizabeth.

came to Canterbury, put on the said copes, and other ornaments upon their backs, and in a Pix, made to reserve the Blessed Sacrament of the Body of our Saviour Jesus, they put a dog's turd; and then beginning at St. George's gate rode in form of procession quite through the city, till they came to Westgate; which done, the very same night they posted back again to Dover.

11. One of these four was Captain Roberts, who presently after carried all the copes, vestments, and other ornaments over the seas to Dunkirk, where he sold them. His miserable and wretched end was, that there leaping out of one small boat into another, to go to his ship, the boat he was in, slipping away, he stepped short of the other, and so falling into the water, pitched his unhappy head upon an anchor, where he beat out his brains.

12. The second, shortly after running mad, cast himself off from Dover pier into the sea, and so was drowned.

13. The third died of John Calvin's disease, that is to say, he was eaten up with lice, being yet alive.

14. The fourth, who afterwards became minister of Maidstone, falling grievously sick, endured God's terrible judgments, for he stunk so abominably, that none, no, not his own wife, could endure to come near him, so that when they gave him meat to eat, they were forced to put it upon the end of a long pole, and so to reach it unto him through a window.

For confirmation whereof there are right credible
and worshipful persons yet alive, who can testify the
same for a certain truth.

15. These are some few, though not the thou-
sandth part, of the malicious dealings of heretics
against the Mass, and of the most remarkable
judgments of Almighty God against them, for their
horrible abuses of the same. O immortal God!
what is there in this divine and dreadful mystery,
which may move any reasonable man to such height
of malice, fury, mischief, and manifest madness?
Do the sacred psalms of Thy servant David, for from
them the Mass doth take its beginning, the humble
acknowledgment of our human frailty, the asking
of mercy for our daily offences, the song of Angels
pronounced at Thy Nativity, petitions unto Thee for
obtaining of graces, the lecture of Thy Prophets, the
Gospels of Thy Evangelists, the Creed of the Apostles,
the Sanctus of Thy Seraphim, supplications for all
sorts of persons, the Commemoration of Thy Passion,
the prayer of all prayers, both made by Thyself, and
taught by Thyself to Thy disciples? And, which is
more to be lamented than all the rest, doth Thy
precious Body and Blood really present in this holy
Sacrifice deserve to be dealt with all in so savage a
sort? Surely no, for such demeanours as these are
most satanical, nor so much as beseeming any
Christians in the world, save only Calvinists.

16. Thou therefore, O Lord, Who art the sole

protector of that which Thou Thyself hast instituted, protect Thyself in this blessed Sacrifice against Thy persecutors. Thou Lord of hosts, defend Thyself in this Holy Host against thine enemies. Permit not, I beseech Thee, Thy precious Body and Blood any longer to be so barbarously abused. Re-establish the same in our Island, mauger * the malice of Thine enemies, and grant that after forty years, wherein Thou hast been grieved with this wicked generation, at the last, this noble Sacrifice may be publicly celebrated by us, to Thine everlasting and perpetual praise.

17. And you, religious Fathers and reverend Priests, to whom is committed the care of this our devastated vineyard, and who are unto us in this our distress, the sole dispensers of this divine Sacrament, venture still I beseech you, as hitherto you have done, the loss of your lives, to distribute unto us this divine Food, and to break unto us this celestial Bread. For in your hands only it is to give unto men this heavenly Manna. In your hands only it is, in this time of dearth, to preserve the lives of your brethren, lest they perish by famine.

18. And we again, my Catholic brethren, let us as boldly adventure our lives to give them harbour and entertainment. Imitating herein our noble patron and protomartyr of England, blessed St. Alban, who presented himself, yea and gave his own

* Notwithstanding.

life, to preserve the life of his priest, Amphibolus. Imitating also in some sort herein, the glorious virgin, St. Catherine of Siena, who, beating and afflicting her body so severely that she drew the blood, the devil appearing unto her, and persuading her that it was both foolish and needless devotion, she made him answer, that her Lord and Saviour had given His Blood for her, and that she would requite and repay him again with blood for Blood. Even so, when either foolish heretics or timorous friends shall condemn you of folly, for losing your goods or exposing your lives, for to harbour priests, consider with yourselves, that you harbour him who bringeth unto you the Body and Blood of Jesus Christ; and that if you shed your blood to receive him who consecrateth in your houses the Blood of Christ, what else do you but render blood for Blood, and spend your blood for the Blood of Christ?

19. Comfort yourselves likewise with this consideration, that when our Lord and Saviour instituted His last supper, and consecrated this mystery, in the house of a friend, even a few days before, did the traitor Judas betray and sell the same most innocent Blood for thirty pence. You, therefore, right Honourable and Worshipful of our English nation, which have bought this holy Sacrifice at a hundred marks; and such as were poor, with the utter deprivance of all the poor little they had in the world; and further, such as have not so much money

as heretics have asked for the price of this Sacrifice, nor any worldly goods at all to give them, and instead of money, have laid to pawn their very carcasses into sundry prisons, gaols, and loathsome dungeons, oh! with what great and unspeakable reward, will our Lord and Saviour one day repay and requite your charity!

20. Never was there any act in the world so vile and abominable as that of Judas, to sell to the Jews for money, the Blood of his Master; ncr ever can there be amongst Christians, any act more honourable, than to buy with such loss of lands and livings the Blood of Christ. That cursed creature sold the Blood of his Master, but only for thirty pence; and yet how hateful is he to all the world, as also to heaven. You pay for the same above threescore pounds. Oh how grateful shall you be both to God and His Angels! Surely this Sacrifice cannot be esteemed by you that love it at any low price, sith * those that hate it, do value it unto you at so high a rate. For that thing must needs be precious, which both the merchant doth set so high, and the chapman is contented to buy so dear. In a word all the sufferings, all the ignominies, all the injuries, all the damages, and all the detriments, which you shall endure for the defence of this Sacrifice, will minister matter to all ensuing posterity of your most noble and heroic acts; which, though you die, will ever live to future memory, resound to your own

* Since.

2

immortal glory and the everlasting renown of our English nation.

21. Finally for as much as I may have just occasion to fear lest I have offended for offering to touch or support with my pen this sacred ark, I therefore here from the bottom of my heart, right humbly crave pardon of the Blessed Trinity, the Maker of this ineffable mystery, of Jesus Christ really present in this mystery, of all the blessed Angels which assist at this mystery, of all Catholic Priests consecrators of this mystery, and of all Catholic people, the true worshippers of this ineffable mystery. And in further satisfaction for this my presumption, I am, and ever will be ready so long as I live, to cast myself under the feet of the meanest Priest in all the world, and to serve him as his footstool, whilst he celebrateth this Sacrifice.

22. And lastly, if peradventure there be anything contained in this treatise, which in the judgment of the Catholic Church, the only elected spouse of Jesus Christ, shall seem contrary either to the faith or good manners of the same Church, I utterly abjure, damn, condemn, and detest the same; protesting myself to be the man, that with the same hands wherewith I writ it, with the selfsame hands to be the first that shall throw the same into the fire.

Thy hearty well-willer and most affectionate countryman

JOHN HEIGHAM.

A WORD OR TWO CONCERNING CEREMONIES.

1. THOSE which make profession of learning, commonly and with very great reason do complain, that arts and sciences have no greater enemy than the ignorant man. And even so, we at this day may justly complain and say the same, that touching the affairs of religion, we find no greater enemies and mockers thereof, and principally of the religious rites and ceremonies belonging to the same, than those who are most of all ignorant of their sense and meaning.

2. And whereas we see in this our cursed and execrable age, a great number of Christians so easily contemn and so impudently mock at such godly ceremonies; so if they rightly understood the reason of them, they would certainly receive them with singular reverence and devotion.

3. Now amongst all the five senses of nature which God hath given us, two especially, to wit, our ears and our eyes, are principally called *sensus doctrinæ aut disciplinæ*, senses of doctrine or discipline, that is to say, whereby we are made capable to re-

2 *

ceive instructions and discipline. For without these
two, it is impossible ever to learn anything, and by
the means of these two principal senses we come to
understand and learn all manner of sciences. All
the ceremonies, therefore, of the Mass are instituted
by the Church principally to instruct the people by
the sense of seeing. And even as they who would
take away preaching out of the Church, do as much
as if they would stop the people's ears, even so they
who would take away the ceremonies out of the
Church do as much as in them lieth to hide or clean
put out the people's eyes.

4. What then may we think or say of the pernicious practices of the arch-heretics of our age?
Yea, and how just occasion have those which are of
their own religion, as well as we, to cry out against
them? For first these malicious masters have quite
rejected a great number of godly ceremonies from
amongst the Christian people in all cities and
countries wheresoever they have lived. And next,
even of those few which still they retain, they as
utterly deprive them of their sense and meaning, as
if there were not so much as any one used in all
their religion.

5. But what suppose you to be the drift and
legerdemain of these deceivers? Forsooth, because
knowing full well that in our Catholic ceremonies
there are comprehended and lie hid so many notable
mysteries, they plainly foresee, that if they should

truly explicate and manifest unto the people the
sense and meaning of some of their own, they
should presently give them a light, and inflame
their hearts with a love of ours.   For which cause,
as by a subtle and crafty device, they for the most
part either conceal them from them, or speak in
contempt and hatred of them.

6. To make this point the more apparent, of how
many thousands of them may you ask these questions
before you shall meet with one that can make you
answer ? For example, ask them why, to the accomplishment of their common service the clerk and
minister must be clad in white rather than in black,
blue or yellow, or in a coat or garment of any other
colour ? Ask them, why, in saying the same service,
the lesson is read out of the Old Testament and not
out of the New ?   And why not all Scripture out of
the Old, or all out of the New ?   Ask them why the
Old Testament is read before the New ; and why not
the New before the Old, seeing it is of far greater
dignity, as themselves do freely confess ? Ask
them, why they kneel at the saying of the Lord's
prayer and rise up at the Creed, rather than rise up
at the Lord's prayer and kneel down at the Creed ?
Ask them, why they set the font near the Church door,
and the Communion table within the chancel, and
why not as well the Communion table at the Church
door and the font within the chancel ? I omit for
brevity's sake the churching of women, the marrying

with a ring, Godfathers and Godmothers in the Sacrament of Baptism, the confirmation of children and so forth. All which, with a hundred more, which I might name, the Protestant clergy do still retain, whereof the people do no more understand the meaning than the man in the moon.

7. Now therefore, forasmuch as all ceremonies, used for the better and more solemn setting forth of the divine service, are of one of these two sorts, that is to say, either commoditative or significative, it followeth that to wear a white surplice rather than a black, or to read for the first lesson, rather part of the Old Testament than the New, or to set the Font at the Church door, rather than within the chancel, or in the bottom of the belfry, are nothing commoditative, neither to the Priest nor yet to the people; therefore they are significative, that is to say, signifying some special mystery, wherein the Christian people ought to be instructed.

8. The holy ceremonies therefore of our religion, if they were explicated unto thee, gentle reader, if thou be a Protestant, as they are unto Catholics, they would assuredly yield thee most singular comfort; wherein I will report me to thine own experience, after thou shalt have first perused the explication only of these which appertain to the holy Mass, whereof thou hast here set down, every word, sentence, and syllable that is in the same. Nothing doubting, but that in the end, thou thyself

wilt freely confess, that the hearers and beholders of the holy Mass enjoy and receive a most incredible comfort, by occasion of the ceremonies which are handled therein; which thou, being a Protestant, canst never enjoy by assisting or being present at thy morning prayer. Try, and then trust, and so farewell.

A DEVOUT EXPOSITION OF

THE HOLY MASS.

CHAPTER I.

OF THE ETYMOLOGY, DERIVATION, AND SIGNIFICATION OF
THE WORD MASS, AND FROM WHAT TONGUE THE SAME
WAS FIRST DERIVED.

To proceed orderly, in the exposition of the holy
Sacrifice of the Mass, it is convenient that we begin
at the etymology or signification of the word. First
therefore it is very probable that the word *Mass* is
neither Greek nor Latin, but pure Hebrew, the
Apostles, who were of the Hebrew nation, having
promulgated the same in that language, and named
it *Missah*, drawn and taken of this Hebrew word
Mas, which signifieth, oblation, tax, or tribute, as
is manifestly to be gathered out of Deuteronomy, *
Kings, † and Isaias. ‡   And in many places of holy
Scripture, it signifieth the sacrifices, and oblations
of the Old Law made of lambs, oxen, turtles,
pigeons and the like. §

* Deuter. ch. 16.   † Kings iii. ch. 8.   ‡ Isaias ch. 13.
§ Numbers ch. 6. Judges ch. 6. Ezech. 45.

For which cause the Catholic Church doth most willingly retain this name, as finding none other more convenient and proper, to signify this most excellent Oblation and Sacrifice, representing that other which was the tax or tribute paid by Jesus Christ unto God His Father for the price and ransom of our redemption.

2. Others will have it to be of the Latin word *Missa, sent*, because in the Mass principally we send up our prayers and oblations to Almighty God :* which some explicate in this manner that this Host was first sent by God the Father, when He sent us His only Son to be incarnate, and to take flesh in the womb of the Blessed Virgin Mary, and afterwards to offer up that bloody Sacrifice upon the altar of the Cross for our redemption; in remembrance whereof, this Sacrifice is celebrated, and is by us again sent and presented to the Eternal Father, for as much as we daily offer it up to His divine Majesty.†

8. Again others think it to be so called of dismissing the people, and so, to signify the same that *Missio*, which signifieth a sending away or dismission.‡ But, howsoever this be, and whether the word be Hebrew, Greek, or Latin, or whether it be contained in the New Testament, or in the Old, it

* Hug. Vict. l. 2, de sacram. ch. 14.
† Innocent III. lib. 3, de Sacrificio missæ, ch. 12; and Bon. op. de Mysterio Missæ.
‡ Bellar. lib. 1, de Missa.

is sufficient for us that in the Scripture is expressed that which this word most truly signifieth. As in the like case and difficulty, St. Augustine told the Arian heretic Pascentius * that he was not to ground his disputation upon the bare word *Homousion*, which the Catholics only used, thereby to give to understand, that God the Son was consubstantial with God the Father, but that he should argue against that which it signified. And the like may be said of many other terms still retained by Catholics, as Trinity, Humanity, Person, Incarnation, Transubstantiation, and the like.

CHAPTER II.

OF THE DIVERS PARTS OF THE MASS, AND BY WHOM THE HOLY MASS WAS FIRST ORDAINED.

THE holy and dreadful Sacrifice of the Mass hath two essential parts. The one is Consecration, the other is, the receiving of the Priest or Communion. Touching these two principal and essential parts of the holy Mass, it is most certain by the Evangelists themselves, † and likewise by St. Paul that they were instituted by Jesus Christ Himself, and by no other, neither man nor angel: our Saviour content-

* Epist. 194.

† St. Matthew ch. 26. St. Mark ch. 14. St. Luke ch. 22. St. Paul, 1 Cor. ch. 11.

ing Himself to institute so much as was of the
nature, necessity and essence of the thing, leaving
other ceremonies and rites requisite to celebrate the
same to the judgment and prudence of His Apostles
and of their successors, to whom He committed the
care of His Church and of all His faithful and
Christian flock : in which respect He said unto His
disciples : *Yet many things I have to say to you, but
you cannot bear them now, but when the Spirit of Truth
cometh, He shall teach you all truth ; and the things
that are to come He shall show you.**

We see the like also performed in other points of
our Religion ; as when our Lord ordained that we
should fast, He contented Himself to institute only
so much as was of the essence of the thing, saying
jejunate, fast ye, prescribing neither how, when, nor
how oft, His holy pleasure was to have it performed : but left all those circumstances to be ordered and accommodated, according to the care and
discretion of His disciples. The like He did and
performed concerning prayer, willing and ordaining
that men should pray, saying : *orate*, pray ye, and
added thereto this word *semper*, ever : but that *ever*
I fear me by many would be turned into *never* if
his spouse, the Catholic Church, had not decreed
and straitly commanded and prescribed the time,
the place, the ceremonies, and the manner, how the
same should be accomplished.

* St. John ch. 16, v. 12, 13.

3. Hence therefore it is, that we affirm and say with very good reason, the holy Mass to have been instituted and ordained by our Lord Himself, for as much as He instituted and ordained the most essential and principal parts thereof, to wit, Consecration and Communion, referring the ceremonies, and other circumstances to the care and discretion of His Apostles and their successors; who in this behalf, have taken such order as might best reduce His Death and Passion into our memories, according to that which He commanded, that so oft as they should do it, they should do it in remembrance of Him. But of all this, we shall speak hereafter more at large.

4. Now, in a word, I may say, that these ceremonies or additions may be reduced to these heads, to wit, to giving of thanks, Confession of sins, Prayer, Doctrine, Profession of faith, and such other parts of our devotion, which, albeit they be no essential parts of this holy Sacrifice, yet are they very requisite and convenient to induce us, the more to reverence and contemplate the majesty and excellency of so great a mystery, to stir up and move our hearts, being present at the same, and to prepare and dispose ourselves before we come to receive so great a Sacrament. For which cause we ought to hold for very laudable these other parts of the holy Mass, annexed to the former, all tending to the greater ornament, reverence, and majesty of so ineffable a mystery.

CHAPTER III.

OF THE EXCELLENCY AND DIGNITY OF THE HOLY MASS;
AND OF THE GREAT WORTHINESS OF THE THINGS THAT
ARE HANDLED THEREIN.

1. Amongst all the things that give testimony of
the sweetness, benignity, and love of God towards
man, one of the chief and principal, is this most
divine and most excellent Sacrament of all Sacraments. The which, because of the great and super-
abundant grace which it containeth, is therefore
worthily called Eucharist, or good grace. For this
most sacred and holy action is of itself, and by itself,
both a Sacrament and Sacrifice, and that the most
noble, divine, and most worthy, that ever was
offered; nor can there possibly be a greater, it
being no other than the only, true, and eternal Son
of God Himself.

2. To prefigure unto us the dignity of this
Sacrifice, our Lord in the Old Testament, would
that the Priest entering into the Sanctuary should
be attired with most rich and precious ornaments,
and those most costly and artificial wrought; to
the end that the people seeing him to enter so
venerably, should know the greatness of God to
Whom he went to speak, and to render due homage.

3. In like manner, the riches and divers ornaments, the magnificent churches, the altars so

sumptuously adorned, the great number of lights, and all other ceremonies which the Catholic Church doth now use in celebrating this Sacrifice, were ordained to this end, to declare the greatness, sanctity and virtue of this mystery. For even as he who entering into a great palace, seeing the walls of the chambers hung with arras or tapestry cometh to know the greatness, the nobleness, and the riches of the personage that dwelleth therein, for as much as poor folks, or people of mean estate cannot be fitted with such costly furniture, even so, and no otherwise happeneth it unto him, who entereth into the Church, and seeth Mass to be celebrated with such curious ornaments: for as much as wise and virtuous men would never be at so great expenses, nor ever labour so much for the performance thereof, if they knew not full well, this work to be the greatest that possibly a man can practise in the world.

4. Another thing which doth most singularly demonstrate unto us the dignity of this Sacrifice is, that it is a perfect epitome or abridgment of all the works of Almighty God, and of the whole Old and New Testament, comprising briefly and summarily all that which is contained therein; the Trinity, Unity, Eternity, Omnipotency, Glory, Majesty, Infinity and excellency of Almighty God; the Creation of Heaven, Earth, Angels, Men, and of all creatures: the Incarnation, Nativity, Preach-

ing, Miracles, Life, Death, Passion, Resurrection, and Ascension of our Saviour Jesus : and consequently, our Redemption, Vocation, Justification, Sanctification and Glorification, together with whatsoever else concerneth the glory of God or salvation of man.

CHAPTER IV.

OF THE GREAT WORTHINESS OF PRIESTS, WHO OFFER THIS HOLY SACRIFICE.

THIS Sacrifice being so excellent a thing, as hath before been shown, it was convenient that the divine Majesty of Almighty God should ordain in His Church, an Order of men, which should be above others, who should both consecrate, and offer the same ; which thing He performed in His last supper instituting the order of Priesthood, unto which He gave power and authority to consecrate, receive, and distribute to others, His most precious Body and Blood, veiled under the forms of bread and . wine.

2. By which it is most manifest, that the Mass is a work, the most great, the most worthy, and most excellent, that possibly a man can undertake or enterprise, seeing the Priest who sayeth it, excelleth in dignity all the Kings, Emperors, and Priests either of the written law or of the law of

nature. And furthermore, he surpasseth in this power, the Patriarchs, the Prophets, yea and the Angels themselves, who neither can consecrate, receive, nor distribute to others, the Body of our Blessed Saviour; whereas the Priest having consecrated It, holdeth It in his hands, receiveth It, keepeth It and imparteth It to others.

3. Rightly therefore do we say that this noble dignity of Priesthood can with no pomp, eloquency or ornament of words be sufficiently extolled. For it surmounteth and surpasseth the tongue of the most subtle philosophers, yea, the top and height of all excellency of every creature. If you compare it to the glory of Kings, or the splendour of Princes' diadems, these are as far inferior thereto, as if we should compare the basest lead to the purest and finest gold that is.

But what need I stand upon earthly comparisons, when the celestial citizens, the Angels themselves dare not aspire to priestly authority. For to which of the Angels hath God at any time said, *whose sins you shall forgive they are forgiven them: and whose you shall retain they are retained* * yea, which is much more: *Do this for the commemoration of Me?* † In a word they admire and tremble to behold that which the Priest may boldly touch, handle and divide in pieces, as being warranted by Christ Himself.

* St. John ch. 20.　　　† St. Paul, 1 Cor. ch. 11, v. 24.

3

5. But to pass yet further from the hierarchies of Angels, and to come to the Lady of Angels, and Queen of all the world, even she, I say, albeit she far surpassed all creatures in the plenitude and abundance of heavenly grace, yet even she herself also giveth place to the orders and hierarchies of the militant church. For having all other honour given unto her by her Son in the highest degree, yet she attained not to this dignity of consecrating or offering this dreadful Sacrifice. True it is, that she in pronouncing eight humble words, *Ecce ancilla Domini fiat mihi secundum verbum tuum, Behold the handmaid of the Lord, be it done to me according to Thy word*, once only, corporally conceived the Son of God, the Saviour and Redeemer of the world. But Priests, as His instruments, are daily the cause, that the self-same Son of God, and of the Virgin, is truly and really present in the Blessed Sacrament.

6. The high King of Heaven, being incarnate in our Blessed Lady, she brought forth to the world a Saviour mortal and passible: the Priests offer to God and give to men the very same Saviour now impassible and most glorious. She gave suck to the new-born Babe with her virginal breasts, handled Him with her hands, bore Him in her arms, and performed such other serviceable offices to Christ's little members.

These Priests receive Him with their mouths, carry Him, and give Him in meat to others, Who is the bread and food of Angels. O venerable sanctity of holy hands ! O high and happy dignity ! O great and only wonder of the world !

7. Nor are any of these comparisons, either arrogant or hyperbolical, but true and justifiable in all propriety and rigour of speech. For as in all rigour of speech it must of necessity be confessed that God is far above His creatures, the soul much more noble than the body, and spiritual things more excellent than temporal, so in all rigour of speech, it must needs be granted, priestly dignity to be the highest dignity and degree of this. life, for as much as it is immediately exercised about the honour of God, and administration of divine and spiritual affairs; whereas the dignity of princes, though in their rank most to be respected, yet their functions and affairs are chiefly touching temporal things.

CHAPTER V.

OF THE END FOR THE WHICH MASS IS SAID OR HEARD, AND OF THE GREAT DEVOTION AND ATTENTION WHERE-WITH THE PRIEST IS TO CELEBRATE THE SAME.

THE end for which the Mass is to be said or heard is most high and excellent, yea, so high, that a higher or greater cannot possibly be invented or imagined. The chief and principal end is only one, the others are diverse. The first is the honour of God, Who being the last and final end of all things,

8 *

of good right willeth and ordaineth that all things be done and referred to His honour.

2. The better to understand this point, it is to be noted, that Sacrifice is an act of worship, adoration or honour, the which is due only to God, with pain of death to all those who shall attribute the same to any other. " *Qui immolat diis occidetur, præter quam Domino soli.*" He that sacrificeth to gods, save only to the Lord, shall be put to death.* The Mass therefore is and ought to be both said and heard chiefly to honour God by and with so divine a Sacrifice.

3. The other ends are diverse, for the which the same may either be said or heard, as for the preservation of the universal Church, the propagation of the Catholic religion, for the Pope's Holiness, for all bishops, pastors, and religious persons, for peace and concord amongst Christian princes, for our parents, friends, and benefactors, for thanksgiving to God for all His benefits, for the preservation of the fruits of the earth, and for our temporal substance, and generally for all manner of necessities either of soul or body.

4. In saying of Mass there is required of the Priest's part a singular attention and devotion, be it either in regard of the thing that is offered, or in regard of Him to Whom the same is offered, which is Almighty God Himself, Who is *King of Kings and*

* Exodus ch. 22, v. 20.

Lord of Lords. Before His presence even the highest Powers of heaven do shake and tremble.

This, St. Chrysostom seriously pondering and weighing with himself, saith : He who is a legate, to treat for a whole city—what speak I of a city ? yea of the whole world, and is an intercessor to Almighty God that He may become propitious unto all men, not only to the living, but also to the dead, what manner of man, I pray you, ought he to be ? Truly I cannot think the confidence of Moses or Elias to be sufficient to dispatch such an embassage or supplication.* And again in the same place he further saith : what hands ought they to be that do administer it ? What the tongue that pronounceth such divine words ? How pure and clean ought that soul to be that doth receive so worthy a Lord ? Thus St. Chrysostom.

6. For further proof and confirmation hereof, the Holy Scripture recounteth a fearful example of the two children of Heli the priest, who were punished by death, for that they did not perform the office of priesthood duly as they ought : what then, may we think, shall be the punishment of such Priests, as should approach unworthily to the altar of our Lord ?

7. It is written of St. Mark the Evangelist, that he had so great reverence of this holy Sacrifice, and so greatly feared his own insufficiency, that he cut off his own thumb, to the end he might be incapable

* St. Chrysos. lib. 6, de Sacerdotio.

and unfit to be made a Priest, which yet was afterwards restored unto him by miracle, as is to be read in the Canons.*

8. It is also testified of the glorious Father St. Francis, that being only a deacon, and purposing to be made Priest, one appeared unto him, holding in his hand a vial of water of most admirable cleanness and said unto him: Francis, seest thou this water? and the blessed Father, having answered he did, he further added: He that will be a Priest must be like unto this in purity: which words struck into the holy man such a deep impression, and such a fear and respect of that sacred function, that he never afterwards would permit himself to be made a Priest.

CHAPTER VI.

OF THE ATTENTION AND DEVOTION OF THE ASSISTANTS, AND HOW THE SAME MAY BE OBTAINED BY HEARING OF MASS.

FORASMUCH as upon all festival days, a man must either say Mass, or at the least hear Mass, by the express commandment of the Church, it is great reason that this work should be well and orderly performed, according as is convenient and as the weight and importance of the thing itself requireth.

First then, we must procure to have an ardent and

*Canon si quis a med. dist. 55.

inflamed desire to hear the same with fruit, and with the greatest attention that possibly we may; which desire ought to be accompanied with a lively faith of the presence of Jesus Christ our Saviour, Who with such exceeding love vouchsafeth to come to visit us.

2. Secondly, it will help very much to think upon the wonderful greatness and dignity of this most holy Sacrifice, whereof I have spoken a little before.

3. Thirdly, to remember our own vileness and abjectness, reputing ourselves most unworthy to be present at so excellent and divine a mystery, in the presence whereof the very Angels do humble and bow down themselves with most divine reverence: wherefore with far greater reason ought a wretched sinner to do the same, and after the example of the publican holding down his head for shame, to knock his breast saying : *God be merciful to me a sinner.*

4. Fourthly, it is also requisite that a man go to Mass out of mortal sin, forasmuch as this greatly hindereth both devotion and due attention, as also the fruit which he might otherwise draw from the same. Yet if a man be fallen into any great sin, he ought not therefore to leave to hear Mass. For albeit it serve him not then to merit eternal life, yet it serveth him nevertheless to satisfy the Commandment of the Church, which is, to hear Mass on the festival days ; which, if he perform not, he doth add another mortal sin to his former.

5. Fifthly, that our end or intention be right; which

is that we purpose to do that which our holy mother
the Church doeth, who in the Sacrifice of the Mass,
maketh an offering and present to the Eternal Father
of His only Son, of His most holy Passion, and of His
merits in satisfaction of the sins of her children.
Whereupon we ought to accompany and join our desires with those of the Priest, and to beseech the
divine Majesty that it would please Him to hear us,
and that He would mercifully pardon both our own
offences, and those of our neighbours, and that He
would graciously assist us in all our necessities, and
that, in the virtue of this most holy Sacrifice.

6. Sixthly, to endeavour to conceive within ourselves a holy fear and a wonderful reverence,
considering that we are present in a place that is
holy, and especially dedicated to the service of God,
remembering how God commanded Moses to put off
his shoes for reverence of the place whereon he
stood.

7. Seventhly, besides the sanctity and holiness of
the place, we ought to consider the presence of our
Lord and Saviour Himself, Who at that time causeth
His blessings and graces to rain down in great plenty
and abundance upon all those who are there present
with pure, unfeigned, and profound attention.

8. Eighthly, when we see the Priest coming towards the altar, we ought to lift up our eyes,
especially those of our understanding, to heaven,
and to imagine that we see descend, as by Jacob's

ladder, a multitude of Angels, who come to present themselves at this most holy Sacrifice, and with their presence to honour it in such wise, that all the Church is filled with Angels, which busy themselves here and there amongst the people, inciting them all to modesty, devotion, and reverent behaviour in the presence of this most holy and dreadful Sacrifice.

9. Ninthly, the great and loving desire that our Saviour Himself hath to come unto us, and therefore to lift up anew our eyes to heaven, and with a lively faith to behold the Son of God, sitting at the right hand of His Father, being ready and prepared to be present, so soon as the words of consecration shall be pronounced, in the hands of the Priest in the Sacred Host, and with a longing desire waiting and attending, in some sort, the time and opportunity to come unto us.

10. Tenthly, consider the cause and end of our Saviour's coming, and so contemplate the greatness of Him that cometh, Who is infinite. The end for which He cometh, which is, to be offered up for us to His heavenly Father. Whither He cometh, into earth, the place and habitation of beasts. The manner wherein He cometh, hidden under the forms of bread and wine.

11. Finally, to maintain the honour of this holy Sacrifice against all enemies, and to use the same aright as we ought to do, we must every day assist thereat, without distraction of spirit, in silence and

decent composition, and be persuaded this to be the
principal and chiefest of all our actions, and which
deserveth that we dedicate unto it the best and most
convenient hour of the morning.   And in so doing,
our merciful Lord will doubtlessly send down His
blessings upon us in great abundance, and the
better prosper all our affairs and business in the day
following.

CHAPTER VII.

OF THE FRUIT AND PROFIT WHICH COMETH, AND IS REAPED BY HEARING OF MASS.

THE fruits which a man may gather by hearing of
Mass are great and many in number.

1. The first is, that a man is admitted unto the
inward familiarity of our Lord Jesus Christ, and to
be near to His person, as His secretary or chamber-
lain, where he both heareth and seeth so many
divine secrets; which places and rooms in the courts
of earthly Princes are so much sought after, even
by the greatest Lords and nobles of this world, and
are so highly esteemed, that oftentimes they are content to serve their whole life for them, without any
recompense at all in the end: whereas our Lord
Jesus Christ, the King of heaven and earth doth
never, unless He be forsaken, forsake him who hath
done Him service, nor leaveth him without reward
and recompense.

2. Secondly, he who is present at Mass, doth participate so much the more of this divine Sacrifice; for as much as in the same, more particular prayer is made for him than for the absent; the Priest saying *Et pro omnibus circumstantibus*, and for all that are standing about. He profiteth also more by the attention and devotion, caused by the real presence of our Lord Jesus Christ: even as the sun doth more heat the countries near unto it, than those that are further from it; and the fire doth more warm those that approach unto it, than those that stand afar off from it. And hence it was that the Apostles received so many graces and privileges, because they were continually in the presence of Jesus Christ. St. Chrysostom also saith, that grace is infused into sundry persons in the presence of the Body of Jesus Christ.

3. Thirdly, in hearing of Mass devoutly, we receive pardon of our venial sins, and obtain remission, at least in part, of the temporal pain, which remaineth after the fault or guilt of our sins is forgiven us, and for the which a man is to endure either in this life or in Purgatory: which is truly a most wonderful benefit, seeing that the very least pain in Purgatory is greater than all the pains of this world together. Insomuch that St. Anselm doubteth not to affirm that one Mass heard by us with devotion in this life, is of greater value than a thousand said for us by others after our departure.

4. Fourthly, in hearing of Mass devoutly, a man

disposeth himself to receive pardon of his mortal sins: for as much as he hath occasion by the memory of the Passion of Jesus Christ, and of His great love and benefits, and of this Sacrifice offered up for our sins, and with the real presence of Jesus Christ, to have repentance, and to be moved to contrition for them.

5. Fifthly, it doth bring us increase of grace, to resist all our evil passions, and to vanquish all sorts of temptations : wherefore well is he that may hear it daily.*

6. Sixthly, it is a strong and assured buckler against all evil spirits, and a singular means to obtain of God safeguard against all dangers, together with many blessings, even corporal, as health and such other like, it maketh us more capable of the visitation and protection of our good Angel, yea and more ready for death, how soon soever it shall assail us.†

7. Seventhly, it is a singular remedy against all superstition, and a most peculiar and effectual means to conserve all faithful Christians in perfect love, charity, peace, and concord, as being particularly instituted to that intent.‡

8. Eighthly, by hearing of Mass cometh another

* S. Hierom. lib. 1 in Joan. S. Aug. contra Petil. lib. 4, cap. 10.
† S. Clement, Can. et Constit. Apost. lib. 8. S. Cyril, Cath. 3. S. Chrys. hom. 13, ad Hebræos.
‡ S. Aug. de civitate Dei, lib. 22, ch. 10. Soz. Hist. Eccles. lib. 9, ch. 8. S. Paul, 1 Cor. ch. 10.

special fruit, to wit, the fruit of instruction which is had and obtained in the doctrine which a man heareth and learneth by being present at the same. Wherein he is taught at the *Confiteor* to ask pardon of his offences ; at the *Misereatur* to pardon the faults of his neighbour : at the *Introit* to laud God : at the *Kyrie eleison* to ask mercy of God. At the *Gloria in excelsis* to magnify God : at the *Dominus vobiscum* to be united with his neighbour : at the *Collects* to present his prayers : at the *Epistle* to think of the contempt of the world : at the *Gospel* to follow Jesus Christ : at the *Credo* to profess that which he ought to believe : at the *Preface*, attention : at the *Canon* devotion : at the first *Memento*, to pray for the living : at the second *Memento* to pray for the departed : at the *Elevation* to adore Jesus Christ : and at the *Communion* to communicate spiritually.

CHAPTER VIII.

OF THE FAULTS AND ABUSES WHICH MAY BE COMMITTED BY HEARING OF MASS.

FIRST it were an intolerable abuse, if any, which God forbid, should go to Mass to content their eyes with wanton and dishonest sights, making the Church a shop of their disordinate appetites, not having any respect either to the presence of God or of His Angels, nor to His divine service, nor to the time in

which is represented the greatest benefit that our
Lord hath done for man.

2. The second abuse were to hear Mass only for
fashion, and much more to spend the time in idle
talk, without any attention or devotion; for this
were not only to depart without fruit, but to lose
much by that, they might gain exceedingly. For
even as you pay not but those who labour in your
vineyard, not those who go thither to see and behold
it, even so our Lord doth not give His hire but to
those who are attentive to the work of His divine
service; but especially upon holy and festival days,
such persons should sin most grievously.

3. The third abuse were to be present with such
distraction and vagation of spirit, that instead of
thinking upon the holy mysteries of the Mass, one
should call to mind his worldly business, bethinking
himself of the means wherewith he should have
prosecuted some negotiations, which therefore came
not to so good effect and issue as he desired; and
discoursing of the circumspection which he must use
for the time to come in some other business, which
he hath yet to do, and so, as we may say, build
castles in the air. Surely the spindle of a wheel or a
mill doth not turn so much, as doth the spirit of such
a man, being present at Mass, suffering himself to
be carried without bridle, whithersoever his wandering fancy shall please to move or to transport him.
And of these I say, as of the former, that they

should offend in the same degree, and lose the fruit and merit which they might reap by hearing of Mass devoutly.

4. The fourth abuse were, to seek for the shortest Masses, and to think the time long that we are present at this divine Sacrifice. For surely this sheweth that our minds are more set upon earthly than heavenly things, since that we find no such irksomeness in corporal banquets, plays or other vain sights. But we should rather consider, how our Blessed Saviour thought not the time of three hours long to hang upon the Cross for our sakes; in which respect, their devotion is very commendable who use to hear more Masses than one every day, according as their other necessary business will permit them. Yea if the fire of the love of God were perfectly enkindled in our hearts, all the while the Mass should last would surely seem unto us very short and little: like as the Scripture saith of Jacob that he served the space of fourteen years to have Rachel in marriage, and that he esteemed all those years but as a few days in respect of the love he bare unto her.

5. The fifth abuse were, to be over-curious in adorning ourselves when we go to Church, and in this women, especially of young years and good calling, must be more wary, because they may otherwise not only hinder their own devotion, but that of others also. It is strange what caveats St. Paul and the holy Fathers give them in this

kind. For surely when they go to Church they should rather seek to please God than men. Neither can they easily excuse themselves if they do otherwise. To conclude, when we repair to the Temple of God to pray, we ought to lay away all toys and vanities, which any way may hinder our devotions, and carefully collect our spirits and drive away all distractions, that we may without any perturbation, freely lift up our hearts to God, and devoutly employ the time in holy, pious, and wholesome meditations, according as shall hereafter be declared. And now to speak of the altar itself.

CHAPTER IX.

OF THE ALTAR WHEREON THE SACRIFICE OF THE MASS IS CELEBRATED, AND OF THE FURNITURE AND ORNAMENTS BELONGING TO THE SAME.

How the Altar made of stone representeth Christ.

1. FIRST, the altar whereon this most divine Sacrifice is celebrated is made of stone; to signify unto us, that Jesus Christ is the head corner-stone as witnesseth the Apostle St. Peter.*

How unity of faith.

The same altar compacted and made of many stones cleaving together doth represent the Church

* 1 St. Peter ch. 2, v. 7.

of God gathered together of divers nations, all coupled and linked in one faith, in one profession and exercise of religion.

How charity.

3. Both in the old law, and now also in the new, some altars were made of beaten gold; to signify the inestimable and pure love wherewith our Lord loved us, and the inestimable and pure love wherewith we ought to love Him again.

How our Lord's table.

This altar also representeth unto us the table whereon our Lord instituted and celebrated His last supper with His disciples.*

How the Mount Calvary.

5. Also the mount of Calvary, whereon He suffered His Death and Passion for the salvation and redemption of all the world.

How the altar-stone representeth the grave.

To the adorning of this altar divers mysterious ornaments are belonging. First there is placed thereon an altar-stone, which representeth the grave or monument wherein the body of our Lord was buried or entombed. And there was nigh the cross a new monument.†

How the linen clothes represent the sindon.

The white linen clothes, wherewith the altar and

.* St. Matthew ch. 26, v. 26. † St. John ch. 19, v. 41.

altar-stone are covered, do betoken the white sindon wherein Joseph of Arimathea did wrap and enfold the body of our Saviour: *Et involvit sindone.* And he put it in a clean sindon.[*]

How the cross representeth the history of the Passion.

There is a cross set upon the altar to signify that the history of our Saviour's Passion is there to be handled. Again to signify that the Sacrifice of the Altar is the same in substance which our Lord accomplished upon the altar of the cross.

How the chalice representeth the cup.

The chalice representeth the cup wherein He consecrated His most precious Blood. *And He took the chalice, saying: This is My Blood.*[†]

How mortification and martyrdom.

Likewise by the chalice is betokened mortification, and a mind always ready to suffer martyrdom for the love of Christ. *Can you drink the chalice, which I am to drink?* to wit, suffer death for My sake, *and they answered, we can.*[‡]

How the Paten representeth the stone.

The Paten laid upon the chalice representeth the stone which was rolled against the door of our Saviour's sepulchre. *And they rolled a stone to the door of the sepulchre.*[§]

[*] St. Luke ch. 23.   [†] St. Matthew ch. 26.
[‡] St. Matthew ch. 20.   [§] St. Mark ch. 15, v. 46.

How the shining of the Corporal representeth Christ's
resurrection and immortality.

The Corporal, the which is most white and shining,
signifieth that Christ by manifold passions was
brought to the brightness of His resurrection; Who
as the Apostle saith, *entered not into glory before He*
had sustained the ignominy of the Cross.

How purity and chastity.

Again the brightness and shining of the same
Corporal admonisheth, that to receive the Body of
Jesus Christ, a man ought to shine with all angelical
purity and chastity both of body and soul. And
that as it shineth with brightness, so the intention
of the offerer ought to shine with simplicity before
our Lord.

The signification of the Candles.

1. Candles are lighted and set upon the altar.
For by candles is signified sometimes the Law,
sometimes the Church, and sometimes Christian
conversation. *Let your light so shine before men, that*
they may see your good works, and glorify your Father,
*which is in heaven.**

How candles signify the light of faith.

2. Again, by the two candles, for commonly there
are so many, is signified the light of faith revealed
to two several people, the Jews and the Gentiles.
Or the two testaments, wherewith mankind is

*. St. Matthew ch. 5, v. 16.

4 *

illuminated, or the two witnesses of the resurrection, Moses and Elias.

How they are a sign of joy.

3. Also Candles are lighted in sign of joy, as testifieth Alcuinus ; and in respect of our Blessed Saviour's presence, Whose divinity is likewise signified by the same. As also to signify the gifts of grace and the light proceeding from the Holy Ghost, wherewith the Church is illuminated.

How the fire of charity.

4. And not unaptly are there fiery lights placed upon the altar to burn, because He is there Who came to send fire into the world, and desireth nothing more than that it burn and be kindled in the hearts of all His faithful.*

Of the curtains.

Lastly for the better adorning both of the Church and altar, there are rich hangings and curtains of divers and sundry colours answerable to the diversity of feasts throughout the year.

Of the signification of the Red.

Upon the feasts of the holy Cross, whereon Christ shed His precious Blood for us, and upon the Apostles and Martyrs, Red is used to signify the bloody martyrdom which they endured for the love of Christ ; for they are those which are come out of

* S. Luke ch. 12, v. 49.

great tribulations, and have washed their stoles in the Blood of the Lamb.*

Of the White.

Upon the feasts of Angels, Confessors, and Virgins we use White, to signify their holiness, chastity, and purity. As also upon the dedication of the Church, which is called by the name of a Virgin. For I have espoused you to one man, to present you a chaste virgin unto Christ.† Again by the White, which is of excellent pureness and cleanness, may be signified the splendour and integrity of good name and fame, especially requisite in any ecclesiastical magistrate. That a Bishop have a good testimony, according to the Apostle, both of those which are within, and of those which are without.‡

The signification of the Black.

Upon the days of prayer for the souls departed is used Black, to signify the dolorous and mournful estate of their souls; of whom it is said, they shall be saved, yet so as by fire.§

The signification of the Green.

Upon other common days, Green is used, for Green is a colour in the midst, betwixt white and black, and signifieth the Church militant, still living in this world, which is sometimes in joy, and sometimes in sorrow; and as it were but yet *in herba*,

---

* Apoc. ch. 7, v. 14.   † 2 Cor. ch. 11, v. 2.
‡ 1 Tim. ch. 3.   § 1 Cor. ch. 3, v. 15.

that is, growing, green, and not ripened; for the harvest of the Church is in the world to come.

The signification of the Purple.

Sometimes is used Purple, to signify the spiritual power and dignity which resideth in the chief Bishop and other Pastors of the Catholic Church, who ought to behave and comport themselves in their places like Kings, not to decline to the right hand, nor to the left, not to bind the worthy, nor to pardon or unbind the guilty.

The signification of the Scarlet.

Sometimes Scarlet is used, which is the colour of fire, by which is signified Pontifical or Priestly doctrine, which, like unto fire ought both to shine and to burn. To shine, by giving light to others, to burn by reprehensions, excommunications, and other censures. *Every tree that yieldeth not good fruit shall be cut down and shall be cast into the fire.* *

The signification of the Hyacinth.

Sometimes Hyacinth or sky-colour is used, by which may be understood the serenity of conscience, which a Bishop or Priest ought always to have both in things prosperous and things adverse. According to the same Apostle: *For our glory is this, the testimony of our conscience.*† As also that his thoughts ought not to be on earthly but on heavenly things,

---

* St. Matthew ch. 7, v. 19.　　　† 2 Cor. ch. 1, v. 12.

according to the same Apostle saying : *Conversatio nostra in cœlis est*, our conversation is in heaven. To conclude, touching the ornaments of the church and altar, Sozomen * and Nicephorus † recount how the Arian Emperor Valens, a great persecutor of Catholics, once upon a Christmas day, entered into the Church of St. Basil, whilst he was at the altar celebrating Mass, assisted by all his clergy, and the people round about with such devotion and reverence, as the quality of the feast and place required. And that he contemplating the goodly order, which was in everything, was so astonished with admiration that he well-nigh fell down in ecstasy. Lo here the proper words of Nicephorus, as they were translated out of Greek into Latin : *Quod ibi omnia miro ordine gererentur ad stuporem delapsus, et totus mutatus, in solum concidisset nisi quidam ex primoribus, tunica correpta, imperatorem jam ruentem retinuisset.* Astonished in admiration, and altogether altered or changed, for that he saw all things governed by so admirable an order, he had fallen down, unless one of the Princes, taking him by the robe, had held him up, being now ready to fall to the ground. Thus he. But in this point, so bare and naked are the churches of heretics and so utterly destitute of all hangings, and other costly ornaments, yea, so empty and quite disfurnished, that, to enter into them is much like as to enter into some empty grange or barn, after all the

* Lib. 6, cap. 16. † Lib. 11, cap. 18.

corn, hay, and straw, are carried out of it. Which is the cause, why some heretics coming over the seas, and contemplating the ornaments, riches, and beautiful ceremonies of the Catholic Church, do so greatly wonder and admire thereat, that when they do depart, they find themselves so marvellously delighted and comforted thereby, as if they had been for the time in some earthly Paradise. Yea, to some this hath been a chief motive of their change and conversion to the Catholic faith. Much more might be said concerning this matter, but I will leave it to the reader's better consideration, and proceed to that which is to follow.

CHAPTER X.

OF THE ORNAMENTS BELONGING TO THE PRIEST.

And first of the Amice.

INNOCENT THE THIRD, speaking of the ornaments belonging to the Priest, saith that the vestments of the Evangelical Priest do signify one thing in the Head, to wit, our Saviour, and another in His members. And for as much as both Head and members are understood in the person of the Priest, therefore these ornaments have sometimes relation to the Head and sometimes to the members.

How by the Amice is signified the cloth that hid and covered our Saviour's eyes.

According hereunto, the Priest putting the Amice

before his face, representeth unto us the mockeries which the Son of God sustained, when His sacred eyes were blindfolded and the perfidious Jews buffeted Him on the face saying: *Prophesy unto us, O Christ, who is he that struck Thee?* *

How the Crown of Thorns.

2. The putting the same afterwards upon his head representeth unto us the crown of thorns, which those most wicked ministers planted upon the head of our Blessed Saviour.

How recollection and attention.

3. Morally, the Amice admonisheth, that as the Priest covereth his head and face therewith, so ought we to be very vigilant, during the time of this divine Mystery, that neither our eyes nor understanding be carried away or busied about any vain cogitations.

How fortitude of good works.

4. The spreading of the same abroad upon the Priest's shoulders doth signify the fortitude of good works. For as the shoulders are made strong to perform hard works, so a man, specially a Priest, ought neither to be idle nor faint in working, but to insist and labour painfully in well doing, according to that of the Apostle: *Labour thou as a good soldier of Jesus Christ.*†

How faith.

6. Lastly, the Priest, putting on this ornament,

---

* St. Matthew ch. 26, v. 68.   † 2 Tim. ch. 2, v. 3.

prayeth saying, *Impone, Domine, etc.* Put, O Lord, the helmet of salvation upon my head, that I may overcome all diabolical incursions. So that, by the Amice is also signified faith, which is indeed the first and chiefest thing that a Christian ought to bring, coming to present himself at so great a Sacrament.

CHAPTER XI.

OF THE ALB.

And how by the same is signified the most pure humanity of our blessed Saviour.

THIS garment is called the Alb, of this Latin word *albedo*, whiteness; whereby the precious Humanity of our Saviour is signified unto us, the Which was formed by the Holy Ghost of the most pure substance of the Virgin Mary, which was most pure, that is to say, without all spot of sin, either original or actual.

How the Incarnation.

2. The putting on of the alb over the head of the Priest, wherewith he is all covered, may put us in mind of the Incarnation of our Saviour, in the womb of the Blessed Virgin, according to the words of the angel spoken unto her: *The Holy Ghost shall come upon thee, and the power of the most High shall overshadow thee.**

* St. Luke ch. 1, v. 35.

How the garment of Innocency.

3. Next this garment may signify unto us the garment of Innocency given unto us by Christ in the Sacrament of Baptism, and may put us in mind of the promise made therein to lead continually a pure, holy, and innocent life : Lay away the old man and put on the new man, which according to God is created *in justice.**

How the garment of mockery.

4. It likewise representeth the white garment which Herod put upon our Blessed Saviour, reputing Him for a fool, and so, mocking and deriding Him, sent Him back to Pilate.†

How the garment of glory.

5. It also signifieth the white garment of glory wherewith we shall be gloriously clothed in the Kingdom of Heaven, where we shall shine more bright than the beams of the sun, as saith St. John: I saw a great multitude clothed in white robes.‡

How penance and mortification.

6. Again, this garment admonisheth us, that even as silk or fine cloth getteth that whiteness by often beating or knocking, which it hath not by nature, even so a man, especially a Priest, should by works of Penance and corporal castigations, attain to that sanctity by grace, which he hath not by nature.

* Ephes. ch. 4, v. 22, 24.   † St. Luke ch. 23, v. 11.
‡ Apoc. ch. 7, v. 9.

How spiritual purity.

7. The Priest in putting on this garment prayeth saying, *Dealba me, Domine, etc.* Make me white, O Lord, and cleanse my heart, that I being whitened in the Blood of the Lamb, may enjoy eternal gladness. So that the Alb also by its whiteness representeth spiritual purity and cleanness of soul, which is most requisite in him that is to administer before our Lord.

CHAPTER XII.

OF THE GIRDLE.

And how by the same is signified the indissoluble bond betwixt Christ's Divinity and His Humanity.

By the girdle wherewith the alb is straightly bound and girded together, is signified the indissoluble bond betwixt the Divinity of Christ and His Humanity, Which, after the Incarnation, were never separated, neither according to His body nor according to His soul, notwithstanding that His soul descended into hell,* and His body remained in the sepulchre.

How His undertaking our human frailty.

The girdle, bringing together the ampleness of the alb doth signify, that Christ, as it were, straightened His high and divine conversation, after our manner of understanding, by taking upon Him our human frailty. And even as the alb is not made less by

* Limbo.

the straightness of the girdle, but only infolded within the same, even so the immensity of Christ remained most entire and perfect in Him, although for our example He seemed to straighten and narrow the same.

How the virtue of chastity.

3. This girdle hath three properties; to gird, to bind, and to mortify, betokening the care and circumspection belonging to a Priest, lest the virtue of chastity, which the white garment representeth in him be remissly and negligently guarded. And that therefore as he girdeth the reins of his body, so should he gird and restrain the reins of his mind, which are his thoughts and desires; to which virtue our Saviour Himself exhorteth saying : *Sint lumli vestri præcincti, etc.* Let your loins be girt, etc.*

How fasting and prayer.

4. The two ends of the girdle that are turned in, the one under the right side, the other under the left, do signify the two means requisite to conserve the virtue of chastity, to wit, fasting and prayer; the one to debilitate and subdue the flesh, the other to strengthen and elevate the spirit. *Pray lest ye enter into temptation.*†

How the cords wherewith our Lord was bound to the Pillar.

5. The Priest in taking the girdle, putteth both his hands behind him at his back, whilst he that

* St. Luke ch. 12, v. 35.   † Ibid. ch. 22, v. 40.

serveth giveth the same into them, representing
thereby, how the most innocent Son of God for our
offences had His blessed hands fast bound behind
Him, whilst He was most lamentably whipped and
scourged at the Pillar.

The Prayer.

In putting on the girdle, he prayeth saying,
Præcinge me Domine, etc. Gird me, O Lord, with the
girdle of purity and quench in my loins the humour
of lust, that there may remain in me the virtue of
continency and chastity.

CHAPTER XIII.

OF THE MANIPLE.

*And how by the same is signified persecution for the faith
of Christ.*

1. THE Priest putting the maniple upon his left
arm doth kiss the same, to put us in mind of the
readiness of heart, wherewith we ought willingly
and gladly to suffer persecution for the faith of
Christ, because *Blessed are they that suffer persecution
for justice, for theirs is the kingdom of heaven.**

How the contempt of earthly things.

2. By the putting thereof upon the left arm, we
are admonished that we ought to be strict and
sparing in seeking after earthly things, but free and

* St. Matthew ch. 5, v. 10.

discharged in seeking after heavenly. According to the counsel of our Saviour, saying, *Seek first the kingdom of God and the justice of Him, and all these things shall be given you besides.*

How Christ's humility, combat for justice, and tender affection towards us.

8. According to some others, the maniple put upon the left arm signifieth the humility of Christ in this life. As also His continual combat for justice, according to S. Bonaventure. And because the left arm is nearest to the heart, it may likewise signify the great love and tender affection which our Blessed Lord and Saviour carried towards us.

How sorrow and contrition for sin.

4. The putting of the maniple upon the left arm may likewise put us in mind of sorrow and contrition for our defects. For as sins are committed by sinister actions, so may they be signified by the left arm; and even as in the soul of a sinner there ought to be continual sorrow and grief for his offences committed against the Majesty of Almighty God, so is it also good reason that on his left arm, the Priest who needeth daily to offer sacrifice not only for his own, but also for the sins of the people, should carry some external sign of the internal sorrow, which both he and they ought to have for this occasion; imitating herein St. Peter, whose abundance

* St. Matthew ch. 6, v. 33.

of tears, which issued from his eyes, in the bewailing
of his offences, was so great, that he had marks of
them, like little gutters in his cheeks, and for this
cause continually carried in his hand or bosom, some
napkin wherewith to wipe them away.

How the cords wherewith our Lord was violently bound.

5. The same being applied to the instruments of
our Lord's most holy Passion, most properly representeth the hard, rough, and boisterous cords wherewith He was rudely and cruelly bound, when He was
led from place to place and from one judge to
another.

The Prayer.

The Priest in putting on this maniple prayeth
saying : *Merear Domine portare, etc.* Let me merit,
O Lord, to bear the maniple of weeping and sorrow,
that I may receive the recompence of my labour
with exultation.

CHAPTER XIV.

OF THE STOLE.

And how by the same is signified the yoke of obedience.

By the stole is signified the yoke of obedience,
whereunto our meek Lord submitted Himself for our
salvation. Take up My yoke upon you.* Which
thing the Priest sheweth himself ready to perform by
kissing the same, both when he putteth it on, and

* St. Matthew ch. 11, v. 29.

when he putteth it off; expressing by this ceremony the desire and resignation, wherewith he willingly submitteth himself under the yoke of our Saviour Christ.

How meekness and humility.

2. In that it extendeth or reacheth to the knees, whose office is to bend and bow, it admonisheth us of meekness and humility. *Discite a me quia mitis sum et humilis corde.* Learn of me, because I am meek and humble of heart.*

How perseverance.

3. The stole, by the length thereof, doth put us in mind of the virtue of perseverance; for he that persevereth unto the end, shall be saved.†

How prudence in prosperity, and patience in adversity.

4. It is folded before the breast in form of a cross from the right side to the left, to admonish us that we must use prudence in prosperity, and patience in adversity, and that we be neither puffed up by the one nor dejected by the other.

How the carrying of the Cross.

5. The resting thereof upon the shoulders may put us in mind of the Cross which, with other instruments of the Passion, our Lord was forced to carry to the place of execution, upon His sore and weary shoulders. Or the rope or cord wherewith

---

* St. Matthew ch. 11, v. 29.   † Ibid. ch. 10, v. 22.

they hastily drew and haled Him forwards to the mount of Calvary.

The Prayer.

The Priest in putting on the same prayeth, saying, *Redde mihi, Domine, stolam immortalitatis,* etc. Render unto me, O Lord, the stole of immortality, which I have lost in the prevarication of our first parent, and although I approach unworthily to Thy holy mystery, I may nevertheless deserve to attain everlasting joy and felicity.

CHAPTER XV.

OF THE VESTMENT OR CASULA.

And how by the same is signified and represented the virtue of charity.

1. THIS vestment covereth both the body and all the other habits, and in Latin is called *casula*, of this word *Casa* a house, because it covereth the whole man, like unto another little house: by which is understood the virtue of charity which, as the Apostle sayeth, covereth the multitude of sins.

How charity towards God and our neighbour.

2. This garment being divided into two parts, doth put us in mind of a double or twofold charity. The one towards God, to love Him above all things, the other to our neighbour, to love him as ourselves.

Thou shalt love the Lord thy God from thy whole heart, and with thy whole soul, and thy neighbour as thyself.[*]

How charity to our friends and to our enemies.

3. This garment is large, ample, and open, neither tied nor girded as the other ornaments are, to give us to understand that charity extendeth itself far off, not only in doing good to our friends but also to our very enemies, never ceasing to do well to all persons, whensoever time and occasion is offered. *If you love them who love you, what reward shall you have, do not also the Publicans this?* [†]

How the Church before and after Christ.

4. Likewise the fore part, which is the lesser, representeth the Church before Christ's Passion, and the hinder part, which is the larger and bigger, and hath the Cross on it, signifieth the increase of Christ's Church since His Passion.

How the uniting of the Jews and Gentiles.

5. The uniting thereof above signifieth the uniting of the two people, the Jews and the Gentiles in the confession of one faith, as it was foretold, saying: and there shall be one Pastor and one flock.

How the Vestment of sundry virtues exercised in the Catholic Church.

6. This garment is commonly rich and curiously wrought with gold, insinuating that which the Royal

[*] Deut. ch. 6, v. 5; and Levit. ch. 19, v. 18.
[†] St. Matthew ch. 5, v. 46.

Prophet saith in the Psalm: *Astitit Regina a dextris tuis*. The Queen, to wit, the Church stood upon Thy right hand in a golden vestment, compassed abou with variety.*

How the purple vestment.

7. It likewise representeth the purple vestment wherewith the Jews clothed our Lord in scorn, and divers and sundry ways abused His holy Person.†

How unity, against schism and heresy.

8. This garment of our Lord, the soldiers would not divide, because it was without seam, to foreshow how great an offence it should be in those, who should presume to rend or divide the unity of Christ's Church by schism or heresy.‡

The Prayer.

The Priest in putting on the same prayeth, saying, *Domine qui dixisti*, etc. Lord, Who hast said, My yoke is sweet, and My burthen is light, grant that I may so bear the same that I may obtain Thy grace.

How by the two crosses upon the stole and maniple is signified the crosses of the two thieves, and by that upon the vestment, the Cross of Christ.

And note that upon three of these ornaments belonging to the Priest, there is commonly made the sign of the Cross. Upon the stole and the maniple there is made two little crosses, and the third upon

* Ps. 44.   † St. Matthew ch. 27.
‡ St. Jchn ch. 19, v. 23.

the Vestment, more large than the rest, whereby is signified unto us a double mystery. First, by the two lesser crosses upon the stole and maniple is understood the crosses of the two thieves, who were crucified, one on the left side, and the other on the right side of our Blessed Saviour, and He Himself in the midst, signified by the Cross made upon the vestment which is greater than the other, as His Cross was greater than theirs.

How more perfection in the Priest than other men.

Secondly, by these three crosses is given to understand that the Priest ought to be of much more perfection than other men, and that he should not only bear the Cross of Christ, signified by the Cross on the vestment, and his own cross signified by the cross on the stole, but also his neighbour's cross signified by the cross on the maniple, which he beareth on his left arm.

CHAPTER XVI.

OF THE COMING OF THE PRIEST OUT OF THE VESTRY ATTIRED AND REVESTED WITH HIS HOLY ORNAMENTS.

How the Priest representeth our Blessed Saviour.

By the Priest, as the Doctors say, is understood our Blessed Saviour; by the people, the world; and by the altar, the mount of Calvary whereon He was crucified for our redemption.

*How his coming out of the vestry representeth our
Saviour coming from heaven.*

The Priest, coming forth of the Sacristy thus re-
vested with his holy habits, signifieth our Saviour
coming forth of the bosom of His heavenly Father,
and entering into the world to take our nature upon
Him.

*How his hands joined upon his breast, represent the
affection wherewith our Saviour prayed for us.*

He proceedeth with his hands reverently joined
before his breast, to represent unto us the great devotion and fervent affection wherewith our Saviour
always prayed unto His heavenly Father for us.
Exauditus est pro sua reverentia. He was heard for
His reverence.*

*How his holy vestments represent our Saviour's holy
virtues.*

His holy vestments and ornaments do signify the
holy virtues, graces, and other perfections, which
most gloriously shined in our Saviour. Of Whom it
is written, saying : *And the Word was made Flesh and
dwelt in us, and we saw the glory of Him, the glory as it
were of the only begotten Son of the Father, full of grace
and verity.†*

The diversity of ornaments do not only signify
the diversity of virtues and perfections which were
contained in our Saviour Christ, but also the diver-

---

* Hebrews ch. 5, v. 7.   † St. John ch. 1, v. 14.

sity of pains and torments which He sustained for us, as hath already been declared.

How honour and reverence in those that receive and handle the Body of Christ.

And for as much as Almighty God gave express commandment to the Priests of the ancient law, that they should not approach to His altar to offer unto Him, but first to be washed and invested, not with their profane, but with their holy ornaments, is it not, then, most convenient that the Priests of the new law should be peculiarly adorned, and thereby dispose themselves with much more reverence to handle and touch the most precious Body of our Redeemer and Saviour Jesus, than the old Priests and Prophets did, the flesh of sheep and oxen or the body of a brute beast?

Our Priests, therefore, going to the altar thus apparelled, do set before our eyes our Saviour Jesus as He was at His Passion, and consequently those that scoff at the Priest, thus representing Christ unto us, do nothing else than, with the wicked Jews, scoff and deride at Christ Himself; and even as those Jews put all these ornaments upon our Saviour for despite, and the more to dishonour Him, yet Christ's holy Mother and His blessed Apostles did both love Him and reverence Him so much the more entirely, for enduring such reproaches and shame for our sakes; so these men, now-a-days, whose minds are wholly set against the Catholic Church, will mock, perhaps, at the Priest standing at the altar in such apparel, but, contrariwise, the true Christian and Catholic people do esteem and honour him so much the more, who is, by the ordinance of God, exalted to so high a dignity as to present unto us so great a mystery.

To conclude, Priestly habits, so much offensive to the heretics of our age, were so highly respected by Alexander the Great, although a Paynim and idolater, going to Jerusalem with deliberation to ruin it, that he, withholden by the only sight of the Pontifical vestments of the High Priest, and touched instantly with the fear of God, did cast himself from his horse upon the ground, as it were to crave pardon for his sinister designs, and granted to the city and country of Jewry all the privileges, franchises, and immunities, that possibly they could desire, as witnesseth Josephus.*

CHAPTER XVII.

OF CARRYING THE BOOK BEFORE THE PRIEST.

And how thereby is represented the Annunciation of the Angel before the Incarnation.

THE Priest, proceeding in reverent wise towards the altar, hath one to go before him to bear the book which containeth the glad tidings of our salvation;

* Jos. lib. 11, cap. 8.

signifying by this ceremony that Christ, entering into this world, sent first an Angel before Him to announce the joyful news of His Incarnation. Let him, therefore, who supplieth this place, consider well whose Person he representeth, and let him see that his carriage be conform to so high a calling.

How the same representeth the dignity and verity of the Gospel of Christ.

Also the book of the Gospel is carried before, to signify the dignity and infallible verity of the Gospel of Christ, which is such, that if an Angel should come from heaven and teach unto us other than this, we ought in nowise to believe him.

How a life conform to the Gospel of Christ.

Again, the Gospel carried before and the Priest following after, is to admonish that every Christian, especially a Priest, ought to conform his life and conversation to the Gospel of Christ.

How the Church built upon a rock.

The book brought and laid upon the altar, which is of stone, signifieth that the foundation of the Church of Christ is built upon a rock, against which the gates of hell shall never prevail.*

How the faith first preached to the people of the Jews.

And it is, therefore, first carried to the right end of the altar, to signify that our Saviour came first to

* St. Matthew ch. 16.

the people of the Jews, according to that of the
Apostle. To you it behoveth us first to speak the
word of God, but because you repel it and judge
yourselves unworthy of eternal life, behold we turn
to the Gentiles.*

Why the book is laid upon the altar shut.

And it is laid upon the altar shut until the Priest
come to open the same, to signify that all things
were closed under shadows and figures until the
coming of Christ our Saviour.

The second reason.

Also to signify that Christ was He Who first
revealed the mysteries of holy Scripture to His
Apostles, saying : *To you it is given to know the mystery
of the kingdom of God.*†   And after His resurrection
He opened their understanding, that they might
understand the Scriptures.‡

The reasons why the Priest hath one to help him at Mass.

Lastly, the Priest hath ever one or more to assist
him at Mass, and this for two reasons. The first is
for that he may have great need of help and aid.
He may fall into some inconvenience or sickness, or
some heretic or some enemy may take the Host out
of his hand, as it happened to St. Matthew, who was
killed at the altar. In which case all good Catholics

---

* Acts ch. 13, v. 46.   † St. Luke ch. 8, v. 10.
‡ St. Luke ch. 24.

ought to succour and defend him, even to the shedding of their blood; which danger was ordinary in the Primitive Church under the heathen persecutors, and therefore the Bishops saying Mass were always guarded with deacons.

The second reason.

The second is in respect of the great majesty and reverence due to this holy Sacrifice, which is such, that the greatest personage in the world need think it no disgrace to wait and attend upon a Priest at Mass; and further, to add thereunto all the humble and respective service he is able.

An example to be noted by such as assist at Mass.

And to the end that each one may assist with the greater reverence, I will briefly recite a history, recounted by St. Ambrose, how a child, which attended upon Alexander the Great when he was about to sacrifice to his idols, holding fire unto him, by chance let fall a coal upon his own arm, which he suffered to pierce through his garments, even to his very flesh, rather than he would make any noise, or give occasion by his cry either to distract the Emperor in his sacrifice, or disturb the people in their devotions. With what attention and reverence then, ought a Christian to assist at this dreadful and most holy Sacrifice, and that offered to no false idol but to the only true and everliving God Himself? *

* St. Ambrose, lib. 3, de Virg.

CHAPTER XVIII.

OF THE PRIEST'S DESCENDING FROM THE ALTAR.

And how thereby is represented the expulsion of Adam out of Paradise.

1. THE Priest having placed the chalice upon the altar presently descendeth and standeth below at the foot of the same, representing thereby the little space of time wherein Adam remained in the state of innocency and original justice, and how, for his transgression, he was presently thrust and expelled out of Paradise.

How his wretched estate after his fall.

2. Again, by his standing below at the foot of the altar, humbly bowing his body towards the earth or falling on his knee, is signified the wretched estate of man after his fall, and the heavy displeasure of God conceived against him for his grievous sin.

How the time before the Incarnation.

3. Mystically also it signifieth the time before the Incarnation of the Son of God, Who for a long season, and for the self-same occasion of sin, stood afar off as it were from all mankind, and would not for some thousands of years approach unto him, to take his nature and substance upon Him, or to open the gates of heaven unto him.

How a soul in mortal sin.

4. Also, that God standeth afar off, and is greatly alienated and estranged from every soul in mortal sin.

How the devout publican and St. Peter.

5. It also representeth the devout publican who, entering into the temple to pray, stood afar of, saying : O God, be merciful to me a sinner ; and that of St. Peter : Go from me, O Lord, for I am a sinful man.*

Why the assistants kneel below.

6. Lastly, the people likewise kneel below, to declare the great honour and reverence which they bear to this holy Sacrifice. For God Himself is present to hear the supplications of His Church. And also many angelical spirits are present, most earnestly desiring that our petitions may be heard, and withal the full and entire remission of our sins obtained.

CHAPTER XIX.

OF THE SIGN OF THE HOLY CROSS MADE AT "IN NOMINE PATRIS," AND OF THE MOST EXCELLENT VIRTUES AND MOST DIVINE MYSTERIES CONTAINED IN THE SAME.

1. As the glory of a fair and sumptuous building is viewed and perceived by the forefront thereof, and as the honour cf a well-ordered army is discovered

* St. Luke ch. 18, v. 13 ; ch. 5, v. 8.

in the comely disposition of the foreward of the
battle, even so, gentle reader, mayst thou easily con-
jecture the excellency of this spiritual building, by
the only beauty which thou beholdest in the forefront of the same.

2. And what else may be expected in this venerable representation of the Death and Passion of
our Saviour Jesus, but that our Holy Mother, the
Catholic Church, should first plant in the forefront
of this excellent Sacrifice, the triumphant banner
and most victorious standard of the Cross, the badge
and livery of her Celestial Spouse, the ensign of
heaven, the consolation of earth, the confusion of
hell, and the royal arms and cognizance of our
Redemption?

3. For this holy sign is the tree of life planted in
the midst of Paradise. It is the wood of the ark
which saved Noe and his family from drowning. It
is the banner which Abraham bore, when he went
to deliver his brother Lot from the captivity of his
enemies. It is the wood which Isaac his son carried
upon his shoulders to the place of sacrifice. It is
the ladder whereon Jacob saw the Angels descend
and ascend up to heaven. It is the key of Paradise,
which openeth and no man shutteth, and shutteth
and no man openeth. It is the brazen serpent
which healeth those that are stricken with the
venomous sting of the devil. It is the rod of Moses
wherewith he caused the stony rock to yield forth

streams of refreshing waters. It is the wood which, being cast by our true Eliseus into the waters that were bitter; made them most sweet and pleasant of taste. It is the stone wherewith David struck Goliath on the forehead and presently slew him. And it is the letter *Thau* marked on the foreheads of all the faithful, which keepeth them and preserveth them from all kind of danger.

4. In a word, no mortal tongue is able sufficiently to express the wonderful virtues of this sign ; for it is the staff of the lame, the guide of the blind, the way of them that err, the philosophy of the un-learned, the physician of the sick, and the resurrection of the dead. It is the comfort of the poor, hope in despair, harbour in danger, the blessing of families, the father of orphans, the defence of widows, the judge of innocents, the keeper of little ones, the guard of virginity, the counsellor of the just, the liberty of servants, the bread of the hungry, and the drink of the thirsty. It is the song of the Prophets, the preaching of the Apostles, the glory of Martyrs, the consolation of Confessors, the joy of Priests, and the shield of Princes. It is the foundation of the Church, the benediction of Sacraments, the subversion of idolatry, the death of heresy, the destruction of the proud, the bridle of the rich, the punishment of the wicked, the torment of the damned, and the glory of the saved. No marvel, then, that the Catholic Church hath so highly

honoured this heavenly sign, as to plant it and seat
it in the forefront of this holy Sacrifice, and to
adorn and beautify therewith this heavenly building,
using, as I may call it, no other key but that which
once opened unto us so high a mystery, to open
unto us now again the highest mystery both of
heaven and earth.

OF " IN NOMINE PATRIS," ETC.

*How " In nomine Patris" is a brief theological protestation
against idolatry.*

First it is to be noted, that the highest and most
supereminent honour which any man can possibly
yield unto Almighty God in this life is principally
included in this holy Sacrifice. And as in the
commandments which were given by God Himself,
He first, before all things, put a difference and ex-
ception betwixt His own honour and the honour of
idols, and of all false gods whatsoever ; even so the
Church in this place, beginning in the name of her
sole and only God, doth evidently give to understand that she utterly renounceth all idolatry, and
that neither idol nor any false god whatsoever, neither
man nor Angel, nor any other creature either in
heaven or earth, ought to be served with this honour
of sacrifice save only God Himself.

In nomine.

In the name. In pronouncing these words we say
" in the name," not, in the names, to signify and to

give to understand thereby that we believe one to be the name and nature, one to be the virtue and power, one to be the divinity and majesty of all the three Persons of the Blessed Trinity.

Patris.

Of the Father. For even as little children in the time either of need or danger do presently break forth into no other cry, but to call for the help of father or mother, which cry of theirs is no sooner heard, but it forthwith bringeth them succour and assistance; even so is it to be understood of this voice and invocation, which is so well known and so willingly heard of our heavenly Father, that no sooner is it uttered by us His children, but He doth presently acknowledge it, and speedily hasteneth to our help and succour.

Et Filii.

And of the Son. After the name of the Father we say, "and of the Son." First, because He as willingly both heareth us and helpeth us as the Father doth; secondly, to declare that albeit this be properly the Sacrifice of the Son, yet that He is equal in glory, co-eternal in majesty, and consubstantial in essence, both to the Father and the Holy Ghost.

Et Spiritus Sancti.

And of the Holy Ghost. Here likewise do we invoke and call for the help, aid, and assistance of the Holy Ghost, to signify that He also proceeding from both, and being equal unto Them both in power, essence, and glory, doth concur with Them to the effecting of this holy and heavenly Sacrifice.

Amen.

And this *Amen* is, as it were, a confident and firm assent of our soul, by which we acknowledge the Persons named to be our one and only God, and, that in trust of His aid, we mean to proceed in offering up of this Sacrifice to His eternal glory. Where you see that this petition, being taken according to its most common and usual sense, doth signify the invocation of the aid, grace, and sanctification of God the Father, God the Son, and God the Holy Ghost, to be infused from heaven into the hearts and minds of all the assistants.

CHAPTER XX.

OF THE PSALM, "INTROIBO" AND "CONFITEOR."

And how by the psalm is signified the desire of the Fathers for the coming of Christ.

1. In the words and mysteries of the Holy Mass, two manner of senses are usually understood, the one literal, the other mystical. According hereunto, the Priest always beginneth with certain verses taken out of the Prophets, to signify unto us mystically the unspeakable sighs and fervent desires of Christ, long time promised unto them and long expected of them.

How the desires of all the world.

2. These verses are not rehearsed of one alone, but of all the choir together, to signify the desire of the Church Universal, and that not only the holy Fathers then detained in Limbo, but that all the world was exiled for sin, and stood in need of the grace and mercy of our Saviour Jesus.

How the excitation of their minds who are present at Mass.

3. According to some of our doctors, this psalm is said of all the choir together, that the spirits and minds of all who are present may be awakened thereby, and, that hearing the noise and sound of the voices, they may understand when the Priest first entereth in to the altar of God; like as in the Old Testament the noise and sound of the bells made known the entry of the High Priest into the sanctuary of our Lord.

OF THE CONFITEOR.

And how the same is a protestation that we are sinners.

This Confiteor is a protestation which we make before God that we are all sinners, and that before the Priest either say Mass, or the people hear Mass, to receive true fruit to ourselves thereby, we ought first humbly to demand pardon and forgiveness of all our offences, which we have committed against His divine Majesty.

Why this Confiteor is called General.

1. This Confiteor is called general and that for divers reasons. First, for that it was briefly instituted for venial sins, which are general and common to all, for as much as no man living is so holy and just, who offendeth not God at the least venially. "For," as the Scripture saith, "a just man shall fall seven times." *

The second reason.

2. Again it is called general, for that it is a declaration, which we make in general, without specifying anything in particular: it being impossible for any man to declare in particular all his venial sins, which moved the holy Prophet to say, "Delicta quis intelligit?" etc. Who can understand sins? from my secret ones cleanse me, O Lord! †

The third reason.

3. Also it is called general, for that it may be made generally before all persons, and generally in all places: in the fields, in the house, within and without the Church, wheresoever.

How the Priest in this confession representeth the Person of Jesus Christ.

4. The Priest in this place, in the Person of Jesus Christ, the Lamb without spot, confesseth unto His

---

* Proverbs ch. 24, v. 16.   † Ps. 18, v. 13.

Father, the sins of all the people, for the which He asketh forgiveness of Him: taking them all upon Himself, with desire to satisfy the justice of His Father for them by His death.

How his bowing or inclination representeth our Saviour's humiliation.

5. His bowing or inclination of himself in saying the Confiteor signifieth how Jesus humbled Himself, taking upon Him the form of a servant, that we, who were made the servants and bondslaves of the devil by reason of our sins, might be made the freemen of God our heavenly Father, through the merits of Christ, His only Son.

How both shame and humility.

6. His inclining or bowing his face, in saying the same, is also to insinuate unto us shame and humility, and that we ought to blush and be appalled to do that in the presence of God, which we would be loath to do or commit in the sight of men.

How a conscience clean even from venial sin.

7. And lastly, this confession teacheth, with how great sanctity and purity this most pure and most holy Sacrifice ought to be handled and received of us : in so much, that if it were possible, we should keep ourselves clean even from venial sins. And now to explicate the words themselves.

Confiteor Deo omnipotenti.

I confess unto Almighty God. First we confess to have sinned against God, because sin is defined to be : Something said, done, or desired contrary to the law of Almighty God.

Beatæ Mariæ semper Virgihi.

To Blessed Mary always a Virgin. Next after Almighty God are recited the names of five of His especial Saints, for five special prerogatives wherein these five surpassed and excelled all other Saints : First, to our Blessed Lady the Virgin, because she it is, who next after God, is the first in glory; who, above all other Saints, is the great and general Patroness of all such sinners, as sorrowfully fly unto her for succour; whose only merits God esteemeth above the merits of all men or angels; whom He especially loveth above all the persons that ever He created; who only among all the children of men never committed any manner of sin.

Beato Michaeli Archangelo.

To B. Michael the Archangel. Secondly to such as have had great conquest and victory over sin and Satan : and this was St. Michael the Archangel, who fought against Lucifer for his sin of pride, conquered him, and lastly cast him out of heaven.

Beato Joanni Baptistæ.

To B. John Baptist. Thirdly to such as did both

preach and do great penance for sin; and this was
St. John Baptist, the first preacher of Penance,
in the entry of the New Law, the Precursor of
Christ, a Prophet, yea more than a Prophet, of
whom Truth Itself did testify, that a greater was
not born amongst the sons of women, who above all
other Prophets, merited to demonstrate the Messias
with his finger, to lay his hand upon His venerable
head, and in the river of Jordan to baptise Him.

Sanctis Apostolis Petro.

To the holy Apostles, Peter. Fourthly, to such as had
chief power and authority in the militant Church:
and this was St. Peter, whom our Lord ordained
chief Pastor over the same, and to whom, for this
purpose, He principally gave and committed in
charge the powerful keys of the kingdom of heaven,
that is, power to remit, or retain sin, as testifieth the
Evangelist.*

Et Paulo.

And Paul. Fifthly, to such as greatly laboured to
convert souls unto our Lord: and this was the B.
Apostle, St. Paul, who in the office of preaching,
laboured more than they all to convert the heathen
and unbelievers to the faith and knowledge of our
Saviour Christ. In which five prerogatives, these
five were most notable patterns, far surpassing all
other Saints.

* St. Matthew ch. 16, v. 19.

Why we jointly confess unto St. Peter and St. Paul.

And therefore do we always jointly confess unto these two Saints together. First, because these two with their blood first founded that invincible Rock, the Church of Rome. Secondly, because that these two Princes of the Church, as in their lives they loved one another most entirely, even so in their deaths they were not separated.

Omnibus Sanctis.

To all Saints. Next we confess to all Saints in general, because it is impossible for us to displease God, but that we must also displease His Saints, by reason of the perfect union that is betwixt them. And further, because God doth use to pardon sins at the intercession and for the merits of His holy Saints, as witnesseth Job.*

Of knocking our breast at Meâ culpâ.

1. In bewailing our sins we knock our breasts three several times, saying these words, "Meâ culpâ. Wherein three things may aptly be observed; the stroke, the sound, and the feeling; to signify three things very requisite unto perfect penance: to wit, contrition of heart, signified by the stroke, confession of mouth, signified by the sound, and satisfaction of work, signified by the hurt or feeling.

2. We knock or smite our breasts to show thereby that we are truly and inwardly sorry, and that we

* Job ch. 5.

could find in our hearts to be revenged of ourselves for our offences.

3. Thereby to make our hard and stony hearts more soft by often beating and knocking.

4. Therefore we now strike them in ourselves, that God may not strike them in us hereafter.

5. And lastly, we knock our breast after the example of the devout publican, who knocked his breast, saying: God be merciful to me a sinner; that so we may depart justified to our own houses.*

Of the ancient practice of the repeating the Confiteor before Mass.

The practice of Confession before Mass is and ever hath been very ancient in the Catholic Church, as appeareth out of Micrologus, who plainly testifieth that Confession was always made at Mass. And the Mass of St. James the Apostle beginneth from Confession. †

CHAPTER XXI.

OF THE PRAYER WHICH FOLLOWETH, COMMONLY CALLED THE ABSOLUTION.

THE Priest having humbly acknowledged himself before the whole congregation to have offended Almighty God, and to be a wretched sinner, the people, the more to move the mercy of our Lord

* St. Luke ch. 18, v. 13.
† Azor. lib. 10, Instit. Moral. p. 1634.

towards him, heartily pray unto God for him, that He would favourably extend His mercy towards him, whom they have chosen at this present, with joint consent to speak unto His majesty in their behalfs, saying *Misereatur*, etc.

Why this absolution was ordained.

This absolution was ordained to shew that the Priest is specially ordained of God to make intercession for the sins of the people. And as the Confession going before was called general, so this absolution following is also general. Which the Priest giveth only by way of Prayer and not of a Sacrament, as that of *Ego te absolvo*, and extendeth itself no further but to the taking away of venial sins.

Why the sign of the Cross is joined with the Absolution.

The sign of the Cross is joined with this absolution, which being made from the head to the heart, and from the left shoulder to the right, may signify the three ways how we offend Almighty God, to wit, by thought, word, and work, but doth chiefly shew that all forgiveness of sin proceedeth from the Passion of our Blessed Saviour.

Of Dominus vobiscum.

Our Lord be with you. This salutation is seven sundry times rehearsed in the Holy Mass.

1. Before the first *Oremus*, which is this. 2. Before the first collects. 3. Before the reading of the

Gospel. 4. After the Creed, or, if the Creed be omitted, before the Offertory. 5. Before the Preface. 6. Before the kissing of the Pax. 7. Before the last Collects : to signify, as some of our devout interpreters say, the sevenfold gift of the Holy Ghost. Which very words with those which follow, St. Paul himself used to Timothy, saying : *Dominus Jesus Christus sit cum spiritu tuo.* Our Lord Jesus Christ be with thy spirit.*

How the words " Dominus vobiscum " are words of admiration.

And they may here be likewise understood as words of admonition, used by the Priest to the people. As if he should say : See that our Lord be with you.

How they are words of consolation.

They may be also taken for words of consolation ; as if he should say unto them : Our Lord dwelleth in you, giving effect to your demands, that with the help of His grace, and by perseverance in the same, you may attain at the last to the happy reward of everlasting life.

Et spiritu tuo.

And with thy spirit. It standeth with great reason that the people should likewise pray for him, and wish that our Lord be with his spirit, who is their speaker and embassador in so important and weighty an affair : which embassage they know he cannot

* 2 Tim. ch. 4, v. 22.

rightly perform, if his mind be otherwise distracted, and be not specially assisted by the grace of God. And for this cause do they often pray that our Lord may be and remain with his spirit.

CHAPTER XXII.

OF THE PRIEST'S ASCENDING TO THE ALTAR.

As before we said that by the descending of the Priest from the altar was understood the fall of man, and the loss of God's favour for his transgression, even so, by his ascending at this present may be understood the accomplishment of the promise of our Lord for his restoring and salvation, according to that of the Apostle, saying: When the fulness of time came, God sent His Son.*

Of Kissing the Altar, and of sundry reasons for the same.

1. The Priest, having finished the prayer aforesaid, approaching the altar, kisseth the same, which he doth in sign of honour and reverence, and in respect, the thing itself is holy, as being sanctified by the Word of God and prayer.†

The second reason.

2. In respect of the precious Body of our Lord

* Gal. ch. 4, v. 4.   † 1 Tim. ch. 4, v. 5.

and Saviour Jesus, Which doth greatly sanctify whatsoever It toucheth.

The third reason.

3. In respect of the Saints' reliques which repose under the same; for never is there altar consecrated without some reliques of Saints, which are put underneath the great stone of the altar within some little vessel, which for this cause is called the sepulchre.*

The fourth reason.

4. Also by this kiss is signified how Christ by His coming hath espoused Holy Church unto Him, according to that of the Canticles,† and that of the Ephesians : ‡ so Christ loved His Church, that He gave Himself for her. For, as a kiss joineth mouth to mouth, so in Christ the Humanity was not only united to the Divinity, but also the Spouse, the Church, was coupled to her Spouse, Christ.

The fifth reason.

5. This kiss also doth signify peace, according to that of the Apostle : Salute one another with a holy kiss, and the God of peace be with you all.

The sixth reason.

6. St. Augustine saith that to kiss the altar is a sign of Catholic communion and unity.

* Concil. Carth. v. cap. 15.　† Cant. ch. 1, v. 1.
‡ Ephes. ch. 5, v. 25.

The seventh reason.

7. Lastly, it admonisheth that at this present, we are to kill all hatred and malice in us towards all persons, be in charity with them, and especially to pray for them. For whosoever is not in perfect charity is not fit to be present at this Holy Sacrifice.

By all which sufficiently appeareth how ancient this ceremony is, and what causes and reasons there are both for the institution and practice of the same. Now besides the performance of this pious ceremony, he jointly with the same reciteth the prayer and petition which ensueth, saying,

Oramus te, Domine, per merita sanctorum tuorum.

We beseech Thee, O Lord, by the merits of Thy Saints. Graces and favours are many times conferred, not only at the request of one friend to another, but many times at the request of a friend to a very enemy. Man, therefore, being become the enemy of God through his sin, interposeth the best beloved friends of our Lord for his intercessors and mediators.

Of the Introit of the Mass, and of sundry pious mysteries to be considered in the same.

The Priest having recommended the people to God by his prayers, and the people, the Priest, he goeth up to the midst of the altar, as we said before, kisseth the same, then turneth him to the right hand of the altar, where the missal is laid, and then beginneth the Introit of the Mass.

How the right end of the altar signifieth the state of innocency.

The right end of the altar, whereunto the Priest addresseth himself, signifieth the life and state of innocency, which our first father Adam lost by his sin, and, consequently, all we his children through his transgression.

How the first going thereto, our Saviour's going first to the Jews.

The going of the Priest first to the right hand or end of the altar signifieth that Christ, Who was promised from the beginning, coming into the world, went first to the people of the Jews before to the Gentiles. For the Jews, by reason of the law, were then on the right hand, and the Gentiles, by reason of their idolatry, on the left.

Of the signification of the word " Introit."

The word "Introit" is borrowed of the Latins, as those that are but meanly learned cannot but know, and signifieth with us a "going in," "an entrance," "beginning" or "prœmium." And for as much as all those who treat of these mysteries do commonly appoint the Sacrifice of the Mass to begin at this place, and for that at this time, the Priest maketh his first entrance unto the altar, and not before, therefore for the proper affinity of the word with the action of the Priest, it is aptly called by the name of Introit. In which sense, both Rabanus and Conradus * and others expound the same.

How the Introit signifieth mystically an earnest desire for the coming of Christ.

This Introit mystically signifieth the earnest desire of the people of all ages for the coming of Christ, which desire He Himself afterwards witnessed, saying : Abraham your father rejoiced that he might see My day, and he saw and was glad.†

How the double repetition signifieth the greatness of the necessity and the fervour of the desire.

The double repetition thereof signifieth the greatness of the necessity and the fervour of the desire, together with the great joy and exultation which was in the world, when He afterwards came Himself in person.

The Gloria Patri, an humble thanksgiving.

The Gloria Patri, which is annexed unto the same Introit, is a most humble and hearty thanksgiving unto the Blessed Trinity for so singular a benefit bestowed upon us.

The Introit of the Mass confirmed by miracle.

Almaricus, Bishop of Treves, testifieth of a miracle, which Almighty God showed in approbation of this part of the Mass. Who writeth, that he heard sung

---

* Lib Ceremoniarum.   † St. John ch. 8, v. 56.

by the holy Angels, for the Introit of the Mass upon the feast of the Epiphany in the Church of St. Sophia, at Constantinople, the 94th Psalm, " Venite exultemus," *etc.**

CHAPTER XXIII.

OF " KYRIE ELEISON " AND OF SUNDRY MYSTERIES TO BE CONSIDERED IN THE SAME.

Three sorts of languages used in the Mass, and what is signified by the same.

IN the holy Mass have long time been used three sorts of languages, sanctified on the Cross of our Saviour Jesus, to wit, Hebrew, Greek and Latin. Of Hebrew these words following, *Amen, Alleluia, Cherubin, Seraphin, Hosanna, Sabbaoth.* Of Greek, *Kyrie eleison, Christe eleison.* Of Latin, all the residue of the Mass, as being the most universal tongue in the West Church. Which three languages represent the title, which was fastened on the Cross of our Saviour, written in Hebrew, Greek, and Latin.

Kyrie eleison, Christe eleison.

Kyrie eleison are two Greek words which signify in Latin *Domine miserere,* Lord have mercy, and *Christe eleison,* Christ have mercy.

* Fortunatus, de Ord. Antiph. cap. 21.

Why Kyrie eleison is nine times repeated.

These devout petitions are nine times repeated, to put us in mind of nine sorts of sins, wherewith we offend Almighty God. The first three by original, mortal, and venial. The second three by thoughts, words, and deeds. The third three by frailty, ignorance, and malice, and particularly in the last three. Wherefore for our sins of frailty we address our prayer to the Father, saying, *Kyrie eleison.* For our sins of ignorance to the Son, saying, *Christe eleison.* And for our sins of malice to the Holy Ghost, saying, *Kyrie eleison.*

The second reason.

Again, these words are nine times rehearsed, to signify the fervent desires of all mankind for the coming of Christ, by Whose coming he should be associated to the nine orders of Angels : which our Lord Himself doth describe by the ninety and nine sheep which He left, to seek out the one lost sheep which was man, to restore him unto His ninety and nine, that is, to the nine orders of Angels.

Why we say Kyrie eleison both to the Father and the Holy Ghost, and not to the Son.

To the Father and the Holy Ghost we say Kyrie eleison, and to the Son, Christe eleison. For the which Innocentius the Third giveth this reason. If you will ask me why we say not to the Son, Kyrie eleison, as well as to the Father and the Holy Ghost; there is but one, and the self-same nature, that is to say, only Divine: but in the Son there is a double nature, to wit, both Divine and human; for that He is both perfect God, and perfect Man, and so is neither the Father nor the Holy Ghost.*

Kyrie eleison confirmed by miracle.

I cannot here let pass to speak of the great and wonderful virtue of these words. St. Basil, by the pronunciation of these words, caused the doors of a Church, which were shut against him, to open of their own accord. And St. Germanus, at the cry of these words, put five Kings to flight. St. Basil, taking unto him a man, which had given himself to the Devil, by a writing under his own hand, which the Devil would in nowise restore, commanded a number of devout people and Religious persons present to lift up their hands to heaven with him, and to cry without ceasing, Kyrie eleison, Christe eleison, Kyrie eleison; which the people performing with many devout tears, in the sight of all that were present, the Devil perforce let fall the self-same writing out of the air into the hands of the holy Bishop.† And these holy words have always been used and highly esteemed amongst devout Christians, as words of singular force and virtue to chase away the Devil,

* Lib. Secundo, de Myster. Miss. cap. 19.
† In Vita St. Basilii.

7 *

and all other malignant spirits that would annoy them.

To conclude, this sacred Canticle is very ancient, as the liturgies of blessed St. James the Apostle, St. Basil, and St. Chrysostom, do make manifest mention; and by the Council of Vase * was brought in the custom to sing the same at Mass, Matins, and Evensong, which Council was holden about twenty-five years before St. Gregory the Great.

CHAPTER XXIV.

OF THE CANTICLE CALLED " GLORIA IN EXCELSIS DEO."

Three hymns in the Mass first invented by the Angels.

THIS Canticle is commonly called *Hymnus Angelicus*, the angelical hymn, as also Alleluia and Sanctus, because the first invention came from the Angels, who have given us example to laud and praise our Lord in this manner. Whereunto accordeth Rupertus saying : This hymn the Church hath taken from the mouth of Angels.

But this is more manifest by the Scripture itself, for we read in St. Luke, that an Angel with a great light appeared to the shepherds, as they were feeding their flocks, and brought unto them tidings that the Saviour of the world was newly born, saying : Behold I evangelize unto you great joy, that shall be unto all

* A D. 529.

people, because this day is born to you a Saviour. And suddenly there was with the Angel a multitude of the heavenly army praising God and saying: Gloria in excelsis Deo, etc.*

Gloria in excelsis, etc., partly composed by men, and partly by Angels. This spiritual hymn consisteth of two parts, the first whereof, as before is said, was composed by the Angels unto these words, *Laudamus te,* etc. Which other words, with the verses subsequent, are said by some to be the words of St. Hilary, Bishop of Poictiers. Some report that he brought them at the return of his exile out of Greece, as namely, Alcuinus.† Others, that it was received into the Church by the institution of the Apostles.‡

Why this hymn is omitted on the Feast of Innocents.

This hymn, as also Alleluia, is omitted upon the Feast of Innocents, to represent the sorrowful mourning for the murder and barbarous cruelty of King Herod, thinking, in killing the infants, to have destroyed and slaughtered our Lord and Saviour.

Why in Septuagesima and Lent.

In Septuagesima likewise, and until Easter, this Canticle is omitted, because then is represented in the Church, the time of Penance, to wit, this life, wherein we cannot participate of the joys of Angels,

* S. Luke, ch. 2, v. 9 to 14.
† Lib. de Divinis Officiis, cap. de Celeb. Miss.
‡ Durand, lib. 4, cap. 13, num. 4.

but are to lament and deplore the miserable estate of our ruin and fall.

Why in the Masses for the dead.

Likewise it is omitted in all Masses for the dead, because, as Almaricus Fortunatus very well noteth, all canticles of joy ought to cease in this Office, which is an Office of tears and lamentations.*

Why this Canticle was first composed and placed in the Mass.

This joyful Canticle, wherein are set forth the ample praises of Jesus Christ, the holy Fathers of the Church first placed in the Mass, to the end to refute and confound the wicked Arians, who had composed sundry ballets and songs to diminish the glory of our Blessed Saviour. For which cause, the aforesaid Fathers by a holy zeal were incited to compose a contrary Canticle, wherein should evidently be set forth the honourable titles and excellences of the same Saviour, by the which, publicly in the Mass, those Arian heretics might be confounded.

Why the Priest standeth before the midst of the altar rehearsing this hymn.

The Priest, in rehearsing this hymn, standeth before the midst of the altar, to signify thereby that Christ is the Mediator betwixt God and man. As also to declare, that it was first pronounced in the

* Lib. 8. de Eccles. Offic. cap. 41.

honour of Him Who is, as it were, in the midst of the Trinity.

Of the lifting up of the hands of the Priest towards heaven.

Standing in the midst of the altar, together with the pronunciation of the words of this Canticle, he devoutly lifteth both his hands to heaven, and then drawing them reverently down, with cheerful voice pursueth on the rest of this angelical hymn, signifying thereby, the ineffable joy which came from above unto men, by the birth and nativity of our Blessed Saviour.

Of the word Amen after Gloria in excelsis.

This word *Amen* is a Hebrew word, wherewith the people make answer at every prayer and benediction of the Priest, and is as much to say, as verily, faithfully, or so be it.   See Rabanus.*

2. Neither is it the custom of the Greeks or Latins to translate this word into their vulgar tongue, no more than Alleluia and other words, which, for their holy authority and the antiquity of the proper tongue, have been religiously observed by the Apostles themselves.

3. And so sacred is this word, that St. John reporteth to have heard the same in heaven.†
Therefore let us not attempt to say it otherwise

* De Institutione Cler. lib. 1, cap. 33.
† Apoc. ch. 19, v. 4.

in earth than it is said in heaven, for that were not only to correct the Church in earth in her doings, but to correct those in heaven also in theirs.

Of the kiss of the altar after Gloria in excelsis.

At the end of this angelical hymn, the Priest boweth him down and kisseth the altar, which he doth in the celebration of the Mass nine several times, and that not without a special mystery. For this kiss is a sign of peace, the which, in this holy hymn, was first announced by the embassage of Angels. The Priest, therefore, in using the same nine several times, insinuateth hereby, that he desireth to be joined and united to the nine orders of Angels, as also, that they would assist him to present his prayers and oblations to Almighty God. Finally, most authors do both agree and confess, that the antiquity of this part of the Mass is deduced at the least from Telesphorus Pope, who lived nigh 1,500 years agone. See Walfridus in Libro de rebus Ecclesiasticis, p. 22; Rupertus, Amalaricus, Rabanus, Berno, and Innocentius tertius.

CHAPTER XXV.

OF THE TURNING OF THE PRIEST TO THE PEOPLE AT "DOMINUS VOBISCUM," AND OF SUNDRY REASONS CONCERNING THE SAME.

The Priest turneth him on the right hand to salute the people, and on the same returneth again unto the altar, all which is not void of singular mystery and signification.

How the Priest's turning on the right hand signifieth an upright intention.

1. First, therefore, it may signify, that the Priest is to have a straight and upright intention to heaven, both for himself and for the people, which is aptly understood by the right hand.

2. Secondly, we also who are present, are hereby premonished, to lift up our hearts to Him Who sitteth on the right hand of His Father, according as we confess in the article of our Creed.

Dominus robiscum.

Our Lord be with you. Having turned himself to the people, he saluteth them, saying : *Dominus vobis- cum,* Our Lord be with you : which he sayeth, that he may conjoin and link the minds of the people to Almighty God, and to make them more attent to His Divine service.

What is meant by extending his arms.

And note, that together with the prolation of the words, he spreadeth and openeth his arms, to signify thereby, how Christ hath His arms always open, and ready to receive those that are truly penitent and do fly unto Him.

Et cum spiritu tuo.

And with thy spirit. In which words the people pray, that with the spirit of man, the Spirit of God

may be present to teach and direct him, without
Whose assistance we can do nothing acceptable to
Him, as Himself hath witnessed by His Apostle,
saying: Without Me you can do nothing.   So that
the answer of the people is wholly to be referred to
the action of the Priest, to wit, to the oblation
which he proposeth to make in their behalf.

*Why after this, the Priest turneth him again to the right
hand of the altar.*

The people having answered *Et cum spiritu tuo*,
the Priest turneth him again to the right hand of the
altar, expressing thereby how our Saviour did not
immediately forsake the Jews for their obstinacy,
but often turned to them, to have turned them to
Him.   As also that we His children should do the
like to our brethren, when at any time they offend
or trespass against us.

The use of this salutation is very ancient in the
holy Mass, as plainly appeareth by the Council of
Vase, and the liturgies of St. James, St. Basil, and
St. Chrysostom.

Of Oremus, and how it signifieth distrust in ourselves.

Let us pray.   The priest, distrusting as it were, in
his own strength, gathereth unto him the prayers of
all the people, saying : Oremus, as if he should say,
assist me with your prayers.   For certain it is that
our merciful Lord will not deny to a multitude their
petitions, Who hath promised to hear the prayers of

two or three that are gathered together in His Name.*

How that our Saviour both prayed Himself, and exhorted others also to pray.

He pronounceth this word *Oremus* with a high voice, to stir up and provoke others to pray and prayeth himself also; for so our Saviour both exhorted His disciples to pray and likewise prayed Himself also.

How elevation of heart in time of prayer.

In saying *Oremus*, he lifteth up hands, to put us in mind that our hearts should be elevated in the time of prayer. For as we read in the 17th chapter of Exodus, whilst Israel fought with Amalech, Moses ascended upon a mountain, and when he lifted up his hands, Israel overcame; but if he slacked or withdrew them, Amalech overcame. Wherein the Priest ought to imitate that holy Moses, to obtain the victory against those invisible Amalechites, the devils.

CHAPTER XXVI.

OF THE FIRST COLLECTS, AND OF SUNDRY REASONS CONCERNING THE SAME.

THE first prayers, which the Priest offereth up to God in the Mass, are commonly called by the name of

* St. Matthew ch. 18, v. 20.

Collects, which is a word borrowed of the Latins, as the learned do very well know, and signifieth a gathering or collection, which, as it may be made of divers and sundry things, so hath it sundry significations.

1. Sometimes it signifieth a collection which is made of tributes and duties to be paid to the Prince; whereof it cometh, that the gatherers thereof are called Collectors.

2. Sometimes it is taken for the collection, which is wont to be made in the Church for the poor, as the 1st Corinthians : *De collectis autem quæ fiunt in Sanctis*, etc. And as touching the collections which are made for the Saints : and again presently after, *Ne cum venero tunc collectæ fiant*. Lest when I come, then collections be made.*

3. Both the Holy Scripture and the ancient Fathers do use this word Collect, to signify an assembly of the people of God, and yet not every manner of assembly, but only of such as are great and solemn, as Leviticus : *Est enim cœtus atque collectæ*. For it is a day of meeting and assembly.† And in Deuteronomy, *Quia collecta est Domini Dei tui*. Because it is the assembly of the Lord thy God.‡ And in the second of Paralipomenon, *Fecitque (Salomon) die octavo collectam*. And Solomon made a collection upon the eighth day. §

* 1 Cor. ch. 16.   † Levit. ch. 23, v. 36.
‡ Deut. ch. 16, v. 8.   § 2 Paralipomenon ch. 7.

So that by this, which hath been already said, it is not hard to understand why the first prayers in the Mass are called Collects; the which Durandus explicateth, saying: Collects properly are prayers, which are so called, for they are said upon the people assembled.*

The second reason.

Again, they may be called Collects, by reason that they are certain brief collections of all the prayers, requests, and supplications of the people of our Lord, which the Priest, who is the speaker for the people, doth collect and gather in one, to present and offer them up to God in their behalf.

The third reason.

And again, they are called Collects, to signify that it is not enough for those who intend to offer up prayers acceptable to God, to be assembled in the self-same place bodily, but that they ought principally to have their hearts united together by perfect love and charity, and to be recollected spiritually. For nothing is more contrary to perfect prayer, than is division or distraction of spirit.

The fourth reason.

As touching the institution of the Collects, it is principally for these purposes, to wit, either in respect of the time wherein they are recited, or of the necessity of the persons for whom they are recited.

* Lib. 4, ch. 15.

Such for example are those, for the most part, of Advent, wherein is desired of God that the coming of Christ our Saviour into the world may be to our salvation. And likewise those in Lent, wherein we pray, that our fasting and abstinence may be profitable unto us, and meritorious for the satisfaction of our sins. Also sometimes they are made for certain persons in particular, as for the Pope, for the Bishop, for the Prince, etc.

The fifth reason.

The matter itself and subject of the Collects is commonly taken out of the Holy Scriptures. As for example, that of the three children, which is recited very often, and namely in the Masses of all the Saturdays, of the four times of the year, and is taken out of the third chapter of the Prophet Daniel; which Collect beginneth as followeth: *Deus qui tribus pueris*, etc. O God, Which to the three children didst mitigate the flames of fire, grant mercifully that we Thy servants be not burned with the flames of our vices, etc. Where you see that this Collect is founded upon that wonderful miracle, which our Lord wrought, in assuaging the flames of the fiery furnace, in the favour and conservation of those His faithful servants; by occasion whereof, we beseech our Lord to assuage in us the flames of our vices and sinful concupiscences.

Likewise that of Sexagesima Sunday is in a

manner the same, wherein the Church taketh occasion to pray unto God, that He would deliver us from all adversity by the help and protection of Blessed St. Paul, whom He graciously preserved from so many perils, saying, *Deus qui conspicis*, etc. O God, Who seest that we do in no wise put our trust in our own actions, grant mercifully, that by the protection of the Doctor of the Gentiles, we may be defended against all adversities, Amen. Sometimes they are taken out of the lives and examples of the holy Saints whose feasts are celebrated. As that on the Feast of Blessed St. Laurence, saying, *Da nobis quæsumus*, etc. Grant us we beseech Thee, O Almighty God, to quench in us the flames of our vices, Who grantedst to St. Laurence to overcome the flames of his torments. And in the self-same manner of divers others.

The sixth reason.

Concerning the different number of Collects, the Church practiseth two or three several things. The first is, that she ordinarily useth disparity of number, either of one alone, or of three, or of five, or else of seven at the most; not for superstition, as heretics do suppose, but for signification and instruction, as shall further appear.

How one, to signify one God and one Faith.

She useth one alone, *propter Sacramentum unitatis*, for the Sacrament of unity, as saith Innocentius III., to signify thereby the unity of God in Whom we believe; as also the unity of faith which we profess, according to that of the Apostle, one God, one faith, one baptism.*

How three for the mystery of the Trinity.

She useth three to signify the mystery of the Blessed Trinity, and in the honour of the three Persons. And after the example of our Saviour, Who prayed three times in the garden.

How five in the honour of the five wounds.

She useth five in honour and memory of the five wounds of our Saviour Jesus, which is a mystery that Christians ought always to have in singular commendation.

How seven in honour of the seven gifts of the Holy Ghost.

And she useth seven to represent unto us the seven gifts of the Holy Ghost; and to conform her proceedings herein to our Blessed Saviour's, Who, teaching His disciples how to pray, comprised all things necessary in seven petitions.

Lastly, these Collects ought to be short, and to comprehend briefly that which we may lawfully desire, hope, and demand, at the merciful hands of Almighty God. They ought also to be pronounced with such humility, attention, reverence, modesty of countenance, and comportment of body, that the assistants may both be edified and made attentive thereby. For he that should pray otherwise, loosely

* Ephes. ch. 4, v. 5.

and swiftly, with the only motion of his lips, should make his prayers barren and unfruitful before God.

Of the conclusion of the Collects, and of sundry reasons concerning the same.

First, all the prayers in the Mass are commonly begun in the Name of the Father, and concluded in the Name of the Son ; the Church having conformed herself in this point to the doctrine of our Saviour Himself, saying : Whatsoever you shall ask the Father in My Name, He will give it you.*

Per Dominum nostrum.

Through our Lord. The Priest, as we have said, concluding the Collects, demandeth all things to be given of our heavenly Father in the Name and for the love of Jesus Christ His Son, our Lord ; because it is He in Whom the Father is well pleased, and to Whom He can deny nothing, for as much as He always accomplisheth His will and pleasure.†

Jesum Christum.

Jesus Christ. At which words the Priest boweth or inclineth himself. For although there be many other honourable names and titles belonging to our Lord, yet at none of these do we bow ourselves ; the reason whereof is, because those names shew what He is in Himself, but this name of Jesus, specially declareth what He is made unto us, to wit, our

* St. John ch. 16, v. 23.   † St. John ch. 6, v. 38.

8

Saviour; for what else is Jesus, as St. Bernard saith, but a Saviour?

Filium tuum.

Thy Son. Thine indeed, neither by grace nor election of creature, but by propriety of kind and verity of substance. Thine truly, not by adoption like unto another, but truly natural, like unto none other.

Qui tecum vivit et regnat, in unitate Spiritus Sancti Deus, etc.   -

Who liveth and reigneth with Thee, in the unity of the Holy Ghost, God, etc. In which words, the Priest admonisheth the people to believe that the Son of God liveth and reigneth for ever without beginning or ending, and is of the same substance and equal power, together with the Father and the Holy Ghost.

Of the word Amen, and of sundry things to be considered in the same.

This word, *Amen,* is very commonly to be read and seen in sundry places of Holy Scripture, as Deuteronomy: * Cursed is he which abideth not in the words of this law, nor doth them in work: and all the people shall say: *Amen.* Also in Tobias, when Gabelus had said the benediction, all answered: *Amen.*†

How Amen signifieth truth or verity.

Sometimes it signifieth the truth or verity of a thing; so Christ answering in the Gospel said: *Amen,*

* Deuteronomy ch. 27.   † Tobias ch. 9.

Amen, that is, *Veritatem dico vobis*, I say the truth
unto you. Wherefore when the Priest concludeth
the Collects, saying : *Who liveth and reigneth with Thee,
God world without end*, the people, to declare that they
do truly and firmly believe the same, answer : *Amen* ;
as if they should say, we do truly, steadfastly, and
verily believe even as thou sayest, of the Son of
God.

What is usually signified by Amen.

·But the most common and usual signification
thereof in all the petitions of the Mass is, that what
the Priest hath faithfully demanded of Almighty
God, we hope undoubtedly shall be given unto us
and truly accomplished in effect.

Why Amen is rehearsed by the people.

And sith in those things which appertain to God,
the people have the Priest as their ambassador, or
speaker, therefore in the end of all his prayers they
give their consent to his demands, saying : *Amen*.
And for this cause it is that all the prayers which
are made by the Priest, although sometimes some of
them be recited in private and silence, yet are they
concluded openly and in the hearing of all the
assistants.

Amen one of the names of Almighty God.

Finally, for the greater honour of this most holy
and sacred word, St. John affirmeth that it is one of
the names of Almighty God, saying: *Thus saith Amen,*

8 *

*the faithful and true Witness.** And so highly doth
St. Augustine honour the same, that he saith it is not
lawful to translate it into any other language.†

CHAPTER XXVII.

OF THE EPISTLE.

And first of the etymology and signification of the word.

FIRST, the word Epistle is a word borrowed of the
Greek word, *Epistellein*, which signifieth, to send
betwixt, as Epistles or letters, which are a speech of
one present to one that is absent. Such was the
Epistle of St. Paul, wherein he saith : I adjure you
by our Lord that this Epistle be read to all the holy
brethren.‡

*The reading of the Epistle representeth the reading of our
Saviour in the Synagogue.*

He which readeth the Epistle, standing upright,
pronounceth the same, the book being open. Because
according to the Evangelist St. Luke,§ Jesus came
to Nazareth where He was brought up, and He
entered according to His custom on the Sabbath day
into the Synagogue, and He rose up to read ; and
the book of Isaias the prophet was delivered unto
Him. And as He unfolded the book, He found the
place where it was written : The Spirit of the Lord

* Apoch. ch. 3, v. 14.   † Tract. 41 in Joan.
‡ 1 Thess. ch. 5, v. 27.   § St. Luke ch. 4, v. 16.

is upon Me, for which the Lord hath anointed Me: to evangelise unto the poor He sent Me.* And when He had folded the book, He rendered it to the minister.

Why the Epistle is read next after the Collect or Prayer.

The Epistle is presently read after the Collect or Prayer, to give us to understand that without humble prayer first made unto Almighty God, never can we read anything to the profit or benefit of our souls.

Why only the Scripture is read in the time of Mass.

Never hath the Church permitted that the lives of any Saints, nor the tracts of any Doctors, how learned or holy soever they were, be read in the office of the Mass, but only the most Holy Scriptures themselves, either of the law, of the Prophets, of the Evangelists, or of the writings or epistles of the Apostles; to signify that this holy Sacrifice doth represent unto us the life of the Saints of all Saints, our sole Redeemer and Saviour Jesus.

Why none of the Old Testament is read upon Sundays.

Never also upon Sundays is read in the Mass any part of the Old Testament, but only of the New, to signify that we are now under the law of grace, which, after the resurrection of our Lord, mystically represented by the Sunday, was publicly preached throughout the world. As also to condemn hereby

* Isaias ch 61, v. 1.

the error of the Jews, who maintain that the law of Moses should remain for ever.

Why the Epistle is always read on the right hand of the Altar.

The Epistle is always read on the right side of the altar, to signify, as often hath already been said, that our Saviour came first to the people of the Jews, who were said to be on the right hand, according to that of the Apostle saying : To you it behoved first to preach the gospel of the kingdom.*

Why the Epistle is read before the Gospel.

And it is read before the Gospel, to declare that all the predictions of the Prophets did only tend to this, to guide and lead men to the true light and understanding of the Gospel of Christ, as also to signify the office of St. John Baptist, who went before the face of our Lord to prepare His ways, as himself testifieth, saying : I am the voice of a crier in the wilderness, make straight the way of the Lord.†
And the Apostles, likewise, were sent before our Saviour into every town and city where Himself was to go.

Why the people sit at the reading of the Epistle.

All the people are permitted to sit at the reading of the Epistle, to signify the imperfection of the old law and the great difference betwixt it and the dignity of the new. And further to declare, that we reserve

* Acts ch. 13, v. 46.   † St. John ch. 1, v. 23.

our greatest and chiefest reverence for the reading
of the Gospel.

The different voices used in pronouncing the Old and New Testament.

But this is much more lively expressed in a High
Mass, by the difference of voices which is used in
pronouncing the Old and New Testament; for the
one is pronounced with a heavy and low voice, but
the other with a cheerful and high voice, which is
done to signify the different estate of the Church
under the two Testaments. For under the old, she
was in servitude and bondage, understood by the low
and heavy voice, but under the new, in freedom and
liberty, understood by the cheerful and high voice.

Why the sub-deacon kisseth the Priest's hand.

After the Epistle is read, if it be in a High Mass,
the sub-deacon presenteth the book to the Priest
closed, who putteth his hand thereon, and then the
sub-deacon kisseth the same, to signify that only
Christ, according to St. John, was the Lamb, Who
could open the seals of that book, wherein both
Christ Himself and His sacred mysteries were
inclosed.

Deo gratias.

Lastly, the Epistle being read, answer is made,
saying : Deo gratias, Thanks be to God. By which few
words are fully signified the consent, gratitude and
thanksgiving of all the people.

The reading of the Epistle in the holy Mass hath no less antiquity than from the Apostles themselves, as appeareth out of Clemens, Justinus, Tertullianus, and Dionysius Areopagita, all whom Durandus* and Azorius† do produce for proof of this point.

CHAPTER XXVIII.

OF THE GRADUAL OR RESPONSE, AND OF SUNDRY REASONS CONCERNING THE SAME.

CONCERNING the Gradual, it is first to be noted that the very word itself is not without some special mystery, signifying steps or degrees, to wit, of perfection, according to the doctrine of our Saviour, saying : Be ye perfect, as your Father Which is in heaven is perfect.

As also to signify, that the end of the doctrine of the Apostles or Prophets, whereunto we have hearkened a little before, is to lead us by little and little to perfection, that we, ascending from virtue to virtue, as the kingly prophet saith, may see the God of gods in Sion.‡

The second reason.

This Gradual doth yet further signify many other notable mysteries. As for example, in a High Mass

* Lib. 2 de Rit. Eccles. Cath. c. 18.
† Instit. Moral, lib. 10, p. 1636.   ‡ Ps. 83.

it is always sung with a grave and heavy voice, to
signify the great pain and difficulty there is in
ascending from virtue to virtue, and in advancing
ourselves in a spiritual life, according to the saying
of our Blessed Saviour: The spirit is willing, but
the flesh is weak.*

The third reason.

Mystically also, the Gradual may be referred to
the vocation of the Apostles, whom our Saviour
calling, and saying: *Venite post me*, Come after Me,
they forsaking all that they had, did forthwith follow
and walk after their Lord, the disciples after their
Master, the children after their most loving Father,
as saith Innocentius the Third.

This Gradual did St. John Baptist first sing, when,
standing with two of his disciples, and seeing Jesus
walking, he said: *Ecce Agnus Dei, ecce qui tollit peccatum
mundi*.† This Gradual did St. Andrew sing, when,
finding his brother Simon, he said: *Invenimus
Messiam*, etc.‡ We have found the Messias, which is
interpreted Christ, and he brought him unto Jesus.

This Gradual did St. Philip sing when he found
Nathanael, and said unto him, *Quem Moyses*, etc.§
Whom Moses wrote of in the Law and the Prophets
we have found, Jesus, the son of Joseph of Nazareth,
come and see.

* St. Matthew ch. 26, v. 41. † St. John ch. 1, v. 29.
‡ St. John ch. 1, v. 41. § St. John ch. 1, v. 45.

The fourth reason.

This Gradual is also called by the name of a Response, because that it hath correspondence to the Epistle. As for example, if the Epistle contain matter of joy, the Response or Gradual doth likewise signify joy. If matter of sorrow, it also is conformable, according to that of the Apostle :* *Gaudete cum gaudentibus, flete cum flentibus.* Rejoice with them that be merry, and weep with them that weep.

The fifth reason.

Innocentius III., and some others, do call the Response, *Lamentum pœnitentiæ,* the song of penance or lamentation, adding further, that it should be sung with a doleful and lamentable voice, to signify the effect of the preaching of St. John. For even as by the Epistle is represented the preaching and doctrine of St. John Baptist, even so this song of lamentation signifieth that St. John preached no other thing than penance, saying : *Pœnitentiam agite,* etc. Do penance : for the kingdom of God is at hand.†

The sixth reason.

To conclude, this Gradual or Response is nothing else but a brief spiritual song, composed of two or three verses at the most, commonly taken out of the Psalms of David. As for example, that of the 17th Sunday after Trinity Sunday is composed of two

* Rom. ch. 12, v. 15.   † St. Matthew ch. 3, v. 2.

little verses taken out of the 32nd Psalm: *Beata est gens cujus est Dominus Deus eorum*, etc. Blessed is the people who have our Lord for their God; and blessed is the people whom our Lord hath chosen for His inheritance. The heavens have been established by the Word of our Lord; and all the power of them by the breath of His mouth.[*] Of the Gradual, Prose, Tract, etc., Walfridus,[†] Rupertus,[‡] Radulphus,[§] Rabanus,[‖] Isidorus,[¶] and others, do make both ample and evident testimony.

CHAPTER XXIX.

OF THE ALLELUIA, AND OF SUNDRY REASONS CONCERNING THE SAME.

THE Alleluia is immediately sung after the Gradual, to wit, the song of joy and of mirth after the song of penance and mourning, to express thereby the great consolation, which is laid up for those which labour and mourn in this life, according to the saying of our Saviour: Blessed are they that mourn, for they shall be comforted.[**]

[*] Ps. 32. [†] Lib. de Reb. Eccles. cap. 22.
[‡] Lib. 1, de Div. Off. cap. 34. [§] De Can. Obser. prop. 2.
[‖] Lib. 2, de Instit. Cler. c. 15.
[¶] Lib. 6, Ety. c. 29; et lib. 1, de Eccl. Off. c. 18.
[**] St. Matthew ch. 5, v. 5.

The second reason.

This word, Alleluia, hath a double signification, the one literal and common to all, the other mystical and proper to Divines. First, therefore, to understand what it signifieth literally, we must know, that Alleluia is composed of two Hebrew words, *Hallelu*, which signifieth in Latin, *Laudate*, in English, Praise ye, and of *ia*, which is one of the ten Hebrew names belonging to God, and signifieth in Latin, *Dominum*, Lord, so that the whole word is as much to say as, Praise ye our Lord.

The third reason.

The mystical or spiritual sense thereof is divers: according to some, Alleluia soundeth as much as spiritual or endless joy, and in this sense, is as much as if the Priest should cry unto the people with these words: Spiritual joy, spiritual joy. Or if we apply it to the latter word, to wit, endless, or perpetual, then it signifieth as much as if he should encourage them with these words: Endless joy, perpetual joy.

The fourth reason.

According to some others, it may be referred to the joy of those which rejoiced in the glorious miracles of Christ our Lord; for then did all the people, in joyful wise, sing forth this Alleluia, when, seeing those miracles, they all gave glory to Almighty God, and rejoiced in those things which were most gloriously and miraculously done by Him, saying : *Quia vidimus mirabilia hodie,* For we have seen marvellous things to-day.* As also when the seventy-two returned with joy, saying : Lord, the devils also are subject to us in Thy Name.†

The fifth reason.

That this Alleluia is sometimes twice repeated is to signify a double joy of the blessed Saints, one of their spirit, another of their flesh, one of their souls, another of their bodies. Of the first joy the royal prophet David saith: *Exultabunt sancti,* etc. The Saints shall rejoice in glory.‡ Of the second, *Fulgebunt justi tanquam sol in regno Patris.* The just shall shine like the sun in the kingdom of their Father.§

The sixth reason.

The use and custom of this word first came from the Angels and from certain holy Prophets. And St. John in his Apocalypse reciteth, that he heard the voice of the heavenly army, as the voice of many waters and great thunders, saying : *Amen* and *Alleluia ;* four times *Alleluia,* and once *Amen.* Wherefore the Church hath thought good to retain these words in earth, and to pronounce them in the Mass by the mouth of the Priest, as they are pronounced in heaven by the holy Angels.

* St. Luke ch. 5, v. 26.   † St. Luke ch. 10, v. 17.
‡ Ps. 149.   § St. Matthew ch. 12, v. 48.

The seventh reason.

And therefore is it left in an unknown language, to denote that we may rather signify obscurely, than any way perfectly express, the greatness of the joys, which our Lord hath promised to all that love Him.

The eighth reason.

Another reason why the Church retaineth this, and other like words, uninterpreted unto us, is because of the great difficulty that there is, well and truly to translate them, being of such virtue and energy, that other languages want proper words sufficiently to express them, and for this cause it is much better to leave them as they are, than to extenuate their force by a strange interpretation. And St. Augustine in his book, *De doctrinâ Christianâ*,* giveth this reason, saying, that in holy writings, many Hebrew words are left without interpretation, because of a certain sanctity that is comprehended under the very words themselves.

Alleluia confirmed by Miracle.

Finally, this Alleluia our Apostle St. Augustine used, when he first entered into our country to convert the same, as witnesseth St. Bede,† whose prayer was in this wise: We beseech Thee, O Lord, for Thy great mercy sake, that Thy fury and Thine anger may be taken from this city, to wit, Canterbury in Kent, and from Thy holy house, because we have sinned, Alleluia.

* Cap. 11.   † Lib. 1, cap. 25.

The same Alleluia also used St. German, Bishop
of Auxerre, in France, who being sent by the Pope's
Holiness into our country to confute the error of
the Pelagians, gave commandment unto certain
soldiers, whom he had placed in a valley, through
which their enemies resolved to pass, that so soon
as they perceived them coming, they should all
forthwith cry out as they heard him cry. The
blessed Bishop, suddenly issuing out before the
enemy, cried out three several times, Alleluia, and
all the rest of the soldiers cried out aloud the same
with him ; wherewith the enemies were so affrighted
and amazed, that they thought not only the hills,
but also heaven itself, to cry out and fight against
them. Whereupon they fled with great fear, and
many of them were drowned in the river which they
were to pass. And so the soldiers that were with
the blessed Bishop, obtained the victory without
any battle, only by the terror which God struck
into them by the sound and echo of Alleluia.*

CHAPTER XXX.

OF THE PROSE, AND OF SUNDRY REASONS CONCERNING THE SAME.

THE Prose is commonly taken for an ecclesiastical prayer, containing the praises of Almighty God,

* St. Bede, lib. 1, cap. 20.

of the Blessed Virgin, and of the glorious Saints; and followeth betwixt the Epistle and Gospel.

The second reason.

The first invention thereof is attributed to Nocherus, Abbot of St. Gaul in Switzerland, afterwards elected Bishop of Liège,* and Pope Nicholas, the first of·that name, greatly moved with the devotion of this holy man, as also with the rhythm, sound, and pleasant melody of the song, permitted the use thereof. But amongst many composed also by others, the Church of Rome hath especially retained in the holy Mass, four for their excellency.

The third reason.

1. The first is *Victimæ Paschali laudes*. The which is said upon Easter-day, in testimony of the joyful Resurrection of Jesus Christ, and thanksgiving for the Redemption of mankind, wrought by His blessed and holy Death. The author is somewhat uncertain, but undoubtedly a man endued with notable piety and devotion.

The fourth reason.

2. The second is *Veni Sancte Spiritus*, and is sung upon Whit-Sunday, to crave of the Holy Ghost to send from above the beams of His celestial brightness, to illuminate the minds of those which are covered with darkness. Robert, king of France, surnamed the great clerk, composed it, the Church having since approved it, and sung it universally

* Durandus, lib. 4, cap. 22, de Ritibus Ecclesiæ.

throughout all the parts of Christendom, as witnesseth Paulus Æmilius, writing of his life.

The fifth reason.

3. The third is *Lauda Sion Salvatorem*, composed
in praise of the Most Blessed Sacrament by St.
Thomas of Aquin, admirable for his learning to the
whole world, which was rather divinely infused into
him, than either attained unto by nature, travail, or
labour of study. Who treated so sublimely of the
Holy Eucharist, as never any since did more set
forth and illustrate the same ; so that God seemeth
purposely to have chosen this great and learned
doctor for a convenient remedy against the heretics
of our times.

The sixth reason.

4. The fourth is *Dies iræ, dies illa*, and this is said
in the holy Mass for the souls departed. The
canticle is very lamentable, and the discourse full of
Christian contemplation touching the apprehension
and fear of the day of general judgment, and was
composed by a noble, famous and religious Cardinal.

CHAPTER XXXI.

OF THE TRACT, AND OF SUNDRY REASONS CONCERNING THE SAME.

THE Tract is so called of this Latin word *Tractus, a
trahendo* by cause, saith Durandus, it is sung *tractim*,

9

and as with a trailing of the voice, as those may easily discern who understand plain song.*

The second reason.

This tract is a spiritual song composed of sundry verses, usually taken out of the Psalms of David, and sometimes out of certain other places of the Holy Scripture, as that upon the Feast of St. Peter's chair. *Tu es Petrus et super hanc petram ædificabo ecclesiam meam.*† And sometimes also composed by the Church, conformable to the Holy Scripture, as: Gaude Maria Virgo, cunctas hæreses sola interemisti in universo mundo.‡

The third reason.

Next it is to be noted, that this tract is always sung either after the Alleluia, or sometimes only in the stead thereof, and further, from Septuagesima till Easter, the Alleluia, which is a song of jubilation, altogether ceaseth both in the Mass and also in the Canonical Hours. The reason whereof is, for that by the time of Septuagesima, the Church would represent unto us the miserable estate of man's nature living in this wretched world, and therefore ceaseth to sing the song of joy, and only singeth the song of sadness and sorrow. Also to signify the difference betwixt our estate, and the estate of the blessed souls in heaven, who sing perpetually without ceasing or

---

* Lib. 4, cap. 41, num. 1.   † St. Matthew ch. 16, v. 18.
‡ Off. B. Virg.

intermission this joyful song of Alleluia, whereas we, who live in this vale of misery, must, whilst we remain here, always intermix our joy with penance and mourning.

The fourth reason.

It likewise signifieth the tears and groans of Christ's Church for her sins, for the prolonging of her felicity, and for the pains and afflictions which she endureth, whilst she liveth in this world; which causeth the Holy Prophet in her person to say, *Hei mihi! quia incolatus meus prolongatus est, multum incola fuit anima mea.** And for this reason, she is often compared in Holy Scripture to a turtle, as in Canticles, the second chapter.

Whereupon St. Bernard saith that the turtle is a bird very solitary, who, having once lost her companion, will never after take any other, but evermore abide solitary, and often mourning upon the top of a dry tree.†

To apply the same to our present purpose; this turtle is the Church of God; her solitude or place of mourning is in the desert of this world. Her companion and spouse which she hath lost is our Blessed Lord and Saviour Jesus, Whom the Jews have killed and put to death: Who, being risen again, is ascended into heaven, the Church often sighing and mourning for His departure, and still desiring to

* Ps. 119. † Hom. 59 in Cant.

9 *

see Him again, and to be there on high in company with Him. And the dry tree upon the which she often sitteth, so mournfully groaning and lamenting, is the Holy Cross, whereon her dearly beloved Spouse was put to death.

To conclude, the first placing of the prose in the holy Mass is attributed to Telesphorus the ninth Pope after St. Peter, as testifieth Durandus.*

CHAPTER XXXII.

OF THE HOLY GOSPEL OF OUR LORD JESUS CHRIST, AND OF SUNDRY WORTHY CEREMONIES WHICH ARE USED BOTH BEFORE AND AFTER THE READING THEREOF.

If I were to explicate unto you all the mysteries of a solemn Mass, I should make mention of many most worthy ceremonies which here of purpose I do omit. Only I will give you by the way a little taste of some of them, because they are so exceeding mysterious, and so contenting and pleasing to every devout and pious person, that loath I am wholly to omit them.

The First Ceremony and its signification.

The Epistle therefore being read by the sub-deacon, the Deacon, disposing himself to pronounce the Gospel, ascendeth to the altar where the book remaineth. The book remaining always upon the

* Lib. 4, cap 4, num. 1.

altar, signifieth that the Sacrifice instituted by our
Blessed Saviour is always joined with the Testament,
which is the Gospel, and that the one shall never be
without the other ; for so long as the Sacrifice shall
endure, the Gospel shall be preached, and when the
Sacrifice shall be abolished, the Gospel shall cease to
be announced, as we see it is at this day in Turkey,
where as there is no Sacrifice offered, so is there no
Gospel preached.

The Second Ceremony and its signification.

And therefore the Deacon, being to pronounce the
Gospel, ascendeth and taketh the book from the altar,
to signify that the place ordained of God to keep the
Holy Scripture is the Catholic Church : as also to
signify that all true and wholesome interpretation of
Holy Scripture ought to be taken from the warrant
and authority of the same Church.

The Third Ceremony and its signification.

Having taken the book from the altar, before he go
to read the Gospel, he reverently prostrateth himself
on his knee before the Priest, demanding his benediction, to shew that none ought to intrude himself,
nor to take upon him the office or charge of preaching, unless he be first lawfully called and sent
thereto.*

The Fourth Ceremony and its signification.

At the taking of the book, the Deacon kisseth the

* Rom. ch. 10, v. 15.

right hand of the Priest, and this for two causes.
First, to signify that he preacheth not his own but
the doctrine of Christ, Whom in this place the Priest
representeth.   And next, that although he preach
the word never so truly or with never so great zeal,
yet that the gift of converting souls doth wholly
proceed from the grace of God.

The Fifth Ceremony and its signification.

At the reading of the Gospel two acolytes go before
the Deacon with two burning lights, to signify that
the assistants ought specially then to have their
hearts inflamed in the desire and meditation of those
heavenly things, which are contained in the Gospel
of Christ.   The custom of lights is most ancient by
the testimony of St. Jerome,* and the causes are
plainly deduced out of St. Isidore.†

The Sixth Ceremony and its signification.

By this that the two acolytes do go before the
Deacon, who is to read the Gospel, carrying wax
lights and incense, is signified that Christ sent before
Him His disciples by two and two into every city
where He was to go, carrying with them the shining
light of miracles and the sweet odour of virtues.‡

The Seventh Ceremony and its signification.

The Deacon lifteth up his voice on high in reading
and announcing the Gospel of Christ, according to

* Adversus Vig.   † Cap. Cleros. sect. Acolith. dist. 22.
‡ St. Luke ch. 10.

that of the Prophet, *Ascend thou upon a high mountain who dost evangelise to Sion, lift up thy voice in fortitude,* etc.* And our Lord saith in the Gospel: *That which I say to you in the dark, tell ye in the light, and that which you hear in the ear, preach ye upon the tops of the houses.*† These worthily pious and sacred ceremonies are seen and performed when High Mass is celebrated, but because my purpose is to treat but briefly of those Ceremonies which are usually to be seen in every low and daily Mass, I will therefore return to speak of them.

The Eighth Ceremony and its signification.

The Alleluia, therefore, or Tract being read, the Priest passeth to the midst of the Altar, where inclining himself, and joining together his hands, he secretly repeateth the prayer following: *Munda cor meum ac labia mea, omnipotens Deus,* etc. Cleanse my heart and my lips, O omnipotent God, who cleansedst the lips of the prophet Isaias with fire; and so by Thy free grace vouchsafe to cleanse me, that I may worthily announce Thy holy Gospel, through Christ our Lord. Amen.

The Ninth Ceremony and its signification.

In the meantime the Clerk or minister removeth the book to the left hand of the Altar, signifying thereby that the Gospel, which was first preached to the Jews, who were on the right hand, was for

---

* Isaias ch. 40.   † St. Matthew ch. 10.

their incredulity transferred from them to the people of the Gentiles, a mystery sundry times represented in the holy Mass, as hath before been mentioned.

The Tenth Ceremony and its signification.

This done, the Priest turneth him to the book, and all the people rise up, whereby two several things are signified; the one, the corruptness of our nature, lying on the ground like unto brute beasts, and wallowing in the uncleanness and ordure of our sins; the other, the virtue of the Gospel of Jesus Christ, which raiseth us up to newness of life, if we receive the same with fruit and worthily express it in our lives.

Again the rising up of the people at the reading of the Gospel doth signify, that they shew themselves ready for the faith of Christ and profession of his Gospel, to give their lives, and to fight even unto the death in defence of the same; remembering the words which our Lord Himself spake, saying: He that hath not a sword, let him sell his coat and buy it.

The Eleventh Ceremony and its signification.

Before the beginning of the Gospel, he saluteth all the assistants, praying that our Lord may be with them; which he doth to render them more attentive to hearken to the Word of Almighty God. For even as to the stomach, which receiveth corporal food, nothing is profitable if it be ill-disposed, so likewise, unless the hearts of the assistants be well disposed and prepared to receive the Word of Almighty God, which is the food of the soul, little will it avail them, though it be announced unto them.

Dominus vobiscum.

Our Lord be with you. The words of this salutation are : our Lord be with you ; as if he should say, I beseech our Lord to send His grace into your hearts, that you may be made attentive and worthy hearers of His sacred Word, which, as the Apostle witnesseth, is able to save their souls.

Et cum spiritu tuo.

And with thy spirit. Then the assistants make answer praying that our Lord may be with his spirit, that is, that with the spirit of man, the Spirit of God may be present to direct and guide him, to the end that he may both faithfully recite the sacred Gospel to the health and salvation of all that are assembled to hear the same, and also himself express in true holiness of life that which he preacheth unto others.

Sequentia sancti Evangelii.

The sequence of the holy Gospel. This done, the Priest saith : *Sequentia sancti Evangelii,* etc. ; thus followeth the holy Gospel of such or such an Evangelist. As touching the word Evangel or Gospel, it is a word which we retain of the Greeks, as many others, and properly signifieth good and joyful tidings ; for what better tidings can there be than these: Do penance for the kingdom of heaven is at hand,* and, All power is given Me both in heaven and earth ?† With divers other things, which are read in the Gospel of the Divinity and Nativity of the Son of God, of His miracles, preaching, passion, resurrection, ascension, and of the salvation and glorification of His elect. Where also note that the name of the Evangelist is always expressed, to the end, that the people may give the more credit as unto the Gospel penned and written by one of the Secretaries of our Saviour Jesus, and received in the Church, to which appertaineth the authority and prerogative to discern the canonical Scriptures and their sense, if by any adversity they should be called in question.

Gloria tibi, Domine.

Glory be unto Thee, O Lord! When he hath thus taught them out of what place of Scripture the Gospel for the day is taken, presently all the people, hearing the name of the Gospel, and making reverence towards the altar, with joyful acclamation, do answer, saying : *Gloria tibi, Domine.* Glory be unto Thee, O Lord! Giving thanks unto God, Who hath made them worthy partakers of the Gospel of Christ. As it is written in the Acts of the Apostles, that all the people glorified our Lord, for that He had sent unto them the word of salvation, saying : God then to the Gentiles also hath given repentance unto life.‡

* St. Matthew ch. 2, v. 3.   † St. Matthew ch. 28, v. 18.
‡ Acts ch. 11, v. 18.

The Eleventh Ceremony and its signification.

In pronouncing the words aforesaid, the Priest maketh the sign of the Cross upon the book, and upon himself. Upon the book, to signify that it containeth the mysteries of our Redemption. Upon himself, to signify that he is an instrument of Christ Jesus, and of Him crucified, and that this Sacrifice doth represent unto us His Death and Passion.

The Twelfth Ceremony and its signification.

The people likewise do make the sign of the Cross in three places. Upon their foreheads, upon their mouths, and upon their breasts. Upon their foreheads, which is the most conspicuous place of all the body, to shew that they are not ashamed of the Gospel of Christ. Upon their lips, to shew that they are always ready, resolutely and constantly to confess their faith, if, at any time, God shall please to call them thereunto. Upon their breasts, to declare that they do stedfastly believe in heart that which they confess with their mouths.

The Thirteenth Ceremony and its signification.

The Priest after the reading of the Gospel, saith : *Per evangelica dicta,* etc. By the evangelical sayings, let our sins be forgiven us. And then he kisseth the book, not closed, but open, to signify that the means to come to the understanding of God's Word is clearly manifested to the Pastors of the Church. And further to signify that it is the

book of Christ crucified, Whom the Apostle affirmeth
to be our reconciliation, and the Maker of our peace
and atonement, which is aptly signified by the
kiss.   As also to show that he preacheth the
gospel of true love and charity for the gaining of
souls, and not for lucre and temporal profit.

Laus tibi, Christe.

Praise be to Thee, O Christ ! The Gospel ended,
all the people make answer, saying : Praise be to
Thee, O Christ, making the sign of the Cross as
before on their forehead, mouth, and breast, to the
end, that the wicked serpent should by no means
hinder their confidence and confession, or dare to
break open the seal of their hearts wherein the
Word of God is sown.   Also to arm themselves
against his malice, who would not that they should
reap any profit by the Word of God.   As is plainly
expressed in the parable of the seed, where it is
said that the fowls of the air came and devoured
one part of the seed which was sown, by which
fowls are understood the foul and unclean spirits.

Miracles wrought by our Catholic church-books.

To conclude, such hath always been the authority
of the holy Gospel, that not only the sacred words,
but also the very books or papers have wrought
sundry strange and notable miracles.   Gregorius
Turonensis * declareth that the city of Averna

* In Vitis Patrum, cap. 6.

being on fire, St. Gallus, going into the church, prayed a long time before the Altar of our Lord, and then rising up, taking the book of the Gospel and opening it, offered himself to go against the fire, and suddenly the flames were extinguished in such sort, that there did not so much as the very sparks remain.

St. Macian, when the flames of fire approached near unto the Church of St. Anastasius, taking into his hands the holy Gospel, he got in through the tiles, and by his prayers and tears, preserved it from burning.

Zonaras also testifieth that the Russians in a great fire, finding the book of the Gospel safe and preserved from burning, by the only motive of this miracle, received and embraced the faith of Christ.

Finally, the reading of the Gospel in the holy Mass, all Liturgies do testify to be very ancient. Also Concilium Laodicenum, * Carthaginense, † Valentinum, ‡ Clemens, § Anastasius writing to the Bishops of Germany and Burgundy, and infinite others, whom here, for brevity sake, I do omit.

* Cap. 16. † Can. 48.
‡ Cap. 3. § Lib. 2, Const. Apost. cap. 16.

CHAPTER XXXIII.

THE Symbol or Creed, immediately pronounced after the Gospel, signifieth the fruit which presently ensued after the preaching of our Lord and His Apostles. And therefore also is it presently pronounced after the Gospel, that by the Gospel we may believe with the heart unto righteousness, and by the Creed we may confess with our mouths unto salvation, as it is written: *Corde creditur ad justitiam, ore autem fit confessio ad salutem,* With the heart we believe unto justice, but with the mouth confession is made to salvation.*

Of the etymology of the word Symbol.

To understand the etymology and meaning of this word Symbol, we must note that it is a Greek word, and signifieth divers things. Sometimes it is taken for a mark or seal, wherewith a thing is marked or sealed. Sometimes again, it is taken for a watchword which a captain giveth to his soldiers, whereby they may know one another, and the better preserve themselves from being surprised by their enemies, so that if they should chance to meet any one of whom they doubted, being asked the symbol or watch-

* Romans ch. 10, v. 10.

word, he should be bewrayed whether he were their friend or foe. In this present place it is taken for a brief form or rule of Christian faith, composed of diverse and sundry sentences, called articles, much like unto so many sinews or joints, binding and tieing together all the parts of the body. Wherefore very fitly may this summary of the Christian faith be called by this name of symbol according to all these significations. For first in very deed, it is a true mark or seal whereby to know and distinguish a Catholic from a heretic ; for never was there a heretic which did not deny some part or other of the Creed.

Secondly, it may well be taken for a watchword given to the faithful, whereby to know one another, and so to keep themselves from the incursion of their enemies.

And thirdly, as in this place, for a brief form or rule of our Christian faith, because it comprehendeth in so short and compendious a manner the sum of all that which we are to believe.*

Three Symbols or Creeds in the Catholic Church.

In the Catholic Church we have three Symbols or Creeds. The first is that of the Apostles, which all good Christians ought to learn by heart, and to say it both morning and evening, for it chaseth away the devils who lie in wait both day and night to devour us.

* Durandus, lib. 4, cap. 25.

The second is that of the Council of Nice, which is usually said in the Mass after the Gospel.

And the third is that of St. Athanasius, which is sung at Prime upon all Sundays. Both which latter are no additions to the former, but expositions or more plain declarations thereof. The reason why the Church admitted these two Creeds, besides that of the Apostles, was for that the heretics, receiving the first according to the words or letter, did not receive it according to the sense and meaning of the Catholic Church. And for that also the Arians and other heretics construed the same so confusedly, that it was hard to discern the Catholics from the heretics any way by the same. In which case the Church was constrained to put to her helping hand, adding the two latter as an exposition or plainer declaration of the former, and hath ever since served to singular good purpose for the conviction of several heresies and heretics, which have sprung up in sundry times and upon sundry occasions.

The Symbol of the Council of Nice was composed under Pope Sylvester,* in the presence of the great and most religious Emperor Constantine, by 318 Bishops assembled from all parts of the world, and kept at his expenses; whereof many had their right eyes put out and their right hands cut off for the defence of the faith and Christian religion in the precedent persecutions, as testifieth Nicephorus.†

* Plat. in Vita Silvestri.   † Lib. 8, cap. 1.

He honoured them with presents condign to their estates, and royally feasted them at his table, causing the principal of them to sit close unto himself, before he would license them to depart to their Churches, kissing also their wounds when he dismissed them.*

This Symbol was made expressly to condemn the blasphemy of Arius, maintaining, against the doctrine of the Church, the inequality of the three Divine Persons in the Holy Trinity. †

By the order of Pope Mark, successor of St. Sylvester, the Clergy and people began to sing it with high voice in the church, for that then the Emperors of the world assisted and constantly defended the Catholic faith. It was also approved in the first Council of Constantinople, but fifty-six years after that of Nice, by one hundred and fifty Bishops assembled under the Emperors Gratian and Theodosius the Elder. ‡

The Symbol of the holy Father Athanasius was composed by him against the aforesaid Arians, when by their audacious pursuit, they exiled him to Trèves, where he laboured by all means to conserve the faith in his former purity. §

The Creed of the Nicene Council, and which is usually sung in the holy Mass, containeth, like as

* Naucler. vol. 2, gener. 11.
† Socrat. lib. 4, Eccl. Hist. cap. 31.
‡ Plat. in Vita Marci.   § Naucler. vol. 2, gener. 13.
10

that of the Apostles, to the number of twelve
articles, which are these that follow.

Credo.

I believe. The first article of this Creed is to
believe, to wit, in God, and is to be opposed against
the ignorance of all Atheists, and of all such as
foolishly say in their hearts: There is no God.*

In.

In. And here note that there is a difference
in belief. For to believe God is to believe only that
God is, but to believe in God is in belief to love
Him, to worship Him, and to serve Him as God;
and this is perfectly to believe in God.

Unum Deum.

One God. For as much as many heathen people
do adore and worship divers vain things instead of
God, calling them their gods, therefore to condemn
their error and to exclude all plurality of gods,
the Creed of the Mass hath adjoined this word
Unum, one, the more plainly to explicate the former,
which is as much as to say: I believe in one only
God and not in more.

Patrem Omnipotentem.

The Father Almighty. Which words ought to
be of most singular comfort unto us. For as He
is a Father, He must needs wish all good things

* Ps. 13.

unto His children. And in that He is Almighty, He is likewise able to help them in all things.

Factorem cæli.

Maker of heaven. By heaven, which is the work of His hands, is understood all heavenly creatures, as Angels, sun, moon, stars, and other elements.

Et terræ.

And of the earth. By earth is understood the whole globe thereof, incredibly enriched with all that is requisite for the ornament and use of all His earthly and mortal creatures.

Visibilium omnium et invisibilium.

And of all things visible and invisible. To this first article of the Creed, the Church hath also adjoined these words against the impiety and heresy of the Manichees, who perversely defended, that God only created things invisible, and that the devil procreated the things which are visible, as witnesseth Nicephorus.* Wherefore to exclude this error, we acknowledge in the Mass that God is the Maker of all things, both visible and invisible.

Et in unum.

And in one. For as much as many took upon them to be called Christ, and would need be so named of the people, as Antichrist likewise shall when he cometh, therefore to exclude this error

* Lib. 6, Eccles. Hist. cap. 31 and 32.

10 *

and to show that there is no true Christ but One, the Church hath likewise here added this word *unum*, one. For as the Scripture foretelleth us, many shall say, Lo! here Christ, lo! there, but expressly commandeth us not to believe them.

Dominum.

Lord. And He therefore is called Lord, to beat down the impiety of those who do hold Him less than His Father in power and authority, yea, and do make Him even a servant, and subject unto Him according to His Divinity, as Calvin,[*] and before him other heretics.

Jesum Christum.

Jesus Christ. With the Name of Jesus, which signifieth a Saviour, there is also imposed upon Him the surname of Christ, which name is a title of honour common to divers estates and dignities, to wit, to Priests, Prophets, and Kings. The office of Priests is to offer prayers and sacrifices to God for the sins of the people. Of Prophets, to foretell things to come to their singular comfort. Of Kings, to reign in sovereignty and puissance of government; all which titles do wonderful well agree to our Blessed Saviour. For He was ordained a Priest by God His Father for ever, after the order of Melchisedech.[†] He was also a Prophet for He foretold the secret counsels of His Father

[*] Lib. 2, Inst. cap. 17, num. 1.   [†] Ps. 109.

unto us concerning our salvation. He is also a King, for as much as by His Providence, He doth accomplish the wonderful endeavours and office of a King in the behalf of His Church, whose King and Governor He shall be to the end of the world.

Filium Dei.

The Son of God. Which words do evidently declare that He is very God. For as a man and woman can beget no child but man or woman of the same substance, even so the Son of God must needs be God and of the self-same substance with God.

Unigenitum.

Only Begotten. Where note that although God hath granted unto those that believe in Him, to be His children and sons, yet this is to be understood by grace and spiritual adoption. But Jesus Christ is His only natural Son, engendered of His own substance, as St. John the Evangelist doth clearly testify.[*]

Et ex Patre natum.

And born of the Father. For as much as this holy Council of Nice was principally gathered to repress the heresy of the Arians, denying that Christ was born and begotten of the substance of God His Father, and equal unto Him, as witnesseth St. Augustine, [†] they were therefore condemned by

---

[*] St. John ch. 1.   [†] Lib. 1, de Trinit. cap. 7.

these very words, and the contrary was there expressly concluded against them.

Ante omnia sæcula.

Before all worlds. And for the more manifest declaration that He is co-eternal with God His Father, there is added in this Creed that He was born of Him before all worlds. True indeed it is that the manner is inexplicable, as St. Cyprian saith,* and therefore we ought simply to believe and devoutly to reverence this His ineffable generation. For who will inquire after that which cannot be found? Of whom shall we learn it? of the earth? It was not subsisting. Of the sea? It was not liquefied. Of heaven? It was not elevated. Of the sun? of the moon? of the stars? They were not as yet created. Of the Angels? He was engendered before they had their being. Briefly therefore we will conclude with St. Basil, saying: We must not inquire after that which hath always been, of that which hath not always been.

Deum de Deo.

God of God. Also, whereas these heretics said that He was not God of God His Father, but only Man of His Mother, therefore the holy Fathers assembled in this Council, concluded that He was God of God, and that He did no whit diminish His

* In Explic. Symboli.

Divine nature by reason of His Incarnation in the Blessed Virgin.

Lumen de lumine.

Light of light. These holy and venerable Fathers, to make this verity more apparent, declared the same by an apt similitude, to wit, that the Son of God was born of His Father, even as the light produceth and casteth forth light of itself without any manner of diminution of its own substance, and can be no more divided from the Father than the sun and the splendour thereof can naturally be separated or divided asunder.

Deum verum de Deo vero.

Very God of very God. The same Catholic Church, further to confound the error of the Arians and Eunomians, denying that He was very God by natural property, but only by grace or communication of name, sometimes given unto them, whom the Psalmist calleth gods for the rareness of their virtues, as Psalm 81, declared that He was very God of very God, that is to say, so verily God as God the Father was God, and truly sprang and issued out of Him.

Genitum non factum.

Begotten not made. And whereas some of these heretics confessed that Christ was indeed of the Father, but yet that He was less than the Father, and not of the same but of another substance than the Father was, therefore to confound this error, there was inserted into this Creed these words: Begotten not made. But with what similitude may a mortal man be able to express this Divine generation? Or what comparison can be made betwixt things created and which have a beginning, and things increated and which have no beginning? St. Irenæus doth hold them for worse than mad who enforce themselves to conceive the same by human reason.* And St. Hilary being not able to comprehend it, comforteth himself with this, that the Angels do not know it.†

Consubstantialem Patri.

Consubstantial to the Father. To prove more clearly that the Son of God was nothing inferior to the Father, this holy Council devised against those heretics this word, Consubstantial, to prove and confirm His coequality with the Father. This also was most clearly pronounced out of the mouth of our Saviour Himself unto the Jews, assuring them that he who saw Him saw the Father also.‡

Per quem omnia facta sunt.

By Whom all things are made. Also, some enemies there were who said that the Father was the Maker of all things, and not the Son. But contrary to this, the Church defended that by the Son also all things were made; not that the Father did aid Him as an

---

* Lib 3, Adver. Hæres. Valent. cap. 48.
† Lib 2, de Trinitate.   ‡ St. John ch. 10.

extrinsical instrument to their production, but as St. John saith,* that without Him nothing was made, no not the world, nor the heavens themselves.

Qui propter nos homines.

Who for us men. In these words the Church proposeth unto us the human nature, which the Son of God took upon Him for our salvation ; whereof He was so desirous and so careful, that He expressly descended from heaven into earth to seek out the strayed and wandering sheep,† and by His Blood to reconcile him to His Father. What other occasion had He so to do? Take away the wounds, saith St. Augustine, and what necessity is there of a surgeon.

Et propter nostram salutem.

And for our salvation. This also was added by the Church, for as much as some there were who affirmed that Christ became man not only to save man, but also to save the Devil, and all those Angels who fell from heaven with him by plain apostacy. For remedy and redress of which error the Church added these words : Who for us men, and for our salvation.

Descendit de cœlis.

Descended from heaven. The better to express the benevolence of our Blessed Saviour towards mankind, it is said that He descended from heaven ; not that He abandoned the heavens or that He had never

* St. John ch. 1.   † St. Luke ch. 19, v. 10.

been on earth, seeing that by His Divine essence He filleth and replerisheth both the one and the other, and is in all places, but for that by taking human nature He was there by a new and miraculous manner of being, to wit, by hypostatical union and conjunction of the Divinity with the Humanity in one Person, after which manner He had never been on earth before.

Et incarnatus est.

And was incarnate. In which words the means of His descending is declared, to wit, by His incarnation. Who will not admire, saith Pope Clement the Sixth, that the same Person remained God as He was from all eternity, and became man which He never was ; He came to be born in earth Whom the Angels adore in heaven.*

De Spiritu Sancto.

Of the Holy Ghost. This article doth confirm us in the belief of the miraculous and supernatural operation of the Holy Ghost, by Whose virtue, the matter was disposed whereof the precious Body of Jesus Christ was organised and formed, to wit, of the most pure blood of the chaste and holy Virgin His Mother, St. Mary.†

Ex Maria.

Of Mary. Some heretics there were, who said that Christ brought with Him a body from heaven,

---

* Cap 6, de Pæn. et Remiss. in Extra. Comm.

† St. Luke ch. 1.

and that He took not His Body of our Blessed Lady, which is refuted by these words, saying, *Of Mary.* Octavius, who in his time ruled all the world, and therefore of the Romans was reputed as a God, did consult with a prophetess to know if in all the world there was to be born a greater than he: and in the same day wherein Christ was born of the Virgin Mary in Judea, Sybilla saw a golden circle near the sun, in which circle a fair virgin did sit, having a most beautiful child in her lap, which she shewed to Octavius Cæsar, and did declare unto him, that at that very time a more mighty King was born than he.

Virgine.

A Virgin. Not only Mary, but of Mary a Virgin; wherein we acknowledge her perpetual virginity to have been no more hurt by His conception than it was by His nativity; her chaste womb being miraculously counterguarded with fecundity, in such sort, that she amongst all others obtaineth the title of Mother and Virgin, which never was nor ever shall be granted to any woman but to herself alone.

Et homo factus est.

And was made man. Again some heretics maintained that Christ had no soul, but that His Godhead was united to His body instead of a soul; and so they inferred that Christ was not man, because man is composed of a body and soul. To refute which error the creed of the Mass saith: *And was made man.* For both these opinions are of like danger, to believe Christ to have been only God and not man, or to have been only man and not God.

Of the genuflection of the Priest at the reciting those words.

These words of the Creed are in effect the same which are read in that Divine Gospel of St. John, viz. *Et verbum caro factum est. And the Word was made flesh.* Words truly full of great majesty and reverence, and therefore both the Priest and the people, at the pronunciation of them, do humbly bow down and incline to the ground in sign of thanksgiving for so excellent a benefit. It is recounted of a certain person, who hearing these words recited, and making no reverence thereat, the devil gave him a box on the ear, saying: If it were read the Word was made devil, all we devils would never have omitted to have bowed our knees at the pronunciation of these words.[*]

Crucifixus etiam.

Crucified also. After His miraculous, supernatural and incomprehensible Incarnation, mention is made of His Death and Passion, with the time, manner, and order of the same. Wherefore, even as our first parents did grievously offend by the wood in eating of the fruit of the forbidden tree, even so would our Blessed Saviour satisfy by the Cross, upon the wood whereof He hath borne our sins in His own Body,

[*] Ludol. cap. 18, part 1.

and hath restored us life by the same means by which death entered into all the world.

Pro nobis.

For us. This punishment of the Cross was always reputed for a death the most ignominious and infamous that could be devised, as is testified in Deuteronomy.* And hereon was Jesus Christ fastened for our sins. O profound wisdom of God! how much more easy is it to admire such mysteries than any way to explicate or utter them with our words?

Sub Pontio Pilato.

Under Pontius Pilate. This Pilate, being Governor of Judea under the Emperor Tiberius, and having sundry times declared Jesus Christ to be innocent of the false accusations, which were imposed upon Him by the wicked Jews, yet in the end did abandon Him for fear to incur the disgrace of Cæsar. But within a while after, this ambitious officer, having for his own advancement and to the oppression of the innocent party, perverted all order of justice, and let loose the bridle to the popular insolency, was himself overwhelmed with so many miseries, that in punishment of this wicked fact, he killed himself with his own hands, much after the example of the traitor Judas, who hanged himself for having betrayed his innocent Master.†

* Deut. ch. 21.　　† Euseb. Eccles. Hist. lib. 2, cap. 2.

Passus.

Suffered. In this His suffering is comprehended all that which He endured to accomplish the mystery of our redemption unto His death; whereunto He offered Himself voluntarily and of His own accord, to satisfy the Divine justice and irrevocable decree of His Eternal Father, which could not otherwise be accomplished, but that the innocent must die for the nocent, and the obedient for the disobedient.

Et sepultus est.

And was buried. Express mention is here made of His burial for an infallible argument and proof of His Passion. Which some, with that execrable heretic Basilides, did deny, maintaining that He came into the world in a phantasy, and that it was not He that was crucified, but one named Simon, and that therefore He was not to be adored, as is testified by Tertullian.*

Et resurrexit.

And He rose again. By this article is declared the glorious mystery of our Lord's Resurrection, which point is so necessary, that all our faith were otherwise merely in vain, as testifieth the Apostle.† Neither is there any one thing which may more comfort and confirm our hope, than to believe that our Head is risen for our justification, as He was dead for our transgression. No resurrection of any person whatso-

* De Prescrips. Hæret.   † 1 Cor. ch. 15, v. 14.

ever is to be compared to His, He being raised by His own proper power without any aid or assistance of others. We read amongst other examples of Holy Scripture * that the body of him who was cast into the sepulchre of Eliseus, was raised to life, but this came to pass by touching the bones of the holy Prophet, for whose sake God restored life to the dead man, and not by the proper force of him that was deceased. This therefore was only reserved to our Lord Jesus Christ, to return from death to life by the only power and virtue of Himself.

Tertiâ die.

The third day. To the end we may believe that this His death was true and not feigned, He was not resuscitated immediately, but remained truly dead until the third day after, which was a time more than sufficient to make assured proof, and to remove away all doubt and ambiguity of the truth of His death. Yet was He not in His sepulchre the space of three whole and complete days, but one day only entire, part of the day precedent, and part of the day subsequent, which, by the figure synecdoche, are called three days and three nights.

Secundum Scripturas.

According to the Scriptures. This clause was necessarily annexed by the Fathers of the Church, for as much as at the beginning it was very hard,

* 4 Kings ch. 13, v. 21.

especially for men of gross capacity, and as yet not thoroughly instructed in the Christian faith, to comprehend so great a mystery as is the resurrection of the dead, which far surpassed the laws of nature; and therefore this was added as an infallible argument why we ought to believe the same.

Et ascendit in cælum.

And he ascended to heaven. Where the question may be demanded, how he ascended up to heaven? True it is that as God He never was absent from thence, but always filled it and all other places with His Divinity: but as man he mounted thither in body and soul, leading with Him captivity captive, as the Apostle saith, which He placed and set in liberty by His excellent victory over death, the devil and hell itself.*

Sedet ad dexteram Patris.

He sitteth at the right hand of the Father. In which words the Holy Scripture doth accommodate itself to our weak understanding, using a metaphorical speech or locution, to instruct us that Jesus Christ hath received of God His Father all honour and advancement of glory in His Humanity, even as we esteem here amongst men, the greatest honour to be done unto those, to whom we give the upper hand. And it was most expedient that He should be most highly exalted, who had so greatly depressed and humbled

* Ephes. ch. 4, v. 8.

Himself, as to endure so manifold defamations, opprobriums and injurious intreatments for our sakes.

Et iterum venturus est.

And He is to come again. Having made mention of our Saviour's first coming into the world to repair the fall and ruin of man, His second coming is next proposed, wherein He shall sit in judgment, and manifestly declare to all the world both His power and justice, rendering to every one according to his deserts. And as His first coming was in great meekness, so on the contrary, shall His second coming be in great majesty and glory.

Judicare vivos et mortuos.

To judge both the quick and the dead. That is to say the good and the bad, the one to bliss and perpetual joy, the other to woe and everlasting pain. Wherein they shall, both the one and the other, perpetually abide, so long as God shall be God, without intermission of joy or pain.

Cujus regni non erit finis.

Of whose kingdom there shall be no end. This is the kingdom, which, as Daniel declared to Nabuchodonosor and Balthasar, Kings of Babylon, should never have end.* This is that kingdom which the Angel foretold to the Virgin Mary should ever endure.† This is that kingdom prepared for the

* Daniel ch. 2.   † St. Luke ch. 1.

11

blessed from the beginning of the world, as testifieth
St. Matthew.* This is that kingdom into which the
good thief, acknowledging his misdeeds, desired to
enter.† This is that kingdom whereof none can have
part, unless he be born anew and be without all
blemish and spot of sin.‡ This is that kingdom
which is celestial and heavenly, not terrene and
worldly, as our Saviour showed unto Pilate, when
he had suspicion that He would make some attempt
against the Estate and Roman Empire.§ Finally, of
this kingdom there shall be no end, for as much as
then all things shall be perpetually established, and
shall never be afterwards changed again.

Et in Spiritum Sanctum.

And I believe in the Holy Ghost. By the name of
Holy Ghost is expressed the third Person of the
Blessed Trinity, who is also called by divers other
names, as Paraclete, Gift of God, Lively Fountain,
Fire, Charity, Spiritual Unction, the Finger of the
right hand of God, His Promise, etc.‖ He is called
Paraclete, which signifieth a Defender, an Advocate,
a Patron, an Intercessor, a Teacher, and a Comforter.
He is called the Gift of God, for that He doth
communicate and impart freely to every one, as He
pleaseth, His gifts and graces. He is called a Lively
Fountain, for that He is the Source and Spring of all
Divine and celestial graces which never dryeth. He

* St. Matthew ch. 25.   † St. Luke ch. 23.   ‡ St. John ch. 3.
§ St. John ch. 18.   ‖ Ex hymno, Veni Creator Spiritus.

is called Fire, for as much as He doth enkindle our hearts in the love of God, and doth warm them like fire. He is called Charity, for that He uniteth all the faithful together in one and the self-same heart, desire, and affection. He is called Spiritual Unction, for that He sheddeth forth upon us His Divine graces in great abundance. He is called the finger of God, for that God doth design all His graces by His operations. Lastly, He is called the Promise of the Father, for that Jesus Christ promised unto His disciples, that His Father would send Him unto them for their instruction and consolation, with abundant infusion of all celestial graces.*

Dominum.

Lord. The third Person of the Trinity is here called Lord, to the end that we acknowledge Him for God, every way coequal with the Father and the Son, of the same might, eternity, and infinite Majesty.

Et vivificantem.

And giving life. Amongst the effects and operations which are peculiarly appropriated unto the Holy Ghost, one is to vivificate or give life. For if He have life in Himself as the Father and the Son have, how shall He not give life unto others, seeing it is the property of life to give life, as it is of light to illuminate, of that which is hot to give and cast forth heat? If also the human spirit doth vegetate the

* St. John ch. 14.

11 *:

body, how shall not the Holy Ghost quicken the soul ?

Qui ex Patre Filioque procedit.

Who proceedeth from the Father and the Son. By this article we are to believe that the Holy Ghost proceedeth eternally from the Father and the Son, as from the same beginning and spiration. Which was added to repress the errors of the Greeks, whereof the heretic Nestorius was the first author, as testifieth Theodosius,[*] denying that the Holy Ghost proceeded from the Father and the Son. For the which he was condemned by the Council of Ephesus, reverenced in the Church as one of the four Gospels. And for the further confusion of heretics, and to the great joy and consolation of all Catholics, the said symbol was publicly sung three several times of all that were present.

Qui cum Patre et Filio simul adoratur et conglorificatur.

Who with the Father and the Son is together worshipped and glorified. To repress the impiety of Macedonius the heretic, who denied the Holy Ghost to be God, holding Him for a simple creature, and to be altogether unequal to the Father and the Son, as witnesseth St. Augustine,[†] the Church hath proposed Him unto us to be adored and glorified together with Them; which doth plainly argue that He is God, because that sort and kind of adoration pertaineth only to Almighty God.

[*] Lib. iv. Eccles. Hist. cap. 8 and 9.
[†] De Trinitate, lib. 1, cap. 6.

Qui locutus est per Prophetas.

Who hath spoken by the Prophets. To avert the people from the false opinion of those which despised visions, revelations, and the sacred predictions of the Holy Prophets, as lies, dreams, and fables, the Church assureth us that the Holy Ghost hath spoken unto us by them, according to the testimony of St. Peter * instructing and teaching us, that prophecy cometh not by the will of man, but that such men have spoken unto us, as they were inspired by God Himself.

Et unam.

And one. There are four special notes or marks of the true Church, gathered partly out of the Creed of the Apostles, and partly out of that of Constantinople. The first is that she is one, the second, that she is holy, the third, that she is Catholic, the fourth, that she is Apostolic. The first property, therefore, is that she is one, because her Head is one to Whom she is united. Her spirit is one, in which, as in one body, all are coupled and coapted which do belong unto her. Her preaching is one, her ceremonies are one, her end is one, and she alone hath means to conserve this unity.

Sanctam.

Holy. For her second mark she is called Holy.

1. By reason of her Head Which is Christ Jesus Himself, Who is the Holy of Holies. 2. In respect

* 2 St. Peter ch. 1, v. 21.

of her instructor which is the Holy Ghost, whom
Christ promised at His departure to send unto her.*
3. In respect of the holy Saints which are in her,
according to our Creed, sanctified by the same Holy
Ghost. 4. In respect of the unity of faith and
absolute obedience to one only chief and supreme
pastor, the Bishop of Rome. 5. In respect of the
holy laws and ordinances wherewith she is governed
and directed. 6. In respect of the holiness of the
Sacraments, which are daily dispensed in her by the
hands of her pastors. 7. And lastly, because only in
her and no way out of her can any one be sanctified
or made holy.

Catholicam.

Catholic. For her third mark she is called Catholic. or universal. 1. For the universality of faith
which she teacheth all men alike to believe. 2. For
the universality of doctrine whereby she instructeth
how to avoid vice and follow virtue. 3. For the
universality of truth which she defineth in General
Councils. 4. For the universality of nations, which
she calleth to the same faith, not excluding any.
5. For the universality of times, because from the
beginning to the ending, from Christ to the consum-
mation of the world, the Christian religion shall ever
continue. So that the Church, to be Catholic, is to
have been extant in all places and in all ages, which
never heretic could say of his Church. Let them,

* St. John ch. 16, v. 7.

saith Vincent of Lerins, shew their errors to have been believed everywhere, always, and of all, and then let them brag that they are Catholics.

Et Apostolicam.

And Apostolic. This fourth mark of Apostolic is also attributed to the Church, for that she is built upon the immovable rock of the doctrine of the Apostles, and hath had a perpetual succession of lawful pastors, without interruption, ever since their days unto this present. This mark no heretic whatsoever once dareth to challenge, it being an absolute prerogative only belonging to our Catholic Roman Church.

Ecclesiam.

Church. The word *Ecclesia* is a Greek word, and signifieth assembly or convocation : and to believe the Church is to believe that she is the lawful assembly of the faithful, universally dispersed in the same profession of faith and Divine worship ; her faith including generally that which is requisite to the salvation of the believers, to whom in many things it is sufficient simply to believe, especially to the unlearned, that which she believeth, without other exact knowledge of all particulars.

Why " in " is here omitted.

And note that the preposition *in*, put in the precedent articles, is here omitted, and it is simply said : I believe the Church, and not I believe in the Church, to discern betwixt the creatures and the Creator of all things in Whom only we must believe, and not in any other.

Confiteor unum Baptisma.

It is here said, *I confess one Baptism,* for as much as it cannot be reiterated under the pains nominated in the holy decrees,* and to the end that none may think himself able to amend the work of the Holy Ghost. Which also agreeth with natural reason itself, according whereunto a man is born but only once.

In remissionem peccatorum.

For the forgiveness of sins. Here ensueth the admirable effect of this most wholesome lotion, wherein all sin, be it original or actual, is pardoned, quite extinct and abolished, as if it had never at all been committed, how enormous and detestable soever it were, together with the pains due to the same; and there is also given us, and that in great abundance, the infusion of Divine graces to render us able to all endeavours and offices of Christian piety.

Et expecto resurrectionem mortuorum.

And I expect the resurrection of the dead. For the more sure establishment of our Faith, there is here set before us the resurrection of the dead, without the which we were of all other creatures the most wretched and miserable, and all our hope planted in

* Cap. Rebaptiz. de Consec. dist. 4.

Jesus Christ were utterly frustrate. Wherefore this article doth teach us to believe that the bodies of all, both men and women, which ever have been born since the beginning of the world, though they be rotten, burnt, eaten of worms, beasts or fowls of the air, yet shall be raised again at the day of judgment and be truly reunited unto their souls.

Et vitam venturi sæculi.

And the life of the world to come. This is the mark whereunto all the faithful ought to direct their designs, and to propose unto themselves as the hire. and recompense of all their labours. Without this no man can but judge himself much more unhappy and accursed than the brute beasts. Finally, if we esteem so much and hold so dear this present life, which is so fickle and so short, that it may rather be called a death than a life, in what estimation ought we to have the life that is eternal, void of all misery, and replenished with all beatitude and perpetual felicity? Of which joy, our Lord of His mercy make us then partakers, what sorrow soever we suffer in this world. Amen.

Of the sign of the Cross made at Vitam venturi sæculi.

The sign of the holy Cross is made at the words, *Et vitam venturi sæculi,* lest having been told of the bliss of the Saints and of the joys of the life everlasting, we should deceive ourselves by thinking to obtain them without any travail, whereas Christ

Himself did not enter into the kingdom of His glory but by the ignominy of His Cross. For from the Church militant unto the Church triumphant, none can enter but by the Cross, as saith Ludolphus.*

Amen.

For confirmation of that which is contained in this present Symbol, there is added for conclusion this word *Amen*, that is to say, in verity, truly, certainly, or without doubt, we believe that which is contained in the precedent articles.

Of the Kiss of the Altar.

After this, bowing down himself, he kisseth the Altar, testifying by this ceremony that he willingly submitteth himself under the Cross of Christ, and that from the bottom of his heart he embraceth the same ; confessing with the Apostle that the miseries of this life are not worthy of the glory, which shall be hereafter revealed unto us.

Dominus vobiscum.

The Creed being ended, the Priest turneth to the people, saying: *Dominus vobiscum*, praying that our Lord be with them, that they may make their profit of that which was repeated and rehearsed in the aforesaid articles. And the people answer :

Et cum spiritu tuo.

And with thy spirit. To the end, that being united together in the same faith and religion, they may

* In Vita Christi.

feel the effects of their salvation. Amalaricus saith, that this salutation of the Priest to the people denoteth an entrance to another office, and Gabriel Biel saith, that the Priest now saluteth the assistants with *Dominus vobiscum*, that God may be with them to receive their oblations.

Oremus.

Having said, *Dominus vobiscum*, next he saith *Let us pray;* because unless our Lord be with us, we cannot pray to our soul's health. And then he turneth him to the Altar, admonishing hereby that now especially every one should return to himself, and diligently search and discuss his conscience, that so he may offer up himself an acceptable sacrifice to Almighty God.

CHAPTER XXXIV.

OF THE OFFERTORY, AND OF THE CONDITIONS OF THE HOST THAT IS TO BE OFFERED.

FIRST, the Offertory taketh its name, *ab offerendo*, of offering, because in this part of the Mass, the people were wont to make their temporal offerings at the altar. Which in a solemn Mass is most melodiously sung, because as the Apostle saith : our Lord loveth a cheerful giver.* Because also it is convenient

* 2 Cor. ch. 9, v. 7.

that after the Gospel there should follow faith in heart, praise in mouth, and fruit in work, as saith Innocentius tertius.

The second reason.

Secondly it is called the Offertory, because at this time, the Priest doth take into his hands, and maketh an oblation of the Hosts that are to be consecrated. As also because it is a most immediate preparation and disposition to the holy Canon.

Of the conditions of the Host.

As touching the conditions of the Host that is to be offered, sundry notable things are signified thereby.

1. This bread is made of wheat, because Christ compared Himself unto wheat, saying: Unless the grain of wheat falling on the ground do die, it remaineth alone.

2. It is made in the form or manner of money, to signify that it is the same penny or reward promised by our Lord in the Gospel to the labourers in the vineyard.*

3. It is round, to put us in mind that God is the Creator of all things both in heaven and earth, Alpha and Omega, without beginning or ending. By which also it denoteth unto us the Divinity of our Blessed Saviour, whereby He filleth the round world.

4. It is white, to represent unto us the most pure

* St. Matthew ch. 20, v. 9.

flesh of our Lord and Saviour, taken of the most holy, perfect, and most pure Virgin.

5. It is thin, to signify that both the Priest and the communicants ought to come fasting to receive the same.

6. It is made without leaven, to signify that our hearts ought to be made clean from all leaven of envy and malice.

7. It must be whole, not cracked or broken, and that to signify two sundry mysteries. The one, that we ought to be always in love and charity with our neighbours. The other, that we ought to live in the unity of the Catholic Church, and never be sundered by schism or heresy.

8. In this Host is written the name and image of our Prince and Sovereign, to signify that we ought to acknowledge ourselves to be His people and the sheep of His pasture, as also that He hath made us to His own image and likeness.

9. Some likewise do form therein the picture of a lamb, to signify that He Which is sacrificed is the true Lamb of God, Which taketh away the sins of the world.

Of the Paten whereon the Host is laid, and why the same is hid or covered under the Corporal.

The Paten is so called, *a patendo*, that is, of patency or ampleness, and betokeneth a heart large, open, and ample. Upon this Paten, that is, upon

this latitude of charity, the Sacrifice of justice ought
to be offered. This latitude of heart the Apostles
had, when Peter said: Though I should die with
Thee, I will not deny Thee; likewise also said all the
disciples. * For which cause our Lord said unto
them: The spirit indeed is prompt, but the flesh is
weak.†

The second reason.

And because this latitude of heart fled from them
and lay hid when they all forsook and abandoned
their Master, therefore after the oblation is made,
the Priest hideth the Paten under the Corporal, or
the sub-deacon, removed from the Altar, holdeth it
covered, whereby the flight of the disciples is signified, who, whilst the true Sacrifice was offered, fled
and forsook Christ, as He Himself foretold them,
saying: All you shall be scandalized in Me this
night.‡

Of the two Palls or Corporals.

And here it is also further to be noted that there
are two Palls called Corporals, the one laid upon the
Altar under the Host and Chalice extended, the other
laid upon the Chalice folded. That extended signifieth faith, that folded betokeneth understanding, for
here the mystery ought to be believed but cannot be
comprehended, that faith may have merit, where
human reason can make no demonstrance.

* St. Matthew ch. 26, v. 35.   † St. Matthew ch. 26, v. 41.
‡ St. Matthew ch. 26, v. 31.

CHAPTER XXXV.

OF THE PREPARATION OF THE BREAD AND WINE FOR THE OBLATION, AND HOW THEREIN IS MOST LIVELY REPRE-SENTED THE ACTION OF OUR BLESSED SAVIOUR IN THE INSTITUTION OF THIS SACRAMENT.

The First Ceremony and its signification.

FIRST, by seeing the Priest prepare the bread for the Oblation, we may be put in mind how the disciples went before our Lord to prepare His Passover, as the Evangelist witnesseth, saying: The first day of the Azymes the disciples came to Jesus, saying: Where wilt Thou that we prepare for Thee to eat the pasch.*

The Second Ceremony and its signification.

His offering up the Host upon the Paten before Consecration, signifieth the great affection, wherewith our Lord and Saviour offered up Himself to His heavenly Father, to suffer His Death and Passion for us. As also the great desire which He had to ordain this holy Sacrament, saying: With a desire have I desired to eat this passover with you before I suffer.†

The Third Ceremony and its signification.

The Priest, preparing himself to perform the Offertory, removeth away the Chalice a little from him, and then holding up the Paten with the Host in both his hands, he saith this prayer following: *Suscipe, sancte Pater,* etc. Accept, O Holy Father,

* St. Matthew ch. 26, v. 17. † St. Luke ch. 22, v. 15.

Almighty and Eternal God, this immaculate Host, which I thy unworthy servant do offer unto Thee, my living and true God, for my innumerable sins, offences and negligencies, and for all here present, as also for all faithful Christians, both living and dead, that it may profit both me and them unto life everlasting. Amen. The removing away the Chalice a little from him doth signify, how our Saviour in the garden went a little aside from His disciples, as the Scripture saith, about a stone's cast. The laying of the Host down upon the Paten representeth the very manner of His prayer, to wit, *Procidit in faciem suam, orans*, as St. Matthew saith :* He fell upon His face, praying.

The Fourth Ceremony and its signification.

The prayer also itself is immediately directed to God the Father, as likewise that of our Saviour's was, saying : *Suscipe, sancte Pater.* Accept, O Holy Father. For even so our Saviour immediately directed that of His, saying : *Pater*, etc. My Father, if it be possible, let this chalice pass from Me.†

Of the mingling of the wine and water, and of sundry notable circumstances concerning the same.

Having ended the former prayer, he maketh the sign of the Cross with the Paten, then layeth the Host upon the Corporal, and afterwards poureth wine and water into the Chalice, of the which, as

* St. Matthew ch. 26, v. 39.   † St. Matthew ch. 26, v. 39.

likewise before of the bread, many notable circumstances are to be considered.

The First Ceremony and its signification.

First, as the bread which is prepared for the Consecration ought to be of pure wheat, so likewise the wine, for the self-same reason, ought to be of the natural grape. Because, as our Saviour compared Himself to bread, saying, *I am the living Bread Which came down from heaven,** so likewise He compared Himself to a vine, saying, *I am the true Vine, and My Father is the husbandman.*†

The Second Ceremony and its signification.

The wine is first poured into the Chalice without the water; and this is done according to the example of Jesus Christ Himself, as St. Cyprian testifieth,‡ to signify the blood which He poured forth at the time of His agony in the garden of Gethsemane.

The Third Ceremony and its signification.

The water is first blessed before it be mingled, but not so the wine. The reason whereof is, for that the wine in this place signifieth Christ, Who needeth no benediction, and water, the people, who in this life cannot be without sin, and therefore have very great need of benediction.

The Fourth Ceremony and its signification.

Next is to be noted, that in this mixtion there is

* St. John ch. 6, v. 51.   † Ibid. ch. 15, v. 1.
‡ Lib. 2, Epist. 3.

more wine put into the Chalice than water; and this
is in signification that the Church ought to be incorporated into Christ, and not Christ into the Church.

And Pope Honorius affirmeth that it should be a
pernicious abuse to do the contrary.*

The Fifth Ceremony and its signification.

In the Chalice of our Lord, wine is not alone
without water, nor water alone without wine, because
both flowed forth together out-of His side at the time
of His Passion, as saith St. Alexander, Pope and
Martyr, the fifth from St. Peter. Which St. Cyprian
very notably confirmeth, saying, *Si vinum tantum
quis offerat*, etc. If any man offer wine alone, the
blood of Christ beginneth to be without us, and if the
water be alone, we begin to be without Christ; but
when both are mingled then is a spiritual and
celestial Sacrament accomplished.† And Theophilus,
upon the nineteenth chapter of St. John, saith that
the Armenians are hereby confounded, because they
do not mingle in the Mysteries water with the wine,
for that they believe not, as it seemeth, that water
issued out of our Lord's side.

The Sixth Ceremony and its signification.

Again, water is mingled with wine to signify the
effect of this Divine Sacrament, to wit, Christ united
to the people believing, and the people believing
united to Christ in Whom they believe. For by water

* Cap. Perniciosus de Cele). Missæ.   † Epist. 65.

is understood the people, as in the Apocalypse :*
Aquæ multæ, populi multi; Many waters are many
people.

The Seventh Ceremony and its signification.

He which assisteth or serveth the Priest neither
layeth the Host upon the Altar, neither poureth the
wine nor water into the Chalice, but both are done
by the Priest himself, insinuating that Christ
Himself first instituted this Sacrament, and after,
recommended the same to His Apostles.   For as the
Evangelist saith : He took the bread and blessed it,
and after, He took the Chalice and consecrated it,
and said to His Apostles, Do this in remembrance of
Me.

Offerimus tibi, Domine.

We offer unto Thee, O Lord.   Having mingled the
water with the wine, as aforesaid, he taketh the
Chalice and offereth it up, saying : *We offer unto
Thee, O Lord, the chalice of salvation, beseeching Thy
clemency, that it may ascend with the odour of sweetness
in the sight of Thy Divine Majesty for our salvation and
that of the whole world.*   Signifying by this ceremony,
how our Blessed Saviour most willingly offered up
Himself unto His Father to be the oblation and
sacrifice for our redemption.   And here offer yourself
to His grace by true and unfeigned contrition of
heart for all your offences.

* Apoc. ch. 17, v. 15.

12*

Then he maketh the sign of the Cross with the Chalice, setteth the same upon the Corporal, covereth it with the pall, and next joining his hands together upon the Altar, he saith, *In spiritu humilitatis et in animo contrito suscipiamus a te Domine*, etc., to wit, in the spirit of humility and in a contrite heart ; for the spirit of humility acknowledgeth the want of virtues, and a contrite heart the number of vices.

Veni Sanctificator, omnipotens æterne Deus.

Come, O Sanctifier, omnipotent eternal God. Elevating his eyes to heaven, and contemplating the greatness and sublimity of this Mystery, which he prepareth himself to offer, he humbly requireth the assistance of the Holy Ghost to sanctify his oblation, from Whom also it is that all good desires and holy inspirations do proceed ; that by his supernatural and miraculous operation, that which he desireth may be effected, saying : Come, therefore, O Sanctifier, come by Thy mercy, come by Thy grace, come by Thy goodness, come by Thy sweetness, come by Thy love, come by Thy benignity, come by Thy piety and infinite bounty.

Et benedic hoc sacrificium tuo sancto nomini præparatum.

And bless this Sacrifice prepared to Thy holy Name. At which words he blesseth the offerings, calling upon the Holy Ghost, Who, albeit He is named alone, yet He cannot be alone, but is even both from and with the Father and the Son.

To conclude, of the Offertory mention is made by Walfridus,* Rabanus,† and others.‡

CHAPTER XXXVI.

OF THE PRIEST'S WASHING HIS HANDS.

HE that looketh diligently and narrowly to the first institution of this ceremony shall find it expressly to be taken from the model and example of our Saviour Himself, when He first ordained this holy Sacrament; for before He consecrated His Body and Blood, or communicated the same to His Apostles, He first prepared them by washing their feet.§

The second reason.

This very custom the Church observed some time, after His example. Tertullian witnesseth that this custom of the Priest, to wash his hands at the altar, was observed amongst the Christians in his time,‖ and St. Ambrose also and divers others make mention thereof.¶

The third reason.

Mystically, this ceremony admonisheth that every

* De Rev. Eccl. cap. 21.   † Lib. 1, de Divinis Off. cap. 2.
‡ Amal. lib. 3, de Eccl. Off. cap. 19. Microlog. de Eccles. Obser. cap. 10. Isidore, lib. 6, Etym. cap. 19. Innoc. lib. 2, de Myst. Missæ, cap. 53.
§ St. John ch. 13, v. 5.   ‖ Ad Uxorem, lib. 2.
¶ Lib. 3, de Sacr. inter opera Sancti.

one ought, with strict examination, to cleanse his conscience, presenting himself at this holy table, if he desire truly to feel the effects thereof to the health of his soul.

The fourth reason.

In particular, the Priest washes his hands at this present, notwithstanding he had washed them before. That if, perhaps by human frailty, he hath admitted into his mind any vain phantasy or imagination, he may now, at the least, cast it from him, and take, as it were, unto him another new cleanness. For he ought to procure so much the more purity, by how much he approacheth the nearer to the work of this most pure and most immaculate Mystery, that so he may touch with the more cleanness the most immaculate and precious Body of our Saviour Jesus.

The fifth reason.

He washeth not His whole hands, but only the tips or ends of his fingers, to signify that our greater faults and grosser offences ought first to be cleansed elsewhere, to wit, in confession, so that at the altar we should not need to wash but the tips of our fingers only, that is to say, some light affections, which may sometimes distract or disturb our spirit.

Then inclining a little before the midst of the Altar, his hands joined thereon, he saith the prayer following :—

Suscipe, sançta Trinitas, hanc oblationem quam tibi
offerimus, etc.

Receive, O holy Trinity, this oblation which we offer
unto Thee. Having now placed the bread and wine
in a readiness to be consecrated, he requireth the
Holy Trinity to accept his oblation, and that in the
memory of the most sublime and high mysteries of
the Passion, Resurrection, and Ascension of our
Saviour Jesus; which points are here proposed as
the most principal articles of the belief and health of
all the faithful.

CHAPTER XXXVII.

OF THE "ORATE FRATRES," ETC., AND OF THE REASON
OF THE PRIEST TURNING UNTO THE PEOPLE UPON
THE LEFT HAND.

THIS done, the Priest kisseth the Altar, and then
maketh one whole turn throughout, from the left
hand to the right, saying: Pray, brethren, that
mine and your Sacrifice may be made acceptable in
the presence of God the Father Almighty.

The first reason.

Touching the reason of the Priest turning to the
people upon the right hand we have already spoken
before, shewing that by the right hand the Priest
representeth the person of our Saviour, as now by
the left hand he representeth his own person; for

by the right hand is understood, virtue and perfection, and by the left hand, frailty and imperfection. The Priest, therefore, representing our Saviour, passeth not to the left hand, to signify that in our Saviour there was no sin nor imperfection. But when he representeth himself, to acknowledge that he is a sinner, frail and imperfect, he passeth to the left hand, saying : Pray for me brethren.

The second reason.

Again, by the right hand is signified mirth and joy, and by the left hand, sorrow and sadness. Wherefore the Priest, turning him to the Altar on his left hand, beginneth to represent the mysteries of the Death and Passion of our Saviour Jesus, a matter full of great sorrow and sadness, and signified by the left hand, as joy by the right hand. For of the Angel which declared the joyful Resurrection of our Saviour Jesus, the Scripture saith, that he sat on the right hand of the sepulchre.*

The third reason.

The good Esther, as we read in her book † before that she would speak to king Assuerus in the behalf of all her nation, was not content to betake her alone to her prayers, but also recommended herself to the prayers of all the people. The Priest, therefore, doth here the very like, considering that at this time he presenteth himself before the King of Kings, to

* St. Mark ch. 16, v. 5.   † Esther ch. 4, v. 16.

speak in the behalf of all his nation, that is to say, in the behalf of all the Church of God.

The fourth reason.

Again, it may be said, that therefore the Priest requireth to be assisted with the prayers of the people, for that he judgeth himself insufficient to consecrate so great a Sacrament, unless he be also holpen and seconded with the prayers and supplications of all the assistants.

Suscipiat Dominus Sacrificium, etc.

1. The people immediately make answer and pray for him, saying: Our Lord receive this Sacrifice of thy hands to the praise and glory of His Name, also to our utility and of all His holy Church. Wherein they imitate the counsel of the holy Scripture, which saith: *Orate pro invicem ut salvemini.* *Pray one for another that ye may be saved.**

2. Secondly, because also it is requisite that both the people pray for the Priest and the Priest for the people; for both the Priest and the people are all sacrificers, though in a far different manner, the Priest sacrificeth by himself, and the people by the Priest, which is his special commission in this behalf.

3. And rightly say they: Our Lord receive this sacrifice of thy hands, etc., to wit, at the hands of the Priest, because it is the self-same Sacrifice, which

* St. James ch. 5, v. 16.

before the celestial Father Himself vouchsafed to receive at the hands of His Son. Wherefore with this
oblation the devout soul may likewise offer herself
to Almighty God.

CHAPTER XXXVIII.

THE SECRET OF THE MASS, AND OF SUNDRY REASONS CONCERNING THE SAME.

FIRST to declare why it is called by the name of
Secret. All agree that it is so called because it
is pronounced in a secret and silent manner, there
being nothing more beseeming this high and
ineffable mystery than silence, as witnesseth
Fortunatus.*

The second reason.

To declare what this Secret is: it is no other
thing than certain petitions, which the Priest
maketh unto Almighty God, that it may please
Him to accept the prayers and sacrifices which
there are presented unto Him in the name of
the Church Universal.

The third reason.

And here let it be noted that these secret
prayers must always agree with the Collects in
number, order, and matter. As for example, if

* Lib. 3, de Eccles. Offic. cap. 21.

the priest do take three Collects, the first of the
Sunday, the second for the peace of the Church,
the third that which is common for the living
and the dead, then must the first Secret also be
of the Sunday; the second for the peace of the
Church, and the third for the living and the
departed; not that either the number or order
maketh so much in this matter, but because the
Church herein followeth the doctrine of St. Paul
saying: *Omnia honestè et secundum ordinem fiant in
vobis. Let everything be done decently and according
to order amongst you.**

The fourth reason.

The Priest reciteth these prayers in secret, and
that especially for five causes. First, to show that
the virtue of the Sacrifice, which our Lord was to
make for the redemption of man, was concealed
and hid from the world, until the time that He
offered Himself upon the Cross.

The fifth reason.

Secondly, to show that the Jews, presently
after the raising of Lazarus, conspired amongst
themselves to kill our Lord; for which cause He
did not walk openly amongst them, as the Scripture saith, but retired Himself in secret into the
city of Ephrem. †

* 1 Cor. ch. 14, v. 40.   † St. John ch. 11, v. 54.

The sixth reason.

Thirdly, to put us in mind what our Saviour did during the time He was thus retired. Whereof Rupertus * rendereth this reason, saying: The Priest, therefore, standing in silence and secretly praying upon the offerings, prepareth the holy Sacrifice; because our Lord, even when He hid Himself, and walked not openly amongst the Jews, prepared for us the wholesome Sacrament of His Passion. Thus He. Neither can the Priest more conveniently represent unto us the mysteries of the Death and Passion of our Saviour Jesus, and the order of them, than by beginning at the conspiration of the wicked Jews, from which He withdrew Himself in secret, because, as the Evangelist saith, His time was not yet come.

The seventh reason.

Fourthly, to represent the great taciturnity and silence which our Saviour used at the time of His examination before the judge, which, as the Gospel witnesseth, was so great that the judge himself did wonder thereat.

The eighth reason.

Fifthly, to put us in mind of the silence which He used at the time of His Passion, when He was led as a meek and innocent lamb unto the slaughter. Which example the holy martyrs do

* Lib. 2, de Divinis Off.

therefore imitate, of whom the Church singeth :
Non murmur resonat, non quærimonia. There is
neither murmur nor complaining heard. *

CHAPTER XXXIX.

OF THE PREFACE, AND OF SUNDRY REASONS CONCERNING THE SAME.

TOUCHING the name, interpretation, and etymology of the word, the word Preface is a word
which we retain of the Latins, as that of Trinity,
Sacrament, and the like, and signifieth no othe
thing than a certain preparation, preamble, or
prolocution, which is used before we come to the
principal narration or matter intended, the better
to prepare and dispose the auditors; like unto the
proems and exordiums which orators use before
they enter into their narrations. And for this
reason, this exhortation and Preface serveth to
prepare and dispose the Christians to devotion,
whilst the Priest addresseth himself to recite the
holy Canon, which containeth the most ineffable
and incomprehensible mystery of the consecration
of the Body and Blood of our Saviour Jesus.

The second reason.

According to the interpretation aforesaid, this

* Roman Breviary.

Preface may be referred to that action of our Lord, where He sent two of His disciples, to wit, Peter and John, saying: Go and prepare us the Pasch that we may eat. Who, as our Lord willed them, went and prepared the same.*

Per omnia sæcula sæculorum.

World without end. The Priest, being come to the end of the Secret, lifteth up his voice, pronouncing his words on high to be heard and understood of all the assistants; to signify that our Saviour having absented Himself from Jerusalem, returned thither again five days before His Passion, showing himself openly to His enemies, and making His entrance into the city with a great multitude of people following Him.

Amen.

Amen. The reply of the people answering *Amen* doth signify the joyful acclamations of the people, who to honour our Saviour, some of them cut down branches from the trees, others cast their garments in the way where He was to pass, and others cried out on high: *Benedictus qui venit in nomine Domini.* Blessed is he that cometh in the Name of our Lord.

Dominus vobiscum.

Our Lord be with you. Then the Priest, to dispose the assistants to be the more attentive

* St. Luke ch. 22.

to that which he goeth about to do, saluteth anew, requiring that our Lord be with them. And that not without need, for great were the misery of man not to be with Him, without Whom he cannot be.

Et cum spiritu tuo.

And with thy spirit. The people, having received this so wholesome a salutation of the Priest, do likewise resalute him again, praying that even as he hath wished, that God may be with them, so also He may be with his spirit, to the end that he may spiritually accomplish his office with all decency.

Joannes Diaconus, in the life of St. Gregory, recounteth that St. Gregory in the time of Mass, saying: *Dominus vobiscum*, and his chaplains, which attended him, being negligent to make him answer, an Angel from heaven supplied their default, saying: *Et cum spiritu tuo.*

Sursum corda.

Our hearts on high. This is another salutation of the Priest to the people, to the end that they should again with new fervour lift up their hearts on high to heaven, to consider the marvellous greatness of the mystery which is there undertaken. Yea, we may truly say that in this salutation, he further exciteth the Angels themselves, and all the celestial hierarchies to laud the majesty of Almighty God.

[4] Joan: Diac. in Vita Greg. lib. 4

Habemus ad Dominum.

We have them to our Lord. Of this *sursum corda*
St. Augustine saith: The hearts of the faithful are a
heaven, because they are daily directed up to heaven,
the Priest saying: *Sursum Corda*, and the assistants
answering him: *Habemus ad Dominum.* Yea this,
the very work of nature itself, and the proportion of
our heart wherewith we pray doth likewise preach
and proclaim unto us; whereof that part which is
turned downwards towards the earth is very little
and picked, and that which is directed upwards to
heaven is large and extended. Which being considered, let those that are present at this dreadful
Mystery, well and duly remember what they have
protested to the Priest at *Sursum corda*, answering
him, *Habemus ad Dominum.*

Gratias agamus.

Let us give thanks. As in the former exhortation it
was needful to crave of the Divine Goodness elevation
of mind, wherewith to pray well, so it is next
expedient, that having received this elevation of
mind, we tender hearty thanks to our Lord God
for the same; and for this cause the Priest admonisheth the people, saying: Let us give thanks.

Domino Deo nostro.

To our Lord God. For He is God Which of nothing
created us. He is Lord Who with His Blood hath re-

* St. Aug. S≀r. 44, de Tempore.

deemed us. He is ours who liberally communicateth Himself unto us. Again He is God, Who in creating, gave us nature; Lord, Who in redeeming, gave us grace; ours, Who in saving us, will give us glory.

Dignum et justum est.

It is meet and just. The people make answer acknowledging that it is meet and just; meet in respect of Him because He is our Lord; just in respect of us, because we are His people and the sheep of His pasture. Again, meet, in respect of His manifold benefits, just, in respect of our gratitude and obligation.

Vere dignum et justum est, æquum et salutare.

It is verily meet and just, right and wholesome. Which words, the Priest repeating after the people, addresseth unto Almighty God, containing so many several mysteries as there be sundry words repeated. For I find, that the learned and holy Doctors of Christ's Church have taken great delight and pleasure, to explicate unto us those five words of the Preface.

First, Albertus Magnus referreth them to five dignities or excellences contained in this holy Sacrament, saying that this Sacrament is a Sacrament of undoubted verity, of a most excellent dignity, of exceeding liberality, of weighed equity, and of most wonderful efficacy. For to the verity thereof answereth this word, *vere*, to the dignity thereof answereth this word, *dignum*, to the liberality

13

thereof answereth this word, *justum*, to the equity thereof answereth this word, *æquum*, and to the efficacy thereof answereth this word, *salutare*.

Others refer these words to four principal benefits which we receive of Almighty God, to wit, our Creation, Redemption, Justification and Glorification. And amongst others Innocent III. thus expoundeth them. Truly meet, because Thou of Thy mere goodness hast created us; just, because of Thy pure mercy, Thou hast redeemed us; right, because gratis Thou justifiest us; healthful, because Thou dost perpetually glorify us.

Nos tibi semper et ubique gratias agere.

That we always and everywhere give thanks unto Thee. By which words, *semper et ubique*, always and everywhere, is understood the greatness and immensity of Almighty God, Who is present everywhere and in all places. Or always, that therefore we ought to render Him thanks in all times and in all seasons. And everywhere, because wheresoever we be, in Him we live, move, and have our being.

Domine sancte, Pater omnipotens, æterne Deus.

Holy Lord, Father omnipotent, eternal God. Which other words express divers most high attributes of His most excellent Majesty. As by the word, *Domine*, that He is a Lord, and therefore to be served. By the word, *Sancte*, that He is holy, and therefore that His servants ought also to be holy. By the word, *Pater*, that He is our Father and we His children. By the word, *omnipotens*, that He is Almighty and able to defend us from the power of Satan and of all our enemies. By the word, *æterne*, that He is everlasting, and can glorify us eternally. By the word, *Deus*, that He is sole and absolute God, our only Maker, Redeemer, and Preserver.

Per Christum Dominum nostrum.

Through Christ our Lord. Which words do give us to understand that we miserable creatures, which have offended a God of such goodness and excellency, a Lord, a holy Lord, an omnipotent Father, a God, an eternal God, being of ourselves nothing else but dust and ashes, and most unworthy to present ourselves before His Majesty, do therefore not only give humble thanks for all His benefits, but also do seek to appease Him for our offences, and that, *Per Christum*, etc., through Christ our Lord.

Per quem majestatem tuam laudant Angeli.

First, this name of Angel is a name of office and not of nature; wherefore when they are sent, they are called Angels or messengers, for as much as they reveal the mind of God unto men. Which name is common to all the celestial spirits, though in this place, it is perhaps understood particularly of those which are of the lowest order; whereof every man hath one for his keeper, unless he drive him away by his evil life. For so St. Augustine saith of them,

18 *

that they love what God loveth, keep what God
keepeth, and forsake what God forsaketh.* Of these
mention is made in the eighteenth chapter of
St. Matthew, the first of St. Mark, and first chapter
of the Epistle to the Hebrews.

Adorant Dominationes.

The Dominations adore.   Dominations are those by
whom the other Angels receive the ordinances of
God, and who do see them executed : of which pre-
eminence and predomination over other Angels they
are called Dominations.   Now then if these so noble
spirits to whom, by reason of their office, adoration
doth seem to be due, do themselves with profound
reverence adore Almighty God, how much more
ought we, who are but dust and ashes, to humble
ourselves under His almighty hand.   Of Princi-
palities, Powers, Virtues, and Dominations, St.
Paul maketh mention, all in one Epistle.†

Tremunt Potestates.

The Powers do tremble.   The Powers are such to
whom the wicked powers are subject : and hereof
they receive their name, because the malignant
spirits by their power are bridled and restrained,
that they cannot do so much hurt as they desire.
Of these it is said that they tremble, not for timorous
fear, being perfectly blessed, but, saith Gabriel Biel,
for obedience, reverence, and admiration of so

* Solil. cap. 7.   † Ephes. ch. 1, v. 21.

ineffable a Majesty, acknowledging their power to be nothing in respect of the Divine and immense power of Him, Who is contained in this dreadful Sacrifice.

Cæli cælorumque virtutes.

And the Powers of the heavens. In this place these words do signify all the company of the celestial spirits which are the intellectual heavens. But some understand them of the material heavens in that sense of the nineteenth Psalm: *Cæli enarrant gloriam Dei: The heavens declare the glory of God.* For as Euthymius * and St. Chrysostom say: the heavens and also the stars, although they want a voice, and have neither life nor soul, yet do they laud and praise the Majesty of God by their greatness, beauty, situation, nature, utility, ministry, perseverance, and by other like means; whereby also they do draw the minds of their beholders into the admiration and praise of their Creator.

Et beata Seraphim socia exultatione concelebrant.

And the blessed Seraphim, with mutual joy do jointly celebrate. Seraphim in Hebrew is interpreted *Ardentes,* burning or inflaming, for that they are enkindled and inflamed in charity above all others; betwixt whom and God there are no other Angels, being so inflamed with the brightness of the divine light, that, as the Prophet Isaias saith,† they cover the face and feet of Him that sitteth on the throne.

* In Ps. 148. † Isaias ch. 6, v. 2.

Cum quibus et nostras voces, ut admitti jubeas deprecamur,
supplici confessione dicentes.

With whom we beseech that Thou wouldst command
our voices to be admitted, with humble confession saying,
For as much as all the celestial orders of Angels
aforenamed are chiefly employed in continual praises
and thanksgivings before the presence of Almighty
God, therefore the Priest maketh his humble petition
to our Lord in the name of them all, that He would
vouchsafe to receive our lauds and praises amongst
the praises of the holy Angels; that so, men associated
with the celestial spirits, as the lower strings of a
harp with the higher, they may jointly sound forth
the heavenly hymn of *Sanctus* following.

Of the sacred hymn of Sanctus, and of sundry reasons
concerning the same.

First, Gabriel Biel, in his exposition of the Mass,
saith that *Sanctus*, is so called of *Sancio*, which is to
consecrate, dedicate, establish, ratify or confirm, and
thus laws, customs, and men also are called holy.

The second reason.

The same author saith that *Sanctus* may be so
called *a sanguine hostiæ*, of the blood of the host, for
amongst the people of the old law, that was called
holy which was consecrated or sprinkled with the
blood of the host, and so *Sanctus* may be as much as
sanguine unctus, anointed with blood.

The third reason.

Cyrillus, or rather Origines saith, that the word *Sanctus* with the Greeks is called *Hagios*, which is, saith he, *extra terram esse*, to be out of the earth,* which thing doth in very deed most perfectly and excellently agree with that most Divine and pure nature of Almighty God.

The fourth reason.

St. Denis, in his seventh chapter of his heavenly Hierarchy, saith that this *Sanctus* is a voice of exceeding praise, full of much dread and reverence. And St. Ambrose saith that we find nothing more precious, wherein we may set forth and extol Almighty God than in that we call Him holy.† Add that Holy is one of the names of Almighty God.‡

The hymn of Sanctus confirmed by miracle.

Gabriel Biel, in his learned exposition upon the Mass, saith that when Constantinople was shaken with an earthquake, and the people for fear prayed in the fields, in the sight of all a little child was taken up into the air for the space of an hour, and afterwards descending again, said that from heaven this angelical hymn resounded in his ears as from a great multitude or choir of celestial singers, and that he was commanded to declare that song of praise to all the people, which as soon as they began to sing, God delivered them from that imminent danger.

* Lib. 11, in Levit.

† Lib. 3, de Sp. Sancto, cap. 12.　　‡ St. Luke ch. 1, v. 35.

Sanctus, Sanctus, Sanctus.

Holy, Holy, Holy. These sacred words thrice repeated may put us in mind of the three Persons of the most Blessed Trinity, the Father, the Son, and the Holy Ghost, every One of which are infinitely holy with the same sanctity. Which sanctity in these three Persons doth far surpass the sanctity of all creatures by many degrees. For first, the sanctity of God is infinite, without bound or measure; secondly, it is independent, and neither springing nor flowing from any other fountain; thirdly, it is to God essential and not participated.

Dominus Deus.

Lord God. The Church in this devout canticle doth most lively declare and set forth unto us her faith in the doctrine of the Blessed Trinity. For the word *Sanctus*, thrice repeated, plainly signifieth the Trinity of Persons, and the words *Dominus Deus*, once repeated, truly declare the unity of essence.

Sabaoth.

Of Hosts. The word *Sabaoth* signifieth as much as *militiarum*, of hosts or armies; for so many armies hath God in earth as there are several Orders in the Church; and so many armies hath He in heaven, as there are sundry Orders of holy Angels. And rightly do we call the Angelical Spirits an army, because they fight against the spiritual powers, to wit, the devils.

Pleni sunt cæli et terra gloria tuâ.

Heaven and earth are full of Thy glory. To wit, Angels and men, replenished with Divine grace. Or heaven and earth are full of His Divine glory, because His Deity is everywhere; above all things, not elated; under all things, not prostrated; within all things, not included; without all things, not excluded. Again heaven and earth are full of His glory; because the self-same Glory, which is in heaven with the Angels, is likewise with us in earth; the self-same Glory which is sitting upon the throne and right hand of the Father, the self-same Glory is upon the altar, and therefore both heaven and earth at one and the self-same time are filled and replenished with the self-same Glory.

Hosanna.

Hosanna in Hebrew is composed of *Hosiach* save, and *anna*, which is an interjection of beseeching, and being put together sound as much as, Save, we beseech Thee. Which Pope Symmachus interpreteth more manifestly, saying, Save me, O Lord, I beseech Thee.

In excelsis.

In the highest. These other words, *in excelsis*, joined to *hosanna* do clearly show what this saving is, which is before understood in the word *hosanna*, to wit, *in excelsis*, in the highest, that is in heaven, because Christ came to give not earthly but heavenly, not temporal but eternal salvation.

Benedictus qui venit in nomine Domini.

Blessed is He that cometh in the Name of the Lord.
Blessed is He Which cometh once to offer Himself for
us in a cruental oblation upon the Cross, and blessed
is He Which cometh daily to be offered incruentally
for us upon the altar; and blessed is He Which
cometh to replenish us with abundance of all spiritual
graces and benedictions.

Hosanna in excelsis.

Hosanna in the highest. This Hosanna is twice
repeated for the two parts of glory, the one of the
body, and the other of the soul; or for the salvation
of two people, the Jews and the Gentiles.

Of the sign of the Cross made at the end of the aforesaid
hymn.

The words *Benedictus*, etc., were, as before was
said, the praises and acclamations of the people,
when our Saviour returned to Jerusalem; at the
pronunciation whereof, the Priest maketh the sign
of the Cross before his face, to signify that this
honourable entry of Christ, with all those high
acclamations of the people, was not to receive the
pomp of a worldly kingdom, but by His Passion and
Death to purchase our redemption. The use of singing sundry prefaces in the holy Mass is very ancient,
as appeareth out of Clemens Romanus, Cyprianus,
Chrysostomus, Basilius, Ambrosius, and sundry
others cited by Durandus.*

* In Lib. de Rit. Eccl. Cath. lib. 2, cap. 30.

CHAPTER XL.

OF THE HOLY CANON OF THE MASS, AND OF SUNDRY NOTABLE MYSTERIES CONTAINED IN THE SAME.

FIRST, Canon is a Greek word which signifieth a rule or a thing regularly composed ; and this part of the Mass is so called, because it containeth certain prescriptions and ordinances for the consecration of so high a Sacrament. As also, because it hath, by the authority of the Church of Rome, obtained the force of a prescript or law. Of the holy Canon do make mention most authors, which ever took upon them to write of the Mass, even from the Apostles unto this present, and therefore it shall not be needful in this place, or in the discourse ensuing, to fill up paper with the particular names of any, either ancient or modern.

Why the holy Canon of the Mass is said in secret.

The holy Canon of the Mass is said in secret, because that which is performed therein is so hidden and secret, that no human reason is able fully to comprehend it.

Durandus saith that the holy Canon of the Mass is said in secret, lest otherwise those sacred words should be made over common, or wax contemptible amongst the simple people, who, by daily use of hearing them, might carelessly recite and sing them in the open streets and other places not convenient.

For as the same author recounteth, when in former times the holy Canon of the Mass was pronounced publicly, almost all manner of persons learned it by rote, and would sing it in the fields and open streets. Whereupon it happened that certain shepherds, singing it for recreation, and laying bread upon a stone, at the prolation of the sacred words, the bread was turned into flesh, but they by God's justice were stricken with fire sent down from heaven. For which cause, the holy Fathers of God's Church have ever since ordained, that these sacred words should always be said in silence.

The like also happened to three little boys, who to make themselves sport, would seem to take upon them to sing Mass. Who first placing a stone instead of an altar, and then laying their bread thereon instead of a host, and after putting water into a wooden dish instead of a chalice, were suddenly stricken to the earth, and their bread and water consumed with fire which fell from heaven; and for the space of three days, to the great amazement of the parents, remained speechless; but after three days, coming again unto themselves, recounted openly all that which had befell then; all which is testified more at large by Joannes Moschus and by many others.

The premisses therefore considered, I am here to pray the gentle reader to pardon me, if I do not turn the words of the sacred Canon, immediately ensuing, into our vulgar tongue, as I have done the former, which I protest, in regard of their dreadful venerableness, I dare not do. Hoping nevertheless sufficiently to explicate their sense and meaning by the ensuing method. Now then, according to St. Jerome let us sprinkle our book and the posts of our houses with blood. And with Zara let us bind a red thread upon our finger, that we may set forth the Passion and Death of our Redeemer, and sorrowfully consider the unspeakable pains which He vouchsafed to suffer for us.

CHAPTER XLI.

OF THE SACRED CANON OF THE MASS.

Te.

FOR as much as in the holy Canon of the Mass special memory is made of the Passion and Death of our Redeemer, therefore perhaps it was ordained by Divine Providence, and not by human industry, that the sacred Canon should take its beginning from that letter, which by its proper form doth lively express the sign of the Cross in the figure of Thau. As the prophet Ezechiel, saith : The figure of Thau in the foreheads of the men which sorrow and mourn.*

* Ezechiel ch. 9.

Igitur.

Which word *Igitur* is a particle illative, connecting the sacred Canon unto the Preface-before rehearsed. As if he should say, after such preamble of prayers, and celebration of praises, at the length we enterprise that which hitherto for reverence we have deferred.

Clementissime.

Clemency by St. Thomas is defined to be alenity or gentleness of a superior to an inferior, and which, out of a certain sweetness and tenderness of affection, doth moderate pains. Seneca in like manner defineth it to be an inclination of the mind to lenity or pity in the execution of punishments. Rightly therefore in this place, our Lord is said to be most clement, because, as for our sins He doth not in this life exact of us to the uttermost farthing, so neither in His Divine service doth He rigorously require at our hands that which is due to so high a Majesty; nay He doth rather greatly tolerate the suppliant's infirmity, supplying his defects with the abundance of His piety.

Pater.

As touching the name and title of a Father, it belongeth to a Father, 1. To produce a child like unto himself. 2. To love it being produced. 8. To provide it of necessaries. 4. To teach and instruct it. All which Almighty God hath most mercifully performed unto us: for He is a Father in creating us, a Father in tenderness of affection towards us, a Father in providing for us, and a Father in instructing us by His Divine and most holy Spirit.

Per Jesum Christum Filium tuum.

In which words is clearly alleged the virtue of the Mediator; the which, of what marvellous operation and efficacy it is, plainly appeareth by the great propinquity which He hath with both parties, between whom He is in the midst as Mediator. For first with God He hath propinquity, because He is the Son of God; also with us He hath propinquity, because He is the Son of man. Whence it followeth, that He first praying to His heavenly Father for us, doth set open His ears to our petitions, and in a sort addicteth them to hear our supplications.

Dominum nostrum.

And worthily is He said in all these to be ours, to wit, our Jesus, our Christ, and our Lord, given for a preservative of our health, in food for our refection, in Sacrifice for our reconciliation, in Sacrament for our sanctification, and in price for our redemption.

Supplices rogamus, ac petimus.

Which two words do somewhat differ in signification, for to ask is simply to demand, but asking joined with beseeching is an obsecration which is made with earnest entreaty and persuasion. And therefore aptly by two divers words the demand is doubled, that so the prayer which is made may be of greater moment.

Why the Priest here kisseth the altar.

This devout ceremony may signify unto us that Christ not only of His humility, obedience, and love to His Father gave Himself to death for us, but also of His exceeding love and charity towards us. For as God so loved the world that He gave His only begotten Son for it; so also His Son loved the same, that He would likewise willingly die to redeem it, not compelled by any necessity, as Himself signified, saying : I have power to lay down My life, and to resume or take the same again.

Uti accepta habeas, et benedicas.

God is said to accept our offerings, not that they are either profitable or delectable to Him, but that according to the accustomed and wonted manner of acceptance, we do beseech Him, that upon those things which we offer unto the glory of His Name, He would pour down the increase of His heavenly benediction. And therefore there is subjoined *et benedicas.*

Hæc + dona, hæc + munera, hæc + sancta sacrificia illibata.

Which three words, *Dona, Munera, Sacrificia,* may be thus distinguished. First, those things are called *Dona,* which are given us of God for our sustenation, as testifieth the Apostle, saying : Every best gift and

every perfect gift is from above.* Furthermore,
Donum, according to St. Isidore, is that which the
superior giveth or bestoweth upon the inferior. Or
as Cyrillus saith, a thing which is given to such as
are in need.† 2. They are called *Munera*, in as much
as they are received of us with a grateful mind. Or
rather, in as much as we, who are poor and inferior,
present them to God as to our superior, expecting in
lieu of them, to receive some better thing from His
blessed hands. 3. They are called sacrifices, in as
much as we offer them up to God, to please and
pacify Him for our sins. Or as they are offered unto
Him, to honour Him with the highest latrial honour.
So that they are to be considered, 1. As they
respect the giver, and so they are called gifts. 2.
As they respect the receiver, and so they are called
rewards. 3. As they respect the offerer, and so they
are called sacrifices. Again some of our holy Doctors
there be, who accommodate these three words, *Dona,
Munera, Sacrificia*, marvellously well to the most
precious Body and Blood of our Saviour Jesus: as
for example, 1. It is a Gift, say they, because God
hath given It us of His mere liberality, and It is of
such excellent greatness that He could not possibly
give or bestow a greater upon us. 2. It is a Reward
or Present, because of all the oblations that we can
present unto Him, we have nothing of price, but His
most precious Body and Blood, which He hath given

* St. James ch. 1, v. 17. † Cyrill. in Collect.

14

unto us that we may give or render again unto Him.
3. It is also a Sacrifice, for that it is the very Lamb
of God Which truly was sacrificed for the sins of the
world.   And lastly, this so worthy a Sacrifice is said
to be *illibata*, for as much as it ought to be offered up
without any spot of soul or body.

*Of the three crosses which are made at the prolation of
the three words aforesaid.*

Concerning the three crosses which the Priest
maketh at the prolation of the three words aforesaid,
Stephanus Eduensis saith, that the bread and wine
are signed with a triple cross, to declare the whole
mystery to be wrought by the marvellous might of
all the Trinity.   According to Albertus Magnus and
Innocentius tertius, by these three crosses may be
understood three derisions or illusions of our Blessed
Saviour.   The first before the High Priest, the second
before King Herod, and the third before Pontius
Pilate.

In primis quæ tibi offerimus pro Ecclesia.

Every Sacrifice ought to be offered up for all, that
is to say, for the Church Universal, for it is great
reason that every Priest pray for all, because Christ
the proper Host of this Sacrifice was offered up for
all, as writeth St. Cyprian.*

Tua.

This word is added to the former by way of

*Epist. 63.

obsecration, wherein we crave that He would be good and merciful unto His Church, not for her own merits, but for His own gifts and many most singular graces, which He hath vouchsafed to bestow upon her, and wherewith He hath marvellously adorned and enriched her. And Gabriel Biel saith that the Church useth this word *Tua*, calling herself *His*, the rather to insinuate herself into His grace and protection. For, as St. Ambrose noteth, every one doth willingly keep and protect his own.*

Sancta.

This Church is called holy for sundry reasons. Holy for her holy religion, holy for her holy laws, holy for her holy Sacraments, holy because her Head is the Holy of Holies ; holy because the Holy Ghost her Ruler and Director is holy ; lastly, holy because she is vowed and consecrated unto Almighty God, and sanctified and washed in the most precious Blood of our Saviour Jesus, as writeth the Apostle.†

Catholica.

Next this Church is called Catholic, that is to say Universal, for as much as she hath been diffused by the splendour of faith even to the uttermost ends of all the world. In which name St. Augustine doth admirably rejoice, because he was contained within the lap of that Church under the sacred name of Catholic.

* Lib. 2, de Pœn. cap. 8.   * Ephes. ch. 5, v. 26.
‡ Epist. quam vocant Fundamenti, cap. 4.

14 *

Quam pacificare.

Rightly in the first place do we pray for the pacification and peace of the Church, this peace being the bond of all concord and the redress of all discord : and which Christ our Saviour, departing from His disciples, last of all bequeathed unto them[*] and after His resurrection first of all preached unto them.[†]

Secondly, aptly is peace here asked of Almighty God, because God is the God of peace and not of dissension.

Thirdly, very well is peace required in the time of sacrificing, because this Sacrifice is a Sacrifice of peace.

Fourthly, because as no community can consist without peace, so neither the Church.

Custodire.

In the next place, we pray that our Lord would keep His Church, especially from the deceitful allurements of the world, the flesh, and the devil. From the dangerous incursions of all ravening wolves, as from infidels, Turks, heretics, wicked pastors, and from all false brethren. Which prayer Christ Himself before His departure made for His Church and chosen, saying : That Thou keep them from evil.[‡]

Again three sundry ways, God preserveth his

[*] St. John ch. 14, v. 27.   [†] St. Luke ch. 24, v. 36.
[‡] St. John ch. 17, v. 15.

from evil. First, by a blessed and happy death, that they live not to see them, as we read of king Joshua. Second, that they escape them by flight, as did St. Paul from Damascus. Third, by giving them fortitude constantly to overcome them, as divers holy martyrs and confessors have done.

Adunare.

And for as much as Christ Himself saith, that He hath other sheep which are not as yet of the same sheepfold,* therefore for these also do we pray, that that they may be brought to the unity of the same Church. In which word, according to St. Augustine, we pray for that which always ought to be prayed for in the Church of Christ, to wit, that faith may be given to infidels, unity to schismatics, and resociation to such, as by the censure of the same Church, are for a time severed to do penance for their offences.†

Et regere digneris toto orbe terrarum.

Which words, together with the other before recited, may be more briefly thus expounded. To pacify from enemies that she be not oppressed, to keep in peace that she be not disturbed, to unite from schisms that she be not divided, to govern in the disposition of her Councils that she be not deceived.

* St. John ch. 10, v. 16.
† St. Aug. contra Julianum, cap. 3.

Una cum famulo tuo Papa Nostro N.

Where note that *Papa* is said of the interjection *Papæ*, which is an interjection of admiration, as admirable for sanctity. And right worthily is this name attributed to the Bishop of Rome, for, whereas in many other seats faith and religion hath failed, to this chair and seat of Rome, never could perfidiousness have access.

Et Antistite nostro N.

A Bishop in this place is termed by the name of *antistes*, so called of these two Latin words, *Ante* and *Stes*, because he standeth and is placed before other Priests. Touching this our Bishop, we ought also to have remembrance of him, for so St. Paul willeth us, saying : Remember your prelates which have spoken the Word of God to you ;* and : Obey your prelates and be subject unto them, for they watch over you, as being to render an account for your souls.† Seeing therefore that they stand answerable and accountable for our souls, should it not be very great ingratitude in us to forget them in our prayers ?

Et omnibus orthodoxis.

Doxa in Greek signifieth sentence or opinion, and *orthodoxos*, as much as right believers. By which word it is most plain that all infidels, heretics and schismatics, separated from the mystical body of our

* Hebrews ch. 13, v. 7.   † Ibid. ch. 13, v. 17.

Saviour Christ, are excluded from the fruit and benefit of this Sacrifice.

Atque Catholicæ et Apostolicæ fidei cultoribus.

Where it is to be noted that to worship the Catholic faith is not only for a man to believe it in himself, but also to declare and express it in his deeds; as, namely, to sustain and defend the same against all such as shall impugn it; all which are truly termed defenders and advancers, protectors and worshippers of the Catholic faith.

CHAPTER XLII.

OF THE FIRST MEMENTO.

Memento, Domine.

HITHERTO the Priest hath prayed for the Church Universal and for her rulers. And now in this place he doth recommend unto the divine clemency his own particular friends, for whom he intendeth to offer up Sacrifice; as his parents, brethren, sisters, kinsfolks, and others benefactors, or such as he hath taken in charge unto him, as speaketh St. Augustine,* saying: *Memento, Domine.* In which words he desireth that our Lord would be mindful of those, whom in his present prayers he offereth up unto Him, because to be had in mind of God is to be holpen of God. And Gabriel Biel addeth that when he asketh

* Epist. 50, Quæst. 5.

that our Lord would remember them, he demandeth
that He would have mercy on them.

Famulorum, famularumque tuarum.

First, as the same author saith, men are set before
women for the dignity of their sex, because, as the
Apostle St. Paul saith, the man is the head of the
woman.* Next he calleth all those for whom he
prayeth unto Almighty God, not simply men, but his
servants, thereby acknowledging Him for their good
Lord and Master, full of all mercy, clemency and
sweetness.

*Why the Priest joineth his hands together and meditateth
awhile in prayer.*

In this place, the Priest meditateth awhile and
calleth to mind all those aforesaid, for whom he is
obliged and bound to pray, as his own parents,
friends, and benefactors, etc. And this truly greatly
moved divers of our holy ancestors to induce some
one or other of their children to the office of Priesthood, because they knew very well that the Priests
were bound to pray and offer Sacrifice particularly
for their parents, friends and benefactors. For how
should the Priest at this present, standing in the
presence of Christ and His Angels, not remember his
faithful and loving friends, their benefits bestowed
upon him, their particular necessities, and their
pious, holy, and devout intentions ? This therefore

* 1 Cor. ch. 11, v. 3.

the Church duly observeth, as being grounded upon the law both of God and nature.

Et omnium circumstantium.

The same holy Mass is further particularly applied to all those, which in fervent faith and attentive devotion, do assist at the same, that they especially may participate of the fruit of the Death and Passion of our Saviour Jesus, who, by particular devotion, have adjoined themselves to assist at the Sacrifice. And well doth he pray for all those that stand about, that is, who stand firm in quietness, inward recollection, and elevation of mind in Almighty God, and not for those who walk or stare about them, for all such do rather stir than stand still.

Quorum tibi fides cognita est, et nota devotio.

Faith, according to St. Paul, is defined to be an argument of things not appearing. To the end therefore, that all those which are present at the Sacrifice of the Mass may reap the fruit which they desire, there is here required in them these two things principally.

1. A firm and unmovable faith, to believe without staggering that the Body and Blood of Jesus Christ, together with His Soul and Divinity, are truly, really, and substantially present under the species of bread and wine, after the prolation of the sacramental words.

2. Devotion, which is defined to be a spiritual act

of the will, readily obeying unto Almighty God.
For it is not enough that the understanding be
united to God by faith, unless the affection likewise
be conjoined unto Him by pure devotion.

Pro quibus tibi offerimus, vel qui tibi offerunt.

The Priest doth pray and offer Sacrifice not only
for those that are present, but for others also which
are absent.   Because some there are, who neither in
body are present at Mass nor yet in intention ; such
are the souls in Purgatory, little infants, and also
many wicked and evil Christians, for whom notwithstanding the Priest doth offer, and that in particular.
Others there be who are present at Mass, either in
intention only and not in body, or both in body and
intention : and these both offer themselves, and the
Priest also doth offer for them, although in a far dis-
tinct and different manner ; for the people offer
spiritually, the Priest properly ; the people in affection, the Priest in function ; the people offer in
heart, holy desire, faithful assistance, uniform
consent and humble prayer, the Priest by actual,
external, and visible ministry, with absolute power
to consecrate and sacrifice.

Hoc sacrificium laudis.

This oblation is here called a Sacrifice, of the
effect, *quia sacros nos efficit*, because it maketh us
holy. And again of praise ; 1. Because Christ
with praise and thanksgiving first instituted the

same. 2. Because He Himself offered it up to
the honour and praise of His eternal Father. 8.
Because there is nothing in this Sacrifice which is
not abounding and full of praise. For if respect be
had to Christ's Divinity, it is here. If His sacred
Humanity be sought for, here is His Soul, here is
His Body, here is His Blood, all most worthy of
praise and honour.

Pro se, suisque omnibus.

In these words, the Priest who maketh this oblation, ought first, according to the well-ordered rule
of charity, to remember himself, and the care and
safety of his own soul. Next that all such as have
any charge committed unto them to rule or govern,
that they do not only commend themselves unto God,
but also all those that are committed to their charge
and oversight; as the Pastor for his flock, the
Prince for his subjects, the Captain for his soldiers,
the Father of a house for his family, the Master for
his scholars, and so of others.

Pro redemptione animarum suarum.

Which words do shew, that the Priest ought not to
pray neither for any earthly appetite nor temporal
gain, but purely and sincerely for the salvation of
their souls; for to do otherwise were with Simon
Magus to buy and sell the gifts of God for money.

Pro spe salutis et incolumitatis suæ.

That is to say, for hope of health as touching the

sick, for hope of safety as touching the healthy, for friends if they be fallen at enmity, for their safe return if they be in journey, and for their amendment if they live viciously.

Tibique reddunt vota sua.

Where note, that a vow in this place is not properly taken for a promise of some spiritual thing made unto God, but for pious intentions, holy desires, and other good works, which the Priest requireth to be accomplished with a most inward affection by the assistants, according to the saying of the Prophet David: Offer up to God the sacrifice of praise, and render thy vows unto the Highest.

Æterno Deo, vivo et vero.

In which three words are plainly excluded, three sorts of creatures which falsely have been taken and reputed for gods, to wit, devils, men, and idols. For the devils, they are living, but not eternal; first, because they had a beginning; and next, because they have lost the life eternal. The second also are living, but neither eternal nor true; not eternal, because they shall have an end; not true, because, as the Scripture saith, Every man is a liar. The third are neither true, nor living, nor yet eternal, as being without all manner of sensibility or motion.

To conclude, concerning the first part of the

holy Canon four things are chiefly to be noted, to wit, to whom, for whom, how, and wherefore we ought to offer up this Sacrifice of praise. To whom? Only to God, that is, to the most Blessed and Undivided Trinity. For whom? For the holy Catholic Church, that is, for all true and faithful believers. How? In the unity of faith, that is to say, in the Communion of Saints. Wherefore? To wit, for all benefits, temporal, spiritual, and eternal.

CHAPTER XLIII.

OF THE COMMEMORATION WHICH IS MADE OF THE BLESSED SAINTS.

Communicantes.

In four things we do communicate with the blessed Saints.

1. In faith, believing whatsoever they believed concerning the verity of this Blessed Sacrament.

2. In hope, because the Saints did hope, and we do hope; for we still hope and expect in patience that which they already possess in full assurance.

3. In charity, for such is the prerogative of charity; that though faith do cease when beatifical vision is present, though hope do desist when pleasant fruition is possessed, yet in heaven charity never faileth, but is more increased and perfected.

4. We do communicate with them, in the use

and oblation of this Blessed Sacrament, whose former viaticum this hath been, to bring them to that most blessed life whereunto they are so happily arrived. Because also it is said of the Saints, that they were persevering in the doctrine of the Apostles, and in the communion of breaking bread.

Et memoriam venerantes.

The first reason why, before the consecration of the Body of Christ, the Church hath ordained the commemoration of the Saints to be made, is because she hath been taught and learned this out of the figures of the Old Testament. For as the legal Priest and Bishop, entering into the Holy of Holies, brought in with him the names of the twelve tribes written upon his Rational, even so the evangelical Priest, entering into the Holy of Holies, bringeth in with him the names of the blessed twelve Apostles.

But besides this, there are sundry other reasons for the commemoration and veneration of the blessed Saints.

1. Because the odour and fame of their virtues is everywhere dispersed throughout the world.

2. Because their holy bodies and relics are had in high veneration, and visited and frequented with many pious pilgrimages.

8. Because both churches and altars of unspeakable riches are dedicated unto God in their names and memories.

4. Because upon the tombs of martyrs, relics, and bodies of the blessed Saints, the Sacrifice of the Mass is daily celebrated.

5. Because at the sepulchres and memories of the blessed Saints, God doth work many marvellous miracles.

6. Because in this the Church doth that which all antiquity was accustomed to do; for it hath ever been the practice of the Church to make commemoration of the blessed Saints in all her prayers and supplications.*

In primis.

First. Where being to speak of our blessed Lady, he well saith, *first*, to wit, before all Angels, before all men, and before all creatures. For to which of the Angels was it at any time said: The Holy Ghost shall come upon thee? Or to what man was it ever said: The power of the Most High shall overshadow thee? Or to what creature was it ever said: That which of thee shall be born Holy, shall be called the Son of God? †

Gloriosæ.

Where note that to this most excellent Queen, four most singular and renowned titles are attributed and given.

1. She is said to be glorious, because she is most gloriously assumpted both in soul and body.

* As Exod. ch. 32; Dan. ch. 3.
† St. Luke ch 1, v. 35.

2. Glorious for the great glory which she enjoyeth in the kingdom of heaven, wherein she far surpasseth all Cherubim and Seraphim, yea, all the Angelical Spirits and orders of Saints being put together.

3. Glorious for the high honour which the Church Militant doth give unto her ; for whereas other Saints are served with the honour which is called *Dulia*, she is worshipped with that honour which is called *hyperdulia*, which hyperdulia is an especial honour due unto her, for the affinity and heroical virtue, even contracted with Almighty God.

Semper Virginis.

In the second place, that most excellent and supernatural gift, to have been always a virgin. For she was a virgin in body, a virgin in mind, and a virgin in profession. A virgin before her child-birth, in her childbirth, and after her childbirth, without any corruption of her virginal chastity.

Mariæ.

The name of Marie hath three interpretations, Star of the Sea, Illuminated, and Empress or Lady. First she is Marie, that is Star of the Sea, for as much as all that are labouring in the bitter sea of penance and sorrow for their sins, she safely bringeth to the secure harbour of health and salvation. She is Marie, that is Illuminated, because those that walk in the darkness of sin and of error are converted by the means of her singular merits. She is Marie, that is Empress or Lady, for she sheweth herself to be Empress and Lady of absolute power over all the devils and infernal spirits, in defending us against them both in our life, and at the dreadful and fearful hour of our departure.

Genitricis.

In the third place, she which before was called a maid is called a mother. A marvellous fecundity is expressed when mother is mentioned; for marvellous truly was the holy Virgin's fecundity, whereat the Prophet admiring saith: A woman shall compass about a man, to wit, Mary, Christ; a maiden, God.*

[Dei et Domini nostri Jesu Christi.

In the fourth place, she is adorned with the supereminent title, not only of a mother, but of the Mother of God, and of our Lord Jesus Christ. For the holy Virgin did not bear or bring forth only a mere man but true God: neither was she only Christipara, Mother of Christ, but also Deipara, Mother of God.

Sed et beatorum Apostolorum.

After the glorious Virgin Marie, mention is made of the blessed Apostles, and that not without just cause. For first, they were the only witnesses of this divine Sacrament, who were present when our

* Jeremias ch. 31, v. 22.

15

Lord first instituted the same. Secondly, they were those who received first authority and commandment to celebrate the same. Thirdly, they were those who first put in practice the celebration of this divine Sacrament. And fourthly, they were those who set down the chief orders and prescriptions to all Christian nations for the administration of the same.

Ac Martyrum tuorum.

After the Apostles, the holy Martyrs are also named, because of their great constancy which they shewed in the hot persecutions, and shedding their blood in the defence of their faith: who therefore were truly martyrs, that is to say, witnesses of the verity of the Christian faith; for martyr properly signifieth a witness, and martyrs are truly witnesses, yea even unto death. For great is the work of martyrdom, and manifold the praises belonging thereto. The first praise is, that it is an act of most noble fortitude. The second, that it is an act of most perfect patience. The third, that it is an act of most firm faith. The fourth, that it is an act of most fervent charity. For as our Saviour saith: Greater charity than this no man hath, that a man yield his life for his friends.* And here in this place may occur a question, why in the Mass, no commemoration is made of the holy Confessors, seeing the Church, amongst the Saints, doth so highly worship

* St. John ch. 15, v. 13.

their memories. The cause whereof seemeth to be this, for that in the Sacrifice of the Mass, in which is represented the Passion of our Lord, the memory of none was to be made, but only of martyrs, who, shedding their blood for the love of Christ, are made thereby perfect imitators of His Passion, which Confessors, though otherwise holy, have not done.

Petri.

Amongst the Apostles, the name of Peter is first expressed, as being the chief and head of the Apostles. He was in great reputation at Rome; the Emperor Nero being angry therewith, caused him to be crucified, with his head towards the earth and his feet upward; the which he himself requested, not thinking himself worthy to be crucified in that manner as his Lord and Master was. The people of Rome, upon this occasion, embraced the faith and Christian religion with great fervour. He was buried on the side of Nero's garden at the Vatican. He held the seat of Antioch, in the time of the Emperor Tiberius, the space of seven years, and twenty-five years that of Rome.

Et Pauli.

St. Paul, a vessel of election, and endued with singular divine graces, was called from heaven to bear witness of the Name of Jesus before kings and potentates. Of whom a religious Father saith: He would have no other university but Jerusalem, no

15*

other school but Mount Calvary, no other pulpit
but the Cross, no other reader but the crucifix, no
other letters but His wounds, no other commas but
His lashes, no other full-points but His nails, no
other book but His open side, and no other lesson
but to know Jesus Christ and Him crucified.   He
suffered innumerable travails in the promulgation
of the Gospel.   He was the same day, that St. Peter
suffered at Rome, beheaded in the seventeenth year
from the Passion of Jesus Christ, and the fourteenth
year of the Emperor Nero.   He was buried in the
way of Ostia, where since is built a most sumptuous
Church and Monastery under his invocation, not far
from whence are to be seen yet at this present, three
fountains of springing waters, which did break forth
of the places, upon which his head leaped thrice after
his decollation.

Andreæ.

Andrew who, at the voice of one only calling,
followed our Saviour Christ.   Who brought his
brother Peter to be instructed of our Saviour.   Who
disputed with the Proconsul Egæus of the verity of
this Blessed Sacrament.   Which Proconsul caused
him to be crucified after the example of Jesus Christ,
but in a manner different, for that he had not his
hands and feet pierced with nails, but straightly
bound with cords, to the end to put him to a most
slow death.

Jacobi.

St. James the greater was a Galilean by nation, the son of Zebedee, and brother of St. John. Both which agreed to follow our Lord with such affection, that they forsook at an instant their carnal father and company of fishers. They were so greatly beloved of our Lord that their mother doubted not to require seats for them on either side of Him in His kingdom. He took them with Him for witnesses of His glorious transfiguration. Also at the raising of the daughter of the Prince of the Synagogue, Jairus, for proof of the inward love which He bore unto them. He was put to the death of the sword by Herod, in the time of the Emperor Claudius. He was the first of the Apostles who exposed his life for the love and faith of his Master Christ. Our Lady and all the Apostles were present at his martyrdom.

Joannis.

St. John, Jesus Christ did most dearly love, and for this respect he was called His Evangelist. He was sent with St. Peter to prepare the Passover. He, only, leaned upon the breast of our Saviour at His last supper, from whence he sucked those divine mysteries, which he hath·left written unto us. At the point of the Death of Jesus Christ, He recommended unto him His Mother, for an assured argument of His confidence and amity. After His Resurrection, he ran the first of the Apostles, to

enjoy the sight of Him. His martyrdom was to
be put into a vessel of oil, but by the Providence of
God, it could not hurt him. Having religiously
preached the Gospel in the lesser Asia, he entered
at the age of ninety-nine years into a sepulchre,
which he was accustomed to frequent, and was
never since seen on earth.

Thomæ.

This Thomas was also called Didymus, which
is interpreted, doubtful, because he doubted of our
Lord's Resurrection, until he first had touched His
wounds, and thereby hath taken from us all wounds
and doubtfulness of infidelity, in such sort, that
since then, the grounds of the Resurrection were
laid in him. He preached to the Parthians, Medes,
Persians, Hircans, Brachmans, and Indians. After
he had well deserved of Christendom, he was thrust
through the side. His memory is yet very much
reverenced in the Indies, not only of the Christians
which dwell there, but of the Jews, Mahometans,
and Paynims, as is declared in the History of the
Conquest of the East Indies, written by the Bishop
of Sylves.*

Jacobi.

To wit, James the less, who was called the brother
of our Lord. He was held for just from his mother's
womb, because of his excellent virtue. He did
never eat flesh, drink wine, nor ever clothed him-

* Lib. 3.

self with cloth dressed or shorn. Moreover he was so assiduous in prayer, that he had his knees as hard as a camel's. He assisted at the first Council held by the Apostles. The Jews, angry at his innocent life, for hatred cast him down from the top of the Temple. He had his head cleft with a fuller's hook. The city of Jerusalem being sacked by Titus Vespasian, this heavy disaster was imputed by some to the cruel and inhuman massacre committed upon the person of this blessed Apostle.

Philippi.

St. Philip received express commandment from Jesus Christ to follow Him, wherein the blessed Apostle promptly obeyed. He also brought Nathanael with him to see our Lord, of whom He was presently acknowledged for the Son of God and King of Israel. He instantly besought Him to show him His Father. Of him our Saviour asked the five loaves, wherewith He miraculously fed as many thousands of people in the desert. He preached in Samaria, and after in Hieropolis of Phrygia, which he cleansed and purged from the worship of idols, yea of the impure and venomous viper there reserved. In the end the vulgar people rose up against him and hung him on a pillar; but after acknowledging him, honoured him with a goodly sepulchre, and embraced with unspeakable fervour the faith and religion which he had preached.

Bartholomæi.

Who only amongst the Apostles is said to have been of noble birth and a philosopher. He preached to the Indians the Gospel of Christ, which he turned into the vulgar tongue, as it was written by St. Matthew. He passed into the Great Armenia, and there converted the king, his wife, and twelve cities to the true worship of Almighty God. Whereupon the brother of the king, being enraged against him, caused him cruelly to be flayed alive in contempt of Christianity, at the instigation of those which adored the idols.

Matthæi.

St. Matthew, called to follow Jesus Christ, was a rich man. Of a common publican, he was made an Apostle, and of a receiver of customs, a distributor of spiritual treasures. The Indians and Ethiopians were by him and by his prayers converted, with their king and his wife, unto the faith, by reason of the miraculous raising of their daughter from death to life. Hirtacus displeased, that by the Apostle's advice she had vowed unto God perpetual virginity, made him pass by the sword, as he was celebrating at the altar. He wrote the Gospel, preached by him, in the Hebrew tongue, whereof the text, written by the hand of St. Barnaby, was found upon his breast, at the invention of his body buried in Cyprus.

Simonis.

St. Simon was the brother of St. James the less. The zeal of this Saint was very great, by which having carefully planted the Word of God in Egypt, Cyrene, Africa, Mauritania, and all Lybia, he was put to death in the reign of the Emperor Trajan, at the age of fourscore years, under pretence that he was a Christian, and of the issue of the royal line of David. Every one marvelled to see a spirit so stout, resolute, and courageous, in a body so crazy, feeble, and decrepit by age.

Et Thaddæi.

St. Thaddeus, called Judas, was the third brother of James the less, and of Simon. Thaddeus is interpreted holding, and this Thaddeus most firmly and constantly held the faith of Christ. He wrote most sharply against the corrupters of the truth, as his Catholic Epistle doth very well testify. He animated the faithful to constancy in the faith once received, by fearful examples of the relapsed Angels, and commemoration of the future judgment. He announced to Mesopotamia and the adjacent countries the Word of God, by the sweetness whereof he mollified and made tractable the minds and spirits of the people, otherwise fearfully barbarous, fierce and wild.

Lini.

To these twelve Apostles are added the number of twelve glorious martyrs, who, in the beginning of the Church, offered themselves to God, living hosts, and shed their blood for the confession of the Name and faith of Jesus.

In the first place is named St. Linus, who was the first Pope after St. Peter, in the government of the Church of God. In which seat he sat until his passion. Having endured sundry kinds of torments for the love of Christ, he rendered up his holy soul unto his Saviour.

Cleti.

St. Cletus succeeded Linus in the Popedom. And albeit the desire to be a Bishop is a thing right laudable,' notwithstanding, St. Cletus could not be won to accept of the Bishopric of Rome but by the persuasion of St. Clement, deputed by St. Peter for his successor. Having religiously ordered the affairs of the Church the space of twelve years, he was martyred under the Emperor Domitian. The seat by the occasion of his death was vacant twenty days, with the unspeakable grief of the people, destituted of their incomparable good Pastor ; having never been touched in his actions but with the zeal of piety, holy and religious devotion.

Clementis.

St. Clement was the disciple of St. Peter, and the fourth Pope after him. He chose him amongst others to be his immediate successor in the Apostolate, but he would not of humility accept the charge, but deferred it to St. Linus and St. Cletus, by whose decease it was committed unto him. The Emperor Trajan offended that by his exemplary life, the Romans were daily converted to Christianity, confined him within an island, in the which two thousand Christians were condemned to saw marbles for the ornament of Rome. The people of the island, in great distress for want of fresh water, were by him refreshed, having found a springing fountain under the feet of a lamb. Whereupon, the Emperor, more offended than before, caused an anchor to be fastened about his neck, and his body to be cast into the sea.

Xysti.

St. Xystus was the eighth Pope after St. Peter. He ordained in the solemnities of the Mass the holy hymn of Sanctus to be sung, and of Agnus Dei. He was greatly given to divine things, as his holy decrees do sufficiently testify. He also received the glorious crown of martyrdom in the time of the Emperor Valerian.

Cornelii.

St. Cornelius was the twentieth Pope, in the time of the Emperor Decius. He transported, by the aid and assistance of St. Lucina, an honourable matron of Rome, the bodies of St. Peter and St. Paul from the place of their burial to put them in safeguard. Whereof the Emperor being advertised, and that he converted many of the people to the faith of Christ,

sent him into banishment, where St. Cyprian often
comforted him by letters, exciting him to constancy.
The which was imputed unto him for treason to the
State, for the participation and intelligence which he
was said to have with the public enemies. For this
he was beheaded, and for not yielding to adore the
idol of Mars. His martyrdom is confirmed by the
testimonies of St. Ambrose and St. Augustine.

Cypriani.

St. Cyprian, Bishop of Carthage, suffered also
under the Emperors Valerian and Galens, in the
eighth persecution raised against the Christians, the
same day that St. Cornelius, but not the same year.
The actions and deportments of this good Father
were such, that there is none, who in reading his
writings, can choose but think to hear speak a true
Christian Bishop, and one designed to martyrdom
for the honour of God. His life and passion are
written by Pontius his deacon. He had at his
death such firm constancy, that at the pronunciation
of the judgment against him, understanding that he
was to suffer by the sword, he cried out aloud in the
consistory of the tyrant, saying : *Deo gratias.* After
his execution, there was found in his heart the
figure of the Cross made in gold, in witness of his
invincible faith.

Laurentii.

St. Laurence was a disciple of St. Xystus, and

Archdeacon of the Church of Rome. He received of him, being prisoner for the cause of religion in the eighth Valerian persecution after Nero, express commandment to distribute unto the poor the treasures of the Church, which he had in his keeping; the which he performed with no less care than fidelity. Upon this occasion he was committed prisoner under the custody of the gaoler Hippolytus, whom he converted to the faith with nineteen more of his family. In the end he was cruelly roasted upon a gridiron, with a slack and prolonging fire, in the presence of the Emperor Valerian.

Chrysogoni.

St. Chrysogonus, having refused the dignity and offices which the Emperor Diocletian offered unto him, to renounce Christianity and to adore the false and counterfeit gods, was, by his commandment, beheaded at Aquila. Nicephorus inserteth in his Ecclesiastical History some epistles written unto him by St. Anastasia, and of him to her. This devout lady did liberally succour and assist him with means during the time of his imprisonment.

Joannis et Pauli.

Sts. John and Paul were brethren, no less zealous of Christian piety than noble and rich; who had been brought up in the court, under the service of the daughter of the great Emperor Constantine, and greatly favoured of her. After his decease, Julian

the Apostate, being come to the Empire, placed
them in the estate of his household servants, knowing that they would refuse this condition by reason
of their religion. Which they having done, he commanded that they should be beheaded; so that the
self-same death and passion made them true brethren,
albeit they were so already by nature. In honour
of their holy and invincible resolution the Church
calleth them Olives and Candlesticks shining before
God in the Epistle of the Mass upon their Feast,
taken out of the eleventh chapter of the Apocalypse.

Cosmæ et Damiani.

Sts. Cosmas and Damian were also brethren, and
Arabians of nation. They were famous in the art
of physic and chirurgery, which art they exercised
freely and purely for the love of God, and were
employed by the true Physician more to cure the
diseases of souls than of the bodies. For this cause
Dioclesian and Maximilian forced them to pass by
water, fire, and sword, in the manner described in
their legend; but God, Who never forsaketh those
that are His, refreshed them, and gave them happy
repose, according to the consolation promised to the
afflicted by the Royal Prophet.

Et omnium Sanctorum tuorum.

Whose number and multitude is so great and
marvellous, that Constantine the Emperor, passing
over the seas, and finding Eusebius, Bishop of

Cæsaria, desired him to ask somewhat of him to enrich his Church. Who answered the Emperor, saying: Sir, my Church aboundeth sufficiently in riches, but I beseech you to send out into all parts of the world, to know and understand the names of the Saints, the times of their passion, under whom, how, and in what places they suffered martyrdom. Which being done, there was found, for every feast in the year, more than five thousand Saints, excepting on the Day of the Kalends of January, in which the Gentiles gave themselves to their banquetings and solemnities, and not to the martyring of the blessed Saints.

Quorum meritis precibusque concedas.

And here, lest any should think it in vain to crave the intercession of the most blessed Saints, or doubt that those holy Saints, whom specially we pray unto, do not again employ their especial protection towards us, St. Gregory, in his thirty-fifth homily, telleth of a certain matron, who often frequenting the Church of the blessed martyrs, Processus and Martinian, upon a day was met withal by the two holy martyrs themselves, who spake unto her, saying: Thou dost visit us now, we will therefore demand thee, in the day of judgment, and all that we are able, we will perform and do for thee.

Ut in omnibus.

To wit, which either in the behalf of the glory of

Thy most blessed Name, or of the salvation of our own souls, is on our part to be believed, desired or to be accomplished.

Protectionis tuæ muniamur auxilio.

In faithfully believing, clearly understanding, heartily desiring and readily accomplishing in all things Thy good Will and holy pleasure, and thereby may be protected against all our enemies, visible and invisible.

Per eumdem Christum Dominum nostrum, Amen.

The aforesaid prayer concludeth like as all others, through Jesus Christ our Lord. Which conclusion plainly declareth, that in the veneration of the blessed Saints, we do not so much worship the Saints as our Lord in the Saints. For whilst in them we praise and magnify the wonderful gifts and goodness of God, what else do we but magnify God Himself, Who, as the Apostle saith, worketh all things in all? To conclude, this part of the holy Canon, as some grave authors affirm, was undoubtedly composed by the instinct and ordinance of God Himself. In confirmation whereof, they report that some Fathers, out of a singular devotion which they bore to some other Saints, added their names to the holy Canon, and removed the names of some of these already added. But the day being passed, on the morrow they found those blotted out, and the former written again in letters of gold.

Of the Priest's spreading his hands over the Chalice.

At this part of the Canon, next ensuing, the Priest lifteth up both his hands from the altar and spreadeth or extendeth them over the Chalice, to signify, that now at this present he ought to lay away from him all temporal cares, and to have his mind wholly fixed and attent to his Sacrifice. All the people, therefore, beholding this ceremony, ought spiritually to imitate his example.

CHAPTER XLIV.

"HANC IGITUR OBLATIONEM."

FIRST he saith : Therefore, to demonstrate that this part of the Canon is the conclusion of that which went before, as if he should say : Therefore, because there is no place to offer the Sacrifice of unity out of the unity of the Catholic Church, we, communicating with the memory of the Saints, and in communion with them, offering up this Sacrifice unto Thee, do beseech Thee that by their intercession, Thou wouldst accept and receive this Sacrifice at our hands.

Servitutis nostræ.

Out of which words it is manifestly to be gathered, that never in the law of the Gospel was it permitted to all men alike to offer sacrifice, but only to such as were Priests, ordained and consecrated by the imposition of the hands of an Apostolical Bishop. These words, therefore, are to be understood of the clergy, which, in all humble service, obedience and subjection, have this peculiar charge committed unto them.

Sed et cunctæ familiæ tuæ.

But because the Priest is the public officer, and that all the prayers and oblations which he offereth are for the Church Universal, whereof he is an officer, therefore he adjoineth, as also of all thy family. Wherefore, as the former words concern the clergy, so these latter comprehend all the laity, which is also a part of the great family of Almighty God.

Quæsumus, Domine, ut placatus accipias.

Here the Priest requireth that God, appeased by the prayers of the Saints, would accept this oblation ; not of the part of the Sacrifice itself, which can no way displease God, because it containeth His only Son, of Whom Himself hath testified, saying : This is My beloved Son, in Whom I am well pleased, but of the part of the sacrificer. In which respect, sometimes it is rejected by reason of his indevotion or profanation, like as the sacrifices of the ancient law unduly offered.

Diesque nostros in tua pace disponas.

In which words may be understood three sorts of peace which we demand of Almighty God. Peace in our souls, peace in our bodies, and peace in our worldly goods or substance. The peace of our souls is disturbed by evil thoughts, desires, and disordinate appetites : the peace of our bodies by sundry sorts of diseases and corporal indispositions : the peace of our goods by wars, famines, sterility, dryness, and such-like calamities. Who then may give us these three sorts of peace, but only He Who hath command and power over our souls, over our bodies, and over our goods, and can deliver us from all evils of mind, from all diseases of body, and from all misfortune of our temporal substance ? And aptly in this place is added the word *Tua, Thy.* For as Odo saith, there are two sorts of peace. There is the peace of the world, and there is the peace of God. The peace of the world is unprofitable, but the peace of God is both wholesome and delectable.

Atque ab æterna damnatione nos eripi.

He which prayeth to be delivered from everlasting damnation, without doubt prayeth also to be preserved from the sin which deserveth damnation. For in vain doth he pray to be delivered from eternal death, who chooseth to abide in deadly sin.

Et in electorum tuorum jubeas grege numerari.

The flock of the elect is double. The one, the Good Pastor hath, upon His proper shoulders, brought already into the fold. The other is as yet preserved and kept in the pastures. Those in the fold are the secure triumphant. Those in the pastures are the doubtful militant. We therefore now pray, that

16 *

through the grace of the Holy Ghost, we may be made of the number of the elect, and be placed in heaven in the society and company of the blessed.

These three petitions before recited were added by St. Gregory, which are very short, but very sweet. For what can be more short, or what can be more sweet, than that which is contained in these three petitions? For to dispose our days in peace, for delivery from everlasting damnation, and for the obtaining of everlasting salvation. Out of these words, therefore, many notable things may be collected. First, that God is sovereign Lord of all things both temporal and eternal, both of earth, hell, and heaven. Of the earth, saying : Dispose our days in peace. Of hell, saying : Deliver us from everlasting damnation. Of heaven, saying : And place us among the number of Thine elect. For if God were not sovereign Lord of the earth, how could He give us peace in our days, and in all our temporal goods and substance? And if He had not all power over hell, how could He deliver us from everlasting damnation? And if He were not Lord of heaven, how could He place us amongst His elect in perpetual felicity and salvation?

Again these words may be expounded in another sense. Dispose our days in peace, to wit, through Him Which for us was betrayed into the hands of those that hated peace. Deliver us from everlasting damnation, to wit, through Him Who for us was condemned to a temporal death. And place us amongst the number of Thine elect or blessed, to wit, through Him Who for our sakes was numbered amongst the wicked.

Per Christum Dominum nostrum. Amen.

This prayer is concluded through Christ our Lord; to the which, saith Albertus, none do answer *Amen*, but only the Priest himself and the blessed Angels who are present in this ministry.

CHAPTER XLV.

OF THE BEGINNING OF THE PRINCIPAL PART OF THE CANON.

Quam oblationem, tu, Deus.

HERE beginneth the principal part of all the holy Canon, which is the Consecration, where the Priest insisteth and beseecheth Almighty God, that the creatures of bread and wine, requisite to the confection of the Holy Eucharist, may be sanctified and blessed, yea, changed and converted into the precious Body and Blood of our Saviour Jesus. This part of the Canon is cited by St. Ambrose, above twelve hundred years agone.*

In omnibus, quæsumus.

Which words, *in omnibus*, in all, may be diversely understood, and first thus: In all, to wit, Thou, O

---

* Lib. 4, de Sacr. (inter opera Sancti), cap. 5.

God, being in all creatures and natures without
definition, in all places without circumscription,
and in all times without alteration, bless, we
beseech Thee, this oblation. Or, in all, to wit,
make this oblation blessed in all ways, in all manners,
and in all circumstances. Or, in all, that it is to say,
vouchsafe to make it blessed above all hosts, by
transferring it into that Host, Which is blessed above
all hosts. Or, in all, to wit, blessed in all degrees,
both clergy and laity, both in the Priest and the
people. Or, in all, to wit, in all our understandings,
in all our powers, in all our thoughts, and in all our
intentions.

Bene + dictam.

The Priest in this word prayeth, that the oblation
made in the beginning of gifts not blessed, God
would make blessed, to wit, by that mystical benediction, wherewith of bread, it may be changed into
the Body of Christ, the cause of all benediction. Or
blessed, to wit, with glory, that it may be made
glorious. Blessed with immortality, that it may be
made immortal. Blessed with incorruption, that it
may be made incorruptible. Blessed with divinity,
that it may be deified.

Adscrip + tam.

Not finite. And in this sense he craveth that his
oblation, which before Consecration is circumscrip-
tible and finite, God would make incircumscriptible

and infinite. For as much as in this most Holy Sacrament, Christ is incircumscriptible, as Divines do teach, and as the Catholic Church doth hold.

Ra + tam.

We call that ratified, which we account for certain, fix and firm. Let it therefore be made firm or ratified, that is, let it not remain instable, and subject to be altered or changed by corruption.

Ratio + nabilem.

The blood of bullocks and of calves, being un-reasonable creatures, was not sufficient to purge man from sin, they being much inferior and less than man. For a reasonable man, therefore, a reasonable Host is requisite, to wit, Christ, that we may offer a true Man for men, and that so for man's sake, God may be propitious and merciful unto men.

Accepta + bilemque facere digneris.

That cannot be but acceptable which hath received the three former species of all sorts of benediction. God cannot hate God ; but because God is charity, God loveth God, and the Host, Which is God, is acceptable to God. Why then pray we, that to be made acceptable, which no way can displease? Because though it be acceptable for itself, yet we may displease in respect of ourselves.

Others, again, have interpreted these words in another sense, as thus : That God would vouchsafe to make our oblation *Benedictam*, blessed, whereby

all that participate thereof are made blessed;
adscriptam, written, by the which we are written
in the book of eternal life; *ratam*, ratified, by the
which we are incorporated in the bowels of Christ;
rationabilem, reasonable, not unreasonable, by the
which we are made clean from all unclean and
beastly desires; *acceptabilemque*, and acceptable,
whereby we, who have displeased Him, may be
made acceptable unto Him in His only Son.

Ut nobis.

That to us; that is, to our health and profit. Or
to us for whom He delivered His Body to death, that
He might give us the same Body in food to everlasting life. Again aptly saith He, to us, that is, to
us worshippers of the Catholic faith, to us communicating, to us worshipping the memory of the
Saints. To us, excludeth Pagans, Jews, Heretics,
and all sorts of infidels.

Corpus et sanguis.

The words aforegoing were dark, obscure, and
hard to understand, but now the gate is opened, all
is made manifest, to wit, that there be made to us
the Body and Blood of Jesus Christ, Which only is a
Host, in all and above all, blessed, adscript, ratified,
reasonable and acceptable.

Fiat.

And worthily in this place is the word *fiat* added,
because now there is required the same almighty

power in this conversion, which was in the Incarnation of the Almighty Word, and in the creation of
the world. For God said, when He was to create
the world, *fiat lux*, and our Lady said to the Angel,
when Christ our Lord was to be incarnate, *fiat mihi*,
and the Priest, therefore, in this place saith, *fiat
corpus*. Again he saith *fiat*, by way of deprecation;
to denote, that the Priest by his own natural ability
cannot work that supernatural conversion. And
therefore he saith not in his own person *facio*,
I make, but *fiat*, let it be made, to wit, by the
omnipotent power of Almighty God.

Dilectissimi Filii tui Domini nostri Jesu Christi.

That of the substance of bread and wine which
are offered unto Thee, may be made, by divine and
miraculous transubstantiation, the Body and Blood
of Thy best beloved Son: the substance of bread to
be converted into His blessed Body, and the substance of wine into His precious Blood.

*Of the five crosses which are made at the prolation of
the five words aforesaid, and what the same do signify.*

You are here to understand, that there is no
ceremony in all the Catholic Church, more proper to
represent the mysteries of the Death and Passion
of our Lord, than is the sign of the holy Cross.
Where it is further to be noted, that commonly the
order and number of the crosses, which are made

upon the Sacrifice, do represent the order and number
of the mysteries of His blessed Passion. Wherefore, if you consider how our Lord and Saviour was
sold for money, you shall see in this sale sundry
persons and sundry practices. You have the Priests,
Scribes, and Pharisees who were the buyers; you
have Judas, who only was the seller; and you have
our Lord, Who only was sold. The three first
crosses, therefore, signify the Priests, Scribes, and
Pharisees who bought Him, the fourth, Judas who
sold Him, and the fifth, our Lord Who was sold by
him.

The second reason.

Again, some of our Doctors have marked the very
manner of making these crosses, and say that the
first three are made together upon the whole
oblation, to signify that the Priests, Scribes, and
Pharisees conspired altogether with one intention
against our Lord and Saviour Jesus. But the
other two are made asunder, the one upon the bread,
the other upon the wine, to signify the different
intention betwixt our Saviour and the traitor Judas;
for the intention of our Saviour was love and charity,
but that of Judas, avarice and treachery.

The third reason.

Again, by these five crosses may be considered five
principal places, wherein our Lord suffered sundry
torments and abuses. In the Garden of Gethsemane,
where He did sweat blood and water for the great

fear and apprehension which He had of death. In the house of Annas, where He received a blow on the face by a wicked varlet. In the house of Caiphas, where He received many outrages, revilings, hiding of His eyes, spittings in His face, and strikings. In the house of Pilate, where He was bound to a pillar, lamentably scourged, crowned with thorns, and clothed in mockery. And upon the mount Calvary, where He was ignominiously crucified betwixt two thieves.

The fourth reason.

Again, these five crosses may be referred to the five principal parts of our Lord's Body, wherein He received His holy wounds, to wit, in both His hands, both His feet, and His blessed side. And the two last crosses, which are made apart, the one upon the bread, the other upon the wine, signify unto us that our Lord truly died for our Redemption, for the blood separated from the body is a most true and certain sign of death.

The fifth reason.

Again, the first three crosses, which are made upon the oblation, may signify three special things, which our Lord did in His last supper concerning the bread and the wine, to wit, He took, blessed, and gave to His disciples. Afterwards one cross is made upon the bread, because He said: *Comedite, hoc est corpus meum*, Eat, this is My Body. Another upon the chalice, because He said: *Bibite ex hoc omnes, hic est sanguis' meus*, Drink ye all of this, this is My Blood. And according hereunto rightly is subjoined that which followeth: *Qui pridie quam pateretur*, Who the day before He suffered.   .

CHAPTER XLVI.

" QUI PRIDIE QUAM PATERETUR."

THE time of the institution of the holy Eucharist is here declared by the ordinance of Pope Alexander I. The day before, that is to say, the fifth feria, which was next unto the holy Feast of the Passover, upon which day this blessed Sacrament was first instituted. Wherefore, the Priest celebrating this holy Mystery, ought to direct his intention to that end which our Saviour Himself then did, sitting in the midst of His disciples. For this very day Jesus Christ, having eaten the Paschal lamb with His disciples for the final accomplishment of the law of Moses, prepared for them a new sort of meat, giving Himself unto them in spiritual food, under the forms of bread and wine.

Accepit panem.

After the observation of the time of this institution, is expressed the matter which He used, to wit, bread truly, not yet flesh. And therefore bread, because as the material bread comforteth the heart of man above all other natural meats, so this holy

Eucharist serveth him to the nourishment and sustentation of his soul, above all other spiritual meats.

In sanctas ac venerabiles manus suas.

By very good right, the Church doth call the hands of her Spouse, Jesus Christ, wherewith He touched the blessed Eucharist, holy and venerable, for as much as the divine and human nature are both in Him conjoined. These are those sacred hands by which the admirable work of the world was formed, without any pattern or example ; man made after His divine image, bread so many times multiplied to his use, the possessed delivered of malignant spirits, the leprous and sick healed, the dead raised, and we daily replenished with divine benedictions.

Et elevatis oculis in cælum.

None of the Evangelists do testify that Christ in His last supper lifted up His eyes to heaven, but apostolical tradition hath delivered this to the Church. For this hath the Mass of St. James the Apostle, and the Liturgy of St. Basil. Where St. James and St. Basil do not content themselves to say, that He lifted up His eyes to God His Father Almighty, but furthermore, that He shewed unto Him the bread which He held betwixt His hands. Whereby they would signify unto us, that our Lord intended to work some such great and marvellous thing, as required thereunto the whole omnipotency and power of Almighty God.

Ad te Deum Patrem suum.

Our Blessed Saviour, about to consecrate His precious Body and Blood, lifteth up the eyes of His Humanity unto God His Father, not those of His Divinity, because He was in nothing unlike or inferior to His Father; Who, as He is co-equal to Him in dignity, so likewise in His everlasting vision and comprehension.

Omnipotentem.

Where special commemoration is made of the Almighty and Divine omnipotency, to settle and confirm our faith, that we fear not the consecration to be a thing impossible, nor doubt of the truth or verity thereof.

Tibi gratias agens.

And hereof it is that this Sacrifice is called a Sacrifice of praise or thanksgiving, because the best procurer of benefits is the mindfulness of benefits, joined with continual giving of thanks. Or, therefore, our Lord gave thanks, being so near His Passion, to teach us to bear all things which we suffer with thanksgiving. Or, He gave thanks to His omnipotent Father for so excellent a grace, for so effectual a food, for so worthy a Sacrament, and for so profound a mystery; yet not for Himself, but for us, that is, for our redemption and reparation, which was to be brought to pass by His Death and Passion, whereof this should for evermore remain a perpetual commemoration.

Benedixit.

After the giving of thanks, He imparted the virtue of His holy benediction upon the bread, and converted the substance thereof into that of His precious Body. The same likewise He did at the creation of the world, when He ordained the increase and multiplication of His creatures, every one according to his kind. Never do we read that He blessed the bread, but that there ensued some notable miracle, as in the multiplication of the five loaves and the two fishes, whereof the fragments were twelve baskets, after the refection of five thousand souls. In pronouncing this word, the Priest maketh the sign of the Cross, because, as St. Augustine saith, from the same all Sacraments do receive their efficacy, and that nothing without it is decently accomplished. Add that the Cross is the only character of all benediction, ever since it touched the blessed Body of our Saviour Jesus.

Fregit.

Which is not so to be understood, that Christ did first break before He did consecrate, but after; like as in the genealogy of Christ, St. Matthew nameth David before Abraham, who yet was not before, but after Abraham.

Deditque.

To wit, His blessed Body unto His disciples, who then were present in body, and now also He giveth the same to all the faithful, to the end, that to those for whom He was to give Himself in price of redemption, He would likewise give Himself in food and refection. For Christ two manner of ways gave Himself for us; once upon the Cross for the sins of all the world, which needed not to be renewed; the other, being miraculously instituted and divinely ordained to preserve the daily memory of His Death, may wholesomely be renewed, the latter being a true commemoration and remembrance of the former.

Discipulis suis, dicens.

Where it is said, to His disciples, to teach us that none can worthily receive this Sacrament, unless he be His true disciple, that it is to say, do faithfully believe what is to be believed of this most high and divine Sacrament. For this cause the Capharnaaites were not His true disciples, who hearing the doctrine of Christ touching this divine mystery, went back saying: How can this Man give us His flesh to eat? This is a hard speech, and the like.

Accipite.

By which word the administration of this Blessed Sacrament is expressed, such being the office of the Priest in the Church, that it is not lawful for any other whosoever, were he king or emperor of all the world, to dispense the holy Eucharist unto the people, Christ having resigned this charge only to Priests, and not to any other, either man or Angel.

Et manducate.

Here is expressed the principal cause of the institution of this most holy and blessed Sacrament, which is not only to be consecrated and honourably reserved, but to the end that the faithful Christians may receive, eat, and employ the same to their necessities, with firm faith, ardent devotion, and exact proof and examination of their conscience, and by this means to be united and dwell in Jesus Christ and He in them.

Ex hoc omnes.

First, Florus Magister saith that these words commend unity and peace unto us, that by this Mystery participating of Christ, we may be all one in Christ. Next these words, Eat you all of this, are not so to be understood, as that divers might eat divers parts of the same, and not each one Christ entirely; for although in respect of the divers species, he may seem to receive one particle, and he another, yet according to the verity it is all one and the same, the whole and entire substance of our Lord's Body Which all do eat; neither do a thousand receive more than one, nor one, less than a thousand, because all receive the whole Body of our Lord, Which now can no more be divided into parts.

Hoc est enim Corpus meum.

As these words of God, Increase, multiply and replenish the earth, spoken once in the constitution of the world, have still as yet their effect unto this present, so that nature, obeying its Creator, engendereth, produceth, and multiplieth in convenient season all things according to their kind, species, property and condition, even so, ever since Jesus Christ in His last supper pronounced these words saying: This is My Body; He gave them such benediction, force and virtue, that they are not only significative, but furthermore effective, and as instruments of His holy Will, to change that which was before common bread, into His true, real, and blessed Body.

Of the worship and adoration of the Blessed Sacrament.

The words of the holy Sacrament being pronounced, the Priest, holding in both his hands the blessed Body of Jesus Christ in the form of bread, doth presently kneel him down and adore the same; shewing herein, that by the virtue of the Divine Word, our Lord, our God, and our Redeemer is there really present. And then rising up, he doth elevate the same on high, to the end that the assistants, also beholding the same, may adore their Lord and Maker, and crave of Him that which may profit them to their salvation.

By which elevation, we also are admonished to hasten us, and forthwith, with trembling and fear, to prostrate ourselves unto the ground, and humbly to beseech of Him, Who sometime being really lifted up upon the Cross, and now truly lifted up under the form of bread, that He, Whose glory and magnificence is lifted up above the heavens, would vouchsafe to draw us up thither to Him Who said: I, when I shall be exalted, will draw all unto Me.

Simili modo.

Where he saith, In the like manner, because the same ought to be understood and done touching the blessed Blood of our Saviour Jesus, which was done before concerning His blessed Body, seeing they are both one and the same Christ; not the one more, and the other less, not His Body in the Host without the Blood, nor His Blood in the Chalice without the Body, but His whole Body and Blood in the one, and His whole Body and Blood in the other: all in heaven, and all upon the altar: sitting at the same time upon the right hand of His Father, and remaining likewise present under the species of the Sacrament.

Accipiens et hunc.

Where it is said that Christ took this Chalice:

17 *

if we should refer the word, this, to the vessel, it is
not the same, as touching the matter and substance
of the metal, but if we refer it to that which is contained in the vessel, then that and this is all one.
Again it is called, this, because it is daily blessed
with the same intention, that it may be made now,
that which it was made then. Again, this, because
this faith is one throughout the whole Church, and
He also One, to Whom both then and now the same
is offered.

Præclarum.

The Chalice, as yet but wine, is called noble, because presently it is made noble by being converted
into blood. As it is written: My chalice inebriating,
how noble is it? Or noble by comparison with
that which Melchisedech, in the law of nature, and
others of the Old Testament offered. Or because
of the great and noble majesty of Him to Whom it
is offered. Whereupon, in that which presently
followeth he saith: We offer to thy noble majesty.

Calicem.

Chalice is taken in three sundry senses: 1. For
sufferance or passion, as in the twentieth chapter
of St. Matthew's Gospel: Can you drink the Chalice
which I am to drink?

2. For the drink contained in the Chalice.

3. For the cup or vessel which containeth the

liquor, and so Christ took the Chalice into His hands. Which vessel, according to 'Albertus, is called *Calix, a calore,* that is to say, of heat or calor, because it enkindleth in us the fire of charity.

In sanctas ac venerabiles manus suas.

Perfectly holy, because of the Holy Ghost and the plenitude of graces infused into Him. Venerable, because of the sundry stupendous miracles which He wrought with them. Perfectly holy, because never was there found in them any kind of iniquity. Venerable, because they were of power to sanctify.

Item tibi gratias agens.

To wit, for the Redemption of mankind, which was to be purchased and wrought by the shedding of His Blood. Again, giving thanks to Thee, to wit, for His infirm and weak servants, who were daily to be refreshed and comforted with this most precious and celestial nourishment.

Benedixit.

The Priest taking into his hands the holy Chalice, giveth thanks as aforesaid, and with the words of Jesus Christ, doth likewise bless the same, making the sign of the Cross thereon, as before upon the bread. And upon the Chalice, as before upon the bread, the sign of the Cross is but once made, because our Lord was but once crucified. And therefore once upon the bread when it is consecrated, and once agáin upon the wine when it is consecrated, because our Lord was crucified for the salvation of two people.

Deditque discipulis suis, dicens.

He gave, and neither sold nor rendered what He had borrowed of others, but as a free gift He gave it freely; that after His example we should not give the same, neither for favour nor any price of money to unworthy dogs or obstinate sinners, but having received freely, we should give it freely to the worthy receivers.

Accipite et bibite ex eo omnes.

Where Jesus Christ commanded all to drink of the said Chalice; but this commandment was made only to His Apostles, ordaining them Priests in His last supper, which is sufficiently demonstrated by the number of twelve, curiously noted by the blessed Evangelists, and namely by St. Mark, witnessing that they all, to wit the Apostles, drank, without expressing that any other drank thereof besides themselves.

Hic est enim calix Sanguinis mei.

In this place is expressed the form which Jesus Christ used in the consecration of the wine, together with the order and manner thereof. Where it is called the Chalice by a metaphor for that which is

contained in the Chalice, as in the promise of the
reward of Him who shall give for, and in the Name
of Jesus Christ, a cup of cold water. Where the gift
is not understood of the cup, but of the water in the
cup.

Novi et æterni.

First, according to Innocentius tertius, it is called
novum, id est ultimum, new, that is, last, as the last
day is called *dies novissima*, a new day. And next,
eternal, not for want of a beginning, but for denial
of the succession of any other; for never shall any
other follow it, for nothing can succeed that which
is eternal, otherwise it should not be eternal. Again,
it is called new and eternal, for the Old Testament
promised only things transitory and temporal, not
permanent and eternal, as doth the New.

Testamenti.

First, Testament is not here taken only for a
writing but for a promise. Next, a testament is the
final distribution of goods, ratified by the death of
the testator. And Christ in this His last Testament
distributed, ordained, and promised everlasting inheritance to His beloved children, that is, to all
faithful people. Again, therefore, is it called a
Testament, because He confirmed all the promises
testified, in His Blood. In figure whereof, Abraham,
having made a league with Abimelech and Phicol,

offered up sheep and oxen, and with their blood confirmed the league. And Jacob flying into Galaad, having made an oath to his uncle Laban, offered sacrifice, that by the blood of the sacrifice the oath of the Covenant might be confirmed. And Moses, that he might confirm the Testament which he received on Sina, sprinkled all the people with the blood of the offerings.

Mysterium fidei.

This word is borrowed of the Greeks signifying a secret, which we must undoubtedly believe by faith, albeit we cannot see it sensibly to the eye, nor apprehend it by human reason. The mystery of faith, because it belongeth to Catholic faith to believe after Consecration that it is true Blood, so that now he is an infidel which believeth not the same. The mystery of faith, because one thing is seen and another thing is believed. *Nam verus sanguis creditur, quod vinum visu sentitur et gustu,* For that is believed to be true Blood, which both to sight and taste seemeth wine ; it tasteth wine and is not, it appeareth not Blood, and yet it is Blood.

Qui pro vobis et pro multis.

For you, to wit, for you that are present. For many, to wit, for all Pagans, Jews, and false Christians. And the words, for many, seem purposely to be added, to the end that this speech should not only be referred to the persons of the Apostles, but generally to all faithful. For although one only drop of the Blood of Christ is in itself sufficient to purge the sins of all, and to give life and salvation to the whole world, yet it is not simply or absolutely shed *pro omnibus*, for all, but only *pro multis*, for many. The reason whereof is, because all do not receive benefit thereby, but only such, who by faith and good works do labour and endeavour to make themselves grateful in the sight of God. Durandus saith that it is shed for the predestinate only, as touching the efficacy, but for all, as touching the sufficiency; for the just, saith he, the Blood of the Just, yet such is the riches of this treasure, that if all universally believed, all universally should be saved.

Effundetur.

Where he speaketh not according to some part thereof, but according to the whole. For liquor which is shed forth of a vessel, according to some part thereof is truly said to be shed, but not to be shed out, because some remaineth within : but of the Blood of Jesus Christ, it is here said not *fundetur*, shed, but *effundetur*, that is, shed out, to wit, wholly and entirely shed out of His blessed Body. And even as the loving pelican doubteth not to shed her own blood to revive her young ones which are dead, even so Christ our Lord feared not for us that were dead by sin, to pour out His precious Blood to restore us to life.

In remissionem peccatorum.

The cause, for the which the aforesaid effusion was made, is the remission of sins, which is done by two manner of ways. The first is by way of laver and washing, the second by way of payment and satisfaction. Touching the first, as he that entereth most foul into a bath of wholesome waters cometh forth most clean by the laver of the same, even so the soul, which is foul by the spots of sin, entering into the bath of Christ's most precious Blood, is purely washed by the virtue thereof. Touching the second, as he that payeth another man's debt, sets the party as free as if he had paid with his own money, even so Christ through His bitter Death, having shed His Blood, hath thereby paid our debt and satisfied the justice of His Father on our behalf, and that much better than if we ourselves had paid with our proper blood.

Hæc quotiescunque feceritis, in mei memoriam facietis.

First, these words are to be referred to both parts of the Sacrifice, as well as to the bread as to the wine, and to the consecration as well of the one as of the other. Next they may also be understood two manner of ways. First thus : So often as you shall eat this bread and drink this Chalice, do it in the remembrance of My Death and Passion ; and this belongeth more generally to all.

Secondly as thus : So often as you shall consecrate this bread and this wine, according to this My institution, do it in the remembrance of Me, and this appertaineth particularly to Priests. And well is it said, In the remembrance of Me. For this truly was one cause of the institution of this most holy Sacrifice in the Church Militant, that it should be a sign, representation, and remembrance of that high and excellent Sacrifice, which Christ offered up upon the Cross. Again, In remembrance of Me, for this last remembrance of Himself, our Lord left and recommended unto us. Even as some one going into a far country, should leave some singular pledge or token of his love to him whom he loved, that as often as he should see the same, he should remember his friendship and kindness ; because if he loved him perfectly, he cannot behold it without very great motion or affection of mind.

Unde et memores Domine.

Mindful, as if he said, this we do according to Thy commandment. After the example of Elias, who praying that God would approve his sacrifice, Hear me, saith he, O Lord, because I have done all these things according to Thy commandment—mindful, because our Lord Himself commanded that we should do this in memory of Him, therefore three things the Church proposeth in the words following to be remembered, His blessed Passion, His Resurrection, and His Ascension.

Nos servi tui.

To wit, we Priests, who, according to the degrees received of clergy, do serve Thee in the oblation of this Sacrifice, and do celebrate the same after Thy example, and in the memory of Thee. For the people perform that only in mind, which the Priest both performeth in mind, and also in external and peculiar manner.

Sed et plebs tua sancta.

The people are also said to be mindful, because Christ died not only for the Priests but also for the people, and ordained this Sacrament for the comfort as well of the one as of the other; and therefore as well the one ought to be mindful of Him as the other. And this people is said to be holy, because having received Baptism and God's holy grace, they are thereby truly sanctified, how far so ever they be dispersed, being firmly linked together in the unity of the same Church.

Ejusdem Christi Filii tui Domini nostri tam beatæ passionis.

And very rightly is the Passion of our Lord and Redeemer Jesus called blessed, because by it we are delivered from all curse and malediction, and by it we receive all bliss and benediction.

Necnon et ab inferis resurrectionis.

Jansenius, in his exposition upon this place, hath very well noted, that because in the words afore-going mention is made of our Saviour's Passion, therefore, saith he, Christ will not have the hinder part of His mortal life to be seen, but passing, like as God shewed Himself to Moses, that is, He will not have His Death to be commemorated, unless we also believe in His Resurrection.

Sed et in cælos gloriosæ ascensionis.

The holy Doctors, who have expounded the mysteries of the Mass, do bring sundry reasons, why in making remembrance of our Lord, we principally do mention His Passion, His Resurrection, and His Ascension. And some say that this is done, because by these three means principally, He hath wrought and accomplished our Redemption. For He died, say they, to deliver us from death. He rose again to raise us to life, and He ascended into heaven to glorify us everlastingly. His Passion exciteth our charity, His Resurrection strengtheneth our faith, and His Ascension rejoiceth our hope. By His Passion He hath blotted out our sins, by His Resurrection He hath spoiled hell, and by His Ascension He hath shewed unto us the way to heaven.

Offerimus præclaræ Majestati tuæ.

That is to God the Father; for often in the Scripture by the titles of omnipotency, glory, majesty, and the like, the Person of the Father is understood, as in the first chapter of the Epistle to the Hebrews, and in sundry other places.

De tuis donis ac datis.

The Body and Blood of Christ are offerings prepared by God for us, yea, true offerings, but placed in heaven: offerings when they are made to God, gifts when they are given in earth to men, yet both here and there truly the same.

Hostiam.

First, some explicating this word, Host, say that it is derived, *ab ostio*, in English a door; because in the old law, the hosts were immolated in the porch or entry of the temple. The Christians do give it the same denomination, because that Jesus Christ, sacramentally immolated at the altar, hath opened unto them the gates of heaven, shut through the prevarication of Adam. Whence the Church at the elevation of the Host singeth this verse: *O salutaris Hostia, quæ cæli pandis ostium, bella premunt hostilia, da robur, fer auxilium,* O saving Host, which openest the gate of heaven, hostile wars oppress us, give strength, bring aid.

The Paynims and Gentiles have derived this term, *ab hoste*, in English, an enemy, because being to make war against their enemies, they did first sacrifice, to the end that they might overcome. And after happy success, they ordained other sacrifices which they called victims, leading their enemies bound even to the altar. Whereupon Ovid composed the distich following:

> *Hostia, quæ cecidit dextra victrice, vocatur.*
> *Hostibus a victis, victima nomen habet.*

And Christ Jesus, being to fight against the enemy of mankind, offered up His Body and Blood in a Host, whereby He hath delivered us out of the bondage and servitude of the devil.

+ *Puram.*

Next, this Host is called Pure, because it is the fountain of all purity, cleansing us from all pollution by the force of its virtue, contrary to those of the Old Testament, which did not cleanse but only bodily foulness.

Hostiam + *sanctam.*

It is also called Holy, because it containeth Jesus Christ, the Holy of Holies, and the only Fountain of all holiness, from Whom the graces of the Holy Ghost pour down upon the faithful in unspeakable abundance.

Hostiam + immaculatam.

Conceived and born without all sin, and lived in this world without all sin, and therefore immaculate. Conceived of a Virgin without the help of a man, and therefore immaculate, only by power Divine, and therefore immaculate.

Panem + sanctum.

Where this holy Host is named bread, not that the substance of bread now any more remaineth after Consecration, but because it is instituted or ordained under the same species. Add that in holy Scripture the creatures are called earth and ashes, because they are formed of such matter. Simon was surnamed leprous of that which he had been and was no more. And this Bread is rightly called *sanctum*, holy, because it truly sanctifieth the receivers.

Vitæ æternæ.

And of eternal life, because, as the Gospel saith, he that eateth of this Bread shall live for ever. Again, of eternal life, because it is no more common as it was before Consecration, but spiritual, celestial, divine, angelical, surpassing all corruptible meat, an incorruptible aliment, a food giving life to our souls, and by virtue of which, in the general resurrection, our bodies also shall be made immortal.

Et calicem + salutis perpetuæ.

The Priest, besides the Eucharistical Bread, offereth to God the holy Chalice, to wit, the Blood of Jesus Christ, contained under the species of wine. The consecration of both which is made separately, and yet nevertheless is but one Sacrament; even as the material food of the body is but one meal or banquet, although it consist both in meat and in drink.

Of the five crosses made at the rehearsal of the five words aforesaid.

Because the Church hath said before that she was mindful of our Lord's blessed Passion, therefore presently after the Elevation of the precious Body and Blood of Jesus Christ, the Priest maketh five crosses in remembrance of His five most precious and principal wounds, to wit, two in His hands, two in His feet, and one in His side. The first three that are made upon the Host and the Chalice together, may signify that Christ truly suffered, truly died, and was truly buried. And the two last which are made, one upon the Host, and the other upon the Chalice asunder, do insinuate the consequence of those His bitter pains, to wit, the separation and disjunction of His holy Soul from His blessed Body.

Supra quæ propitio ac sereno vultu respicere digneris.

Upon the which, to wit, Bread of eternal life and

Chalice of perpetual health, vouchsafe to look with a merciful and gracious countenance. Which is to be understood in respect of us, lest we put any impediment which may hinder the benefits and graces, that otherwise we should receive of Almighty God.

Et accepta habere.

Not of His part Who is offered, Who no way is, nor no way can be unacceptable unto Thee, but of his part who is the offerer. For it cannot be that the only Son of God, in Whom He is well pleased, and Who resteth in the bosom of the Father, should not be most acceptable to Him.

Sicuti accepta habere dignatus es munera.

Where it is to be noted, that we do no ways mean by these words to equalise the sacrifice of those, who are immediately to be named, with this of ours, which is infinitely more worthy and acceptable than all other sacrifices that ever were or ever shall be ; for they offered sheep and lambs, but we, the Lamb of God; they, creatures, but we, the Creator; they, the figure, we, the verity ; but the sense is, that God would receive as acceptable this Sacrifice at our hands, like as He did the sacrifices of those holy Fathers, who, for the sincere devotion of their hearts, were acceptable unto Him.

Pueri tui justi Abel.

Two titles are here given to Abel ; the one to be a

child, the other to be just. 1. To be a child in holy
Scripture is often taken to be harmless, and to
live in simplicity and innocency. Whereupon our
Saviour said in the Gospel, Unless you become like
little children, you cannot enter into the kingdom of
heaven.* 2. This title of Just is given unto Abel by our
Saviour Himself, saying : That all the blood of the
just which is shed upon the earth may come upon
you, even from the blood of Abel the just.† Add
that Abel was a figure of our blessed Saviour ; for
the blood of Abel was shed by his brother Cain, and
the Blood of Jesus Christ by His brethren the Jews.
Abel was a Priest, a martyr, a virgin, and the first
shepherd, and Christ was a Priest, a Martyr, a
Virgin, and the Chief Shepherd or Pastor of our
souls.

Et sacrificium Patriarchæ nostri Abrahæ.

In the second place is proposed the example of the
sacrifice of Abraham, who, through singular faith
and obedience, offered to God his only son. For the
patriarch Abraham was of such singular faith and
obedience, that at the commandment of Almighty
God, without any manner of doubt or hesitation, he
had presently sacrificed his only son, if the voice of
an Angel from heaven had not speedily prevented
the execution.

* St. Matt. ch. 18, v. 8.   † St. Matt. ch. 28, v. 35.

18 *

Et quod tibi obtulit summus sacerdos tuus Melchisedech.

Melchisedech is placed in the third place, who is here called the High Priest of God for two respects. The one, because his priesthood was preferred before that of Aaron, and for that he gave his benediction also to Abraham; the other, because he was the first that ever we read to have offered sacrifice in bread and wine, the true figure of this blessed Sacrament. In the sacrifices of these three holy men aforementioned, is truly represented unto us the conditions requisite for all such persons, as will offer up sacrifice agreeable to God: 1. Innocency of life, signified by Abel. 2. Faith and obedience, signified by Abraham. 8. Sanctity and religion, signified by Melchisedech.

Sanctum sacrificium.

The sacrifice of Melchisedech is called holy, not absolutely, nor as touching itself, but in respect of that of the New Testament, the which it represented more expressly than did all the other oblations. And it was foretold in the law of nature, that Jesus Christ should be established a Priest for ever after the order of Melchisedech.

Immaculatam Hostiam.

The same sacrifice is also for the selfsame reason called immaculate for the which before it was called holy, to wit, because it was the figure of the verity of the same that was to be offered in the Church, without any manner of spot or blemish; and it may be very well, that these last two clauses are rather meant of the present Sacrifice than of that of Melchisedech.

Of the Priest's inclination, joining his hands, and laying them upon the altar.

The first ceremony and its signification.

First, the Priest here lowly boweth or inclineth himself towards the altar, to signify how our blessed Lord and Saviour, giving up the ghost, inclined His head upon His breast, saying: O Father, into Thy hands I commend My spirit.

The second ceremony and its signification.

Next he joineth his hands before his breast, to signify that humble prayers, denoted by his foresaid inclination, are then especially heard when they proceed by faith from the bottom of our heart.

The third ceremony and its signification.

And he layeth them upon the altar, to signify that not every faith, but only that which worketh by love, is acceptable to God, which work is well understood by the hands.

Supplices te rogamus omnipotens Deus.

Together with the performance of the aforesaid ceremonies, he jointly pronounceth the words of the holy Canon, saying, *Supplices*, etc. We humbly beseech Thee, O omnipotent God, we heartily pray Thee, we prostrate ourselves before Thee, we meekly intreat Thee, etc. For prayer is an act of subjection and submission, as noteth Cajetan upon St. Thomas.

Jube hæc perferri.

But what is all this which is desired with so great instance? Verily this, that God by the ministry of His Angels, which attend both upon us and upon the holy Mysteries, would command the Body of His Son our Lord to be carried up before Him, not according to changing of place, or local mutation of the Sacrament, but according to His gracious acceptation of our service.

Per manus sancti Angeli tui.

This place Hugo de St. Victore expoundeth to be of the Angel-keeper of the Priest, and Thomas Waldensis, who wrote so learnedly against Wickliffe, calleth this Angel, *angelum vernaculum sacerdotis*, the proper or peculiar Angel of the Priest; signifying hereby, that every Priest, as he is a Priest, hath an Angel deputed to him by Almighty God to aid and assist him in the discharge of his function.

In sublime altare tuum.

As the Church hath a visible altar below in earth, so hath she an invisible altar above in heaven. And because the Angels are said to be ministering

spirits, therefore we pray that by the hands of the
holy Angels, the Hosts, which we have here upon the
altar in earth, may be presented above upon the
altar in heaven. For as St. Chrysostom saith, at
the time of Consecration, there are present many
thousands of Angels, who environ the altar, and do
honour and homage unto our Saviour Jesus.

In conspectu divinæ Majestatis tuæ.

To wit, the same first entering and going before,
we also, by means thereof, may be admitted to follow
after, and to enter in before the sight of the same
Majesty.

Ut quotquot ex hac altaris participatione.

The Church, as we said before, hath a visible altar
here in earth and an invisible altar above in heaven,
and because we do participate of Christ's Body and
Blood two manner of ways, sacramentally and really,
or by faith and spiritually, therefore all good
Christians have often recourse to these two altars,
sometimes to the one, sometimes to the other; and
so we participate of the same Body and Blood both
upon the altar in earth and upon the altar in heaven.
When we receive our Lord from the one, we go up
by faith unto Him, and when we receive Him from
the other, He descendeth and cometh down unto us.

Of the Kiss of the Altar.

The Priest at the prolation of these words doth

kiss the altar, by which ceremony is represented
unto us our reconciliation with God, made in the
death of Jesus Christ by the commemoration of this
Sacrifice; for a kiss, as before we have said, is a
true representation and sign of peace.

Sacrosanctum Filii tui cor + *pus et san* + *guinem*
sumpserimus.

To express the excellency of the holy Communion,
the Body and Blood of Jesus Christ is called sacro-
sanct or most holy. Which prayer doth not only
concern the Priest who doth celebrate, but the
people also who do communicate by faith and
devout assistance in time of Mass, with intention
to communicate often, and at the least on the times
appointed by the Church.

+ *Omni benedictione cælesti et gratia repleamur.*

The end of this present petition tendeth to this,
that as well the Priest communicating sacramentally,
as also the people spiritually, by religious assistance
at this holy Sacrifice, may be replenished with all
celestial benediction and grace, to carry from this
holy Communion fruit profitable to their salvation.

Per eumdem Christum Dominum nostrum. Amen.

Wherein we desire that God, for the love of His
Son, would both hear us, and have mercy on us; as
though God should seem little to regard His Son, if

He should not mercifully hear us for His sake. And as if the Son ascend not to the Father, if our devotions ascend not unto Him and be accepted of Him.

Of the three crosses which are made at the three words aforesaid.

By the first, which is made at *corpus*, is commemorated the cold and stiff extension of the Body of Jesus Christ, which according to the saying of the prophet was such, that they might dinumerate all His bones. By the second, which is .made at *sanguinem*, the abundant effusion of His precious Blood; whence it followed, that all the humours being quite exhausted, His Body was wholly parched and withered. By the third, which is made at *omni benedictione*, is designed the fruit of His holy Passion, from whence all benediction floweth forth upon us; for which cause, the Priest maketh the third benediction or cross upon himself.

CHAPTER XLVII.

OF THE SECOND MEMENTO.

Memento etiam Domine.

As before Consecration mention was made of the living, for some in particular, but for all in general, even so after Consecration, commemoration is made

for the departed, for some in particular, but for all
in general, saying: Remember also, O Lord: to wit,
remember to comfort them, remember to have mercy
upon them, remember to deliver them, remember to
take them out of their pains, and to glorify them.

Famulorum, famularumque tuarum.

Where they are called His servants, that is to say,
of His family, because whilst they lived in their
bodies, they were true members of the Church,
which is the family or house of God. And also when
they died, they died in the same Church, and therefore are rightly called His servants or family.

N et N.

These letters, put in this place of the Canon, do
serve for a mark to reduce particularly into memory
the names of those, for whom the Priest doth
specially pray or celebrate Mass, as his parents,
benefactors, friends, and others committed unto his
charge, for whom he prayeth secretly.

Qui nos præcesserunt cum signo fidei.

Which sign of faith is to have been regenerate of
water and the Holy Ghost, and signed with the
triumphant sign of the holy Cross, the peculiar
mark or character of Christians, whereby they are
distinguished from all infidels. Sign of faith, to wit,
for those who, before they departed, received the

holy Sacraments, and were not separated from the unity of the Catholic Church by any note or mark of heresy. Sign of faith, in which words, as well noteth Gabriel Biel, is touched the devotion and piety of the departed, to wit, that when they were living, there appeared in them evident signs that they were both faithful and true believers.

Et dormiunt in somno pacis.

That is, are departed in peace of conscience without mortal sin, and in the friendship and grace of Almighty God. Who, therefore, are said to sleep in peace, because as those that do sleep in peace awake again, so those that are departed out of this life in peace shall arise again. And as those which depart out of this life, without the sign aforesaid, are truly said to die, so they that depart with the same sign are not said to die, but rather to sleep or to rest than to be dead; for they are properly said to be dead, which never shall be raised to the life of glory.

Ipsis Domine.

To wit, to those of whom before he hath made particular commemoration; taught so to do by the Church instructed by the Holy Ghost, that the souls departed are aided by the suffrages, prayers, alms, and other works of piety, and principally by the acceptable Sacrifice of the Mass.

Et omnibus in Christo quiescentibus.

After particular commemoration of his friends and parents, he maketh his general prayer for all the departed, wherein he assisteth those, who have no particular friends to be mindful of them. Who also are said to rest in Christ, because they died in charity, having yet some defects to be purged, for that either they have not fully satisfied for their venial sins, or for the pain due to their mortal sins.

Locum refrigerii.

By the which is understood the kingdom of heaven, where all the Saints do daily draw out of the springs of the Lamb, the pleasant and cooling waters of everlasting comfort, after their long labours and torments sustained either in this life or in the fire of purgatory.

Lucis.

That is to say, such a place which needeth neither the light of the sun, nor of the moon, nor yet of the stars, because the splendour of God's Presence doth face to face illuminate it, and the glorious Lamb of God is their perpetual lantern.

Et pacis, ut indulgeas deprecamur.

In which place of light most perfect, full, secure, and sempiternal peace doth reign, where is neither faintness nor sadness, nor fraud, nor fear of foes, but one everlasting and joyful harmony of voices;

in which place of peace our Lord Himself doth dwell, Who doth guard and keep it, so that nothing can enter therein, which may disturb their peace.

Per eumdem Christum Dominum nostrum. Amen.

To wit, into this most blessed city, into this place of refreshing, of perpetual light, and of peace, we humbly beseech Thee, that the souls of them that are departed, having their offences forgiven them by the virtue of this Sacrifice, may be brought to repose and dwell for ever, through Him Whom now we offer up unto Thee in their behalfs, Christ Jesus. Amen.

Of the Ceremonies used in this Memento.

In this Memento three Ceremonies are observed :

1. The silent prayer of the Priest with his hands joined together.

2. The disjoining of them asunder. And 3. The conjoining of them again together.

The first ceremony and its signification.

At the first joining of his hands, he meditateth awhile and prayeth for his friends departed. And by this same may be understood the descending of our Saviour into *Limbo Patrum*, to comfort the souls of His dear friends, who had long sat in darkness and in the shadow of death.

The second ceremony and its signification.

At the disjoining or spreading of his hands abroad,

he prayeth for all the departed in general. And by
this may be understood how our Lord, in triumphant
and victorious manner, led forth with Him out of
Limbo all that company of holy souls.

The third ceremony and its signification.

At *Per Christum*, etc., he conjoineth them again
together. And by this may be understood that both
they and we, as members of one body, shall one day
be inseparably united to our Sovereign Head, Christ
Jesus.

CHAPTER XLVIII.

OF THE COMMEMORATION OF THE SAINTS.

Nobis quoque peccatoribus.

The first ceremony and its signification.

AT the recital of these words there are two ceremonies to be observed. The first, that the Priest
interrupteth his silence which he used a little before,
representing thereby, how the good thief reprehended
his companion, saying : We receive worthy of our
doings, but this Man hath done no evil. And
presently, after, with contrition and sorrow for his
sin, he said to Jesus : Lord, remember me when
Thou shalt come into Thy kingdom.*

The second ceremony and its signification.

The second, that in pronouncing the words afore-

* St. Luke ch. 23, v. 41, 42.

said he smiteth his breast; expressing thereby that of the centurion and others, who were present at the death of our Saviour, who seeing what had happened were sore afraid, saying : Indeed this was the Son of God.* And the people who were present at this spectacle departed sorrowful, and knocking their breasts.

In saying *nobis quoque peccatoribus*, he knocketh his breast, because as Alexander Hales saith, albeit we ought at all times, from the bottom of our hearts, to acknowledge ourselves sinners, yet that, chiefly it is to be done in the time of the Sacrifice of the Mass, which is celebrated in the remission and forgiveness of sins.

Famulis tuis.

In which words there may seem to be a certain contrariety, to wit, to be sinners, and yet to be God's servants. But as because of our proclivity and proneness to sin, we may justly affirm ourselves to be sinners, so having been contrite and confessed of those wherein by frailty we have fallen, we are nevertheless bold and confident to call ourselves His humble servants.

De multitudine miserationum tuarum sperantibus.

In the multitude of His mercies, not in our own justifications, do we prostrate our prayers before

* St. Matt. ch. 27, v. 54.

Him. For holy David, albeit so great a king and prophet, yet that his prayer might be heard, he grounded it only in the mercy of God, saying : According to Thy great mercy, do Thou remember me, O Lord for Thy goodness.*

Partem aliquam.

Titlemanus expoundeth this word *partem,* a part, wherein we desire to have some part of the kingdom of heaven with the blessed Saints, not for a piece, but for participation ; for else our petition were absurd, if we should think that the kingdom of heaven were divided amongst the Saints by parts or pieces.

Et societatem.

The learned Doctor, Gabriel Biel, explicating this word, saith that they are said to have society, because in that place of beatitude, to each one in particular the goods of all the Saints are made common. Add that by the name of society is insinuated the singular peace, charity, and unity of the blessed Saints. And Alexander Hales very well noteth, that in the commemoration of the Saints made before the Consecration of Christ, their prayers and suffrages are implored ; but in this which is made after Consecration, the society of the Saints is required ; to signify that before the coming of the

* Psalms.

kingdom of Christ, we have need in this life of the suffrages of the Saints, but after that the Body of Christ is consecrated, that is, after this kingdom is manifested, we shall enjoy their company and society, nor shall any longer stand in need of their prayers or supplication.

Donare digneris.

And it is said *Donare* not *Reddere*, that is, to bestow or give of his bounty and liberality, not to pay or render as a thing due in rigour.

Cum tuis sanctis Apostolis et Martyribus.

So oft as there is any occasion to speak or make mention of the blessed Saints, first the Apostles are named, and next the Martyrs; the one because of the singular dignity of their office, wherein they excelled all others, the other, because of their unspeakable patience in their torments, wherein they surpassed all others.

Cum Joanne.

Amongst the Saints that are specified in this part of the Mass, St. John is first named. Some there be that suppose it to be meant of St. John Baptist, who, although he could not be named before amongst the Apostles, yet may now be mentioned amongst the Martyrs. Others think it more probably to be understood of St. John the Evangelist, amongst whom is Innocentius tertius, saying, that although St. John was mentioned in the first commemoration, yet that he is here again rehearsed in this, because Christ upon the Cross commended His Mother to His disciple, the Mother a virgin to the disciple a virgin.

Stephano.

Next after St. John is named St. Stephen. The one excellent for the prerogative of Apostleship and virginity, the other excellent for martyrdom and virginity. He was the very first that suffered for Jesus Christ. In imitation of Christ, he prayed for his enemies at the time of his passion. To him was especially deputed by the Apostles the charge of the devout widows. In him shined the singular praise of sanctity, of whom it is said: Stephen, full of grace and fortitude did great wonders and signs amongst the people. Of whom it is farther said, that all that sat in the council, beholding him, saw his face, as it were, the face of an angel. At the time of his disputation with the Jews, being full of the Holy Ghost, looking steadfastly up to heaven, he saw the glory of God, and Jesus standing on the right hand of God.

Matthiâ.

St. Matthias was divinely elected by lot into the Apostleship to supply the sacred number of twelve, diminished by the disloyal prevarication of Judas. Having commission to announce the gospel in Ethiopia, he accomplished the same with exceeding labour. His enemies attempted to stone him to

death, which not being able to take effect, he was in
the end martyred with a chopping-knife.

Barnabá.

St. Barnabas was a native of Cyprus, and one of
the seventy-two disciples of Jesus Christ. He was
also by the ordinance of the Holy Ghost separated
with St. Paul, for the execution of the ministry
whereunto he was called. He was put to death in
the seventh year of the Emperor Nero. His bones
were found in Cyprus under a tree, having upon his
breast the Gospel of St. Matthew written with his
hand, as is before noted. To him and to St. Paul
is attributed to have been the first Apostles of the
Gentiles.

Ignatio.

St. Ignatius was companion of the Apostles,
disciple of St. John the Evangelist, and second
successor of St. Peter in the bishopric of Antioch;
the footman or page of the glorious Mother of God,
the Virgin Mary, and her chaplain. Who, as
Dionysius writeth of him, had nothing else in his
mouth but *Amor meus crucifixus est*, My love is crucified. He was condemned under Trajan, the Emperor of Rome, to be devoured with wild beasts.
He affirmed that if they refused to hurt him, as
they had done other martyrs, he himself would provoke them, saying, that he was Christ's corn, and
must be ground betwixt the teeth of lions. When

he was dead, the Name of Jesus was found written in his heart in letters of gold.

Alexandro.

St. Alexander was Pastor of the Universal Church, the sixth Pope from St. Peter in the seat of Rome. He gave himself wholly to advance the worship and service of Almighty God, as his laudable institutions do very well witness. He added to the Canon these words: *Qui pridie,* etc. Having virtuously ruled the space of ten years in Rome, and converted Hernetus and Quirinus, he was there martyred together with Eventius and Theodulus his deacons, under Adrian the Emperor. Whose blessed body lieth in St. Sabin's under the high altar.

Marcellino.

St. Marcellinus was a Priest of the Church of Rome in the time of the Emperor Dioclesian. He baptised Paulina the daughter of Artemiras, keeper of the prison of the city, whom St. Peter the exorcist delivered of a malignant spirit that possessed her, together with her father, mother, family and neighbours, who ran to see the miracle. For which he was most strangely tormented, and in the end beheaded by the order of the judge Serenus, who could neither bend nor move him from the holy and invincible resolution of the observation of the Christian faith and religion.

Petro.

This St. Peter was ordained an exorcist in the Church of Rome, to impose, according to the form there observed, his hands upon those which were vexed with unclean spirits, either to cast them out, to repress them, or to appease them. Who for having dispossessed the keeper's daughter and assisted at the baptism aforesaid, performed by St. Marcellinus, suffered like martyrdom with him and upon the same day. Their holy souls, Doretheus, who beheaded them, saw clothed in most bright and shining garments, set with most rich jewels, and carried up into heaven by the hands of Angels, whereupon he also became a Christian.

Felicitate.

St. Felicitas was a noble woman of Rome, who not only obscured the lustre of all the ladies of her time, but also far surpassed them in all virtue. She was mother of seven sons, who endured sundry kinds of torments in her sight for the faith of Jesus Christ, all which she beheld with wonderful constancy and more than manly courage, and gave unto them many wholesome admonitions and exhortations. And a little after, she herself followed them with the same courage and constancy. For which St. Gregory saith that she suffered eight times, seven times in her children and once in herself. She made such proof of her immovable and inflexible resolution, that all were filled with astonishment and admiration. By the commandment of Publius, ruler under Antoninus Augustus, she was commanded to be beheaded.

Perpetua.

Amongst the perfections wherewith St. Perpetua was adorned, she is highly praised, for that she always strongly resisted the passions and provocations of the flesh, having vowed to God her chaste virginity. She suffered martyrdom in Mauritania under the Emperor Severus, whereby she happily arrived to heaven, where she gloriously shineth with a double diadem. Tertullian and St. Augustine make honourable mention of her in their writings.

Agatha.

St. Agatha was, amongst the noble virgins of her time, very famous both for her virtue and beauty, and for this cause was extremely loved of Quintianus Governor of Sicily, even to the attempting of her virginal chastity. But she, not enduring any breach nor blot in her honour, strongly withstood him. Whereupon he was so discontented, that his disordered affection was changed into a marvellous hatred and extreme desire to revenge himself by all the means he might possibly devise. After many insupportable torments she was martyred, having first both her breasts cut off by the commandment of the said Quintianus, ruler under the Emperor Decius. In the time of her imprisonment she was visited by St. Peter the Apostle, and healed of her wounds. Finally, this holy virgin received in her sepulchre a testimony of her sanctity by the hands of Angels.

Lucia.

St. Lucy was of a very noble family, and from her infancy wholly given to piety. Having by her prayers, made at the sepulchre of St. Agatha, obtained of God the healing of her mother, extremely afflicted with a flux of blood, she distributed by her consent, unto the poor that which she had assigned for her marriage. Whereupon he to whom she was betrothed, greatly offended, brought her before the Justice for a Christian. Paschasius, Provost of the city, not being able by infinite horrible torments to divert her from her religion, commanded her throat to be cut.

Agnete.

St. Agnes was a Roman by birth and born of noble parents, exceeding beautiful of mind and body. The governor's son of the city, falling greatly in love with her, desired to have her for his wife, whom she constantly refused, saying that she would have none other but Jesus Christ to be her husband. The father of the young man, understanding that she was a Christian, thought by that means to constrain her to marry with his son. Which she absolutely refusing, he commanded her to be led to the common brothel or stews. But God so provided, that her hair grew so thick and so long, that it covered her all over, and seemed to adorn her more than her apparel. In the said brothel house where she was put, an Angel of our Lord came unto her to defend h that she should not be abused or defiled. She was cast into a great fire to be burned, but the flames had no power to touch her chaste body. At the last, Aspasius caused her to be beheaded. She suffered in the year 317. St. Ambrose wrote of her.

Cæcilia.

St. Cecily was also of the lineage of the noble citizens of Rome, in the time of the Emperor Marcus Aurelius. She was wholly devoted to the honour of God and to His divine service. She was married against her will to Valerian, a citizen of Rome. Whom she warned in the first night of her marriage, that he should not touch her, for that she was committed to an Angel of God, who would preserve her from all pollution, and sharply revenge the wrong which he should do her. Whereunto he willingly accorded, and was converted to the faith by the exhortation of St. Urban, of whom he was baptised, together with one of his brethren. Afterwards persevering constantly in the faith, they were all three martyred by the fire and the sword. St. Cecily had her head cut off: and being dead, was found to have a hair-cloth under her precious habits of golden tissue.

Anastasia.

St. Anastasia was the daughter of a noble citizen of Rome, called Prætextus. She was wonderfully charitable to the poor, amongst whom she liberally distributed all her substance. Whereupon Publius her husband, who was an infidel, was greatly offended, and caused her straightly to be restrained in a most hideous prison, and not being able to divert her from her faith, caused her to be burnt alive. During her imprisonment, she received sundry consolatory letters from St. Chrysogonus, which, together with her answers, are inserted in the Ecclesiastical History of Nicephorus.

Et omnibus sanctis tuis.

To avoid prolixity, the Priest comprehendeth in general all the Saints, after the special commemoration of those which are expressed in the Canon. Always insisting to be admitted unto their number, and to come with them unto everlasting glory by imitation of their virtues. And therefore he proceedeth, saying,

Intra quorum nos consortium non æstimator meriti sed veniæ.

In which words the Church doth not simply deny God to be the esteemer of merits, but the sense and meaning is, that God will not barely reward every godly man according to his merit, but, of His goodness and liberality, will add to him above his deserving : nor rigorously punish the defects of him that sinneth, but always reward the one above his merit, and punish the other less than his desert.

Quæsumus largitor admitte, per Christum Dominum nostrum.

Not to be refused in this request, he maketh it and concludeth it through Jesus Christ. For what exterior show soever our works may have, they are not agreeable to God but by His Son working in us. Who hath so greatly loved us, that He would descend from heaven unto earth to be our Mediator, and finally to place us amongst His Saints.

Of the joining of the Priest's hands.

In saying, *per Christum Dominum nostrum,* he joineth his hands together. By which ceremony, used at the commemoration of Saints, may be understood the same that before was said concerning the souls departed, to wit, that through the merits of Christ our Lord, Who is our Head, we hope to be joined with Him and His Saints in everlasting glory.

Per quem.

For as much as the confection of the holy Eucharist is attributed to Jesus Christ, Who is the Author of this holy institution, therefore the Priest giveth thanks and praiseth God the Father, for that by Him He hath created the matter, to wit, the bread and the wine, under the forms whereof, He doth exhibit unto us, truly and really, His Body and Blood in food and nourishment of our souls.

Hæc omnia Domine semper bona.

To wit, all the Hosts which the Church doth immolate through the whole world. Which, if we consider the sensible qualities, are of infinite number, but if the substance, all is one Body and all is one Blood, which is daily made present in this holy Sacrifice by Him, by Whom, as saith St. John, all things were made, and without Him was made nothing that was made.*

Creas.

Here a question may be moved why the Priest doth not make the sign of the Cross at the word *Creas,* Thou dost create, as well as at the other words following, *Sanctificas, vivificas,* etc. Whereof Alexander Hales giveth a very sufficient reason, saying that the sign of the Cross is a representation of our Lord's Passion; and because the creation of man was no cause of His Passion, but the fall of man was thereby to be repaired, therefore when sanctification, vivification, and benediction are mentioned, the sign of the Cross is made, but when creation is named, the Priest doth not then make the sign of the Cross, because the creation of man was not painful to our Saviour, but his Redemption. And St. Thomas, in his Exposition of the Mass, saith that this was ordained by the admirable Providence

* St. John ch. 1.

of Almighty God, to signify that man had not that by
nature in his creation, which since he hath obtained
by the Cross of Christ in His Redemption.

Sancti+ficas, vivi+ficas, bene+dicis.

These three words may be considered three manner of ways. They may either be referred to the
bread and wine, or to our Saviour, or to ourselves.
If you consider them as spoken of the bread and
wine, then it is most easy to conceive their sense.
Dost sanctify, to wit, according to their sacramental
causes: vivificate, by converting them into Thy
Flesh and Blood: bless, by pouring down and mul-
tiplying Thy graces upon them. If you refer them
to Christ, then are they thus to be understood, to
wit, those creatures which before were but earthly,
void of life, and of all benediction, are by the blessing of Christ made heavenly, lively, and every way
most blessed. If we apply them unto ourselves,
then may they thus be taken, to wit, that this
sacred Host is sanctified in respect of us, that it
may be our sanctification from all sins; vivificated,
that it may be the life of our souls, to quicken us in
spirit to newness of life; blessed, that we may by
the same attain the abundance of all spiritual grace
and perfection.

*Of the three crosses which are made at the three words
aforesaid.*

As touching the three crosses which are made in

this place upon the Host and the Chalice together, they are made to signify unto us that our Redemption, wrought by Christ by the virtue of His Cross, was with the consent of all the Blessed Trinity. Or, according to Albertus Magnus, three crosses are made in this place, to signify that all things are sanctified, vivificated, and blessed by the virtue of the Cross and Passion of our Redeemer.

Et præstas nobis.

The thing, which in these words we desire of God may be given unto us, is the precious Body and Blood of Christ His Son for our refection, Who lying hid under these species giveth Himself to us to eat, that so He may be in us and we in Him. And Titlemanus saith, that this holy Host is given us to our utility and health; it is given us in meat, it is given us in drink, it is given us in life, it is given us in nourishment, it is given us in preservation, it is given us in defence, it is given us in remission of our sins, it is given us for the obtaining of good things, it is given us against the assaults of our enemies, it is given us for the subduing of our flesh, it is given us in commemoration of the Death of Christ and of all His benefits.

Per ip + sum et cum ip + so et in ip + so.

Then uncovering the Chalice, bowing his knee, and holding the Host in his right hand and the Chalice in his left, he maketh three crosses, from

side to side of the Chalice, saying, *Per ipsum*, as by
the Mediator betwixt God and man ; *et cum ipso*, as
every way equal with the Father ; *et in ipso*, as consubstantial and co-eternal both with Him and the
Holy Ghost. Again, *per ipsum*, by Whom Thou hast
created all things, *et cum ipso*, by Whom Thou go-
vernest all things created ; *et in ipso*, in Whom Thou
consummatest all things.

Est tibi Deo Patri + *omnipotenti*.

Not called Father only by name, honour, and
veneration, as we call our elders and betters,
fathers, but by nature and origin, so that truly and
properly the Divine generation appertaineth unto
Him.

In unitate Spiritus + *Sancti*.

That is to say, in the communion of the Holy
Ghost, Who is the knot and love of the Father and
the Son, in Whom they communicate as in one
common gift, proceeding from both.

Omnis honor et gloria.

Be all honour as to our Lord, and all glory as to
our God. Where in the same order that God the
Father doth send His graces and blessings unto us,
which is by the means of Christ His Son, even so
in the same order, all honour and glory return
again by the means of Christ unto the Father, and
that evermore, in the unity of the Holy Ghost.

*Of the five crosses which are made at the five words
aforesaid.*

As touching those three which are made with the
Host over the Chalice at these words, *Per ipsum*, etc.,
divers things may be signified by the same. First,
they may signify the three hours wherein our Lord
and Saviour hung upon the Cross, in most unspeakable pain, alive.

The second reason.

According to St. Thomas, these three crosses are
made to signify the triple prayer of Christ upon the
Cross. First, Father, forgive them. Secondly, My
God, why hast Thou forsaken Me. Thirdly, Into
Thy hands I commend My spirit.

The third reason.

The other two crosses, which he maketh betwixt
the Chalice and his breast at these words, *Est tibi
Deo Patri omnipotenti*, etc., do signify the mystery of
the Blood and water which issued out of the side of
our Blessed Saviour, hanging upon the Cross, and the
two Sacraments which were instituted in virtue of
the same, to wit, Baptism and this Blessed Sacrament of the altar. According to the testimony of
St. John, one of the soldiers with a spear opened
His side, and incontinent there came forth blood
and water.*

* St. John ch. 19, v. 34.

The fourth reason.

At the words, *omnis honor et gloria*, the Host is held above, and the Chalice beneath, and both a little elevated. Which ceremony doth very aptly signify the Death of our Saviour, to wit, how in His Passion, His Blood was truly separated from His Body, and consequently also His blessed Soul.

Of other Ceremonies performed after the short elevation.

The Priest, having performed this short elevation, layeth the Host down upon the corporal, covereth again the Chalice, and then adoreth.

The first ceremony and its signification.

First, the Host is laid upon the corporal, because Joseph and Nicodemus, begging of Pilate the Body of Jesus, took it down from the Cross, wrapped it in a fine sindon, and after buried it.

The second ceremony and its signification.

And because they rolled a great stone before the door of the sepulchre, therefore the Priest with the pall covereth the Chalice. And because those holy men worshipped the Body of Christ in the sepulchre at their departure, therefore the Priest adoreth our Lord in this holy Sacrament.

The third ceremony and its signification.

This done, the Priest lifteth up his voice and pronounceth on high these words, saying, *Per omnia sæcula sæculorum.* And the people answer, *Amen.*

Our Doctors here do say, that this lifting up of the voice of the Priest representeth the strong cry of our Lord and Saviour, when He yielded up His spirit into the hands of His Father. And that the answer of the people signifieth the lamentation and pity of the devout women, which were present at this spectacle. In this manner, Innocentius tertius interpreteth the same. Because Jesus, saith he, crying with a high voice, rendered up His spirit, therefore the Priest lifteth up his voice saying : *Per omnia sæcula sæculorum.* And because the women lamenting, bewailed their Lord, all the choir, as lamenting, do answer : *Amen.*

CHAPTER XLIX.

OF THE END OF THE SECRET PART OF THE CANON.

Per omnia sæcula sæculorum.

World without end. By the words themselves are commonly understood one of these two things: either that all honour and glory appertaineth to God, world without end, or that the Son doth live with the Father and the Holy Ghost, world without end. Again, *per omnia sæcula sæculorun,* that is, throughout all ages of the world, for *sæculum* is taken for a time somewhat long, and so is called *sæculum* of this word *sequor* to follow, because time followeth time.

Oremus.

Let us pray. The Priest having gotten, as it were, a good opportunity, having now before him the Lord and Maker both of heaven and earth, and that according to His corporal presence, he exhorteth all the people heartily to pray, saying: *Oremus,* let us pray.

Præceptis salutaribus moniti, et divina institutione formati.

Admonished by wholesome precepts, and formed by divine institution. And therefore the Priest sayeth that it is by precept and divine institution, that we are admonished to say this prayer, because both our Lord instituted the same, and also commanded His Apostles to use the same, saying: Pray always, and be not weary. Again, pray without intermission. Which prayer Christ Himself taught His Apostles to say in the holy Sacrifice of the Mass, as St. Jerome witnesseth.[*]

Audemus dicere.

We dare to say. The reason why we here affirm, that we are bold to speak unto the Majesty of God Almighty, is because this selfsame prayer, which we pour forth before God, the selfsame prayer proceeded out of the mouth of God; so that in this prayer we recommend ourselves unto God with no other than the very words of God. For, as St. Gregory well saith, it were very unmeet that upon the holy

[*] Hieron. lib. 3, contra Pelagianos.

Eucharist, any prayer should be recited, of the scholars' composing, and that omitted, of the Master's making.

The praises of the Pater noster.

This prayer for many causes doth very far excel all other prayers. For the authority of the Teacher, for brevity of words, for sufficiency of petitions, fecundity of mysteries, utility, efficacy, and necessity. For the authority of the Teacher, for, as we said before, it proceeded out of the mouth of Almighty God. For brevity of words, because it is easily learned and soon recited. For sufficiency of demands, because it comprehendeth the necessities of both lives. For fecundity of mysteries, because it containeth innumerable sacraments. In utility, because Christ being our Advocate with the Father for our sins, we, praying unto Him, do pronounce and use the very words of our Advocate. In efficacy, because, as St. Augustine saith, it taketh away our venial sins. In necessity, because, as St. Clement saith, all Christians are bound to know it, and often to rehearse and say it. Lastly, this prayer anciently was held in so great reverence, that it was not permitted but to such as were baptised, either to write or to pronounce the same.

Pater.

Father. I will here set down for this first point a right worthy consideration of St. Leo the Great, saying : Great, my beloved, is the gift of this Sacrament,

20 *

and this gift exceedeth all gifts that God should call man His son, and man name God his Father. Hence also St. Augustine admonisheth the rich and noble of this world, not to wax proud or contemn the poor and ignoble, because they pronounce and say that together to God our Father, which they can never truly say, unless they acknowledge themselves to be brethren.

Noster.

Our. As by the word *Pater* we understand the grace of adoption, so by the word *noster* we understand brotherly union. For, as St. Cyprian saith, our Lord, Who is the Master of peace and unity, would not that when any one prayeth, he should pray for himself only, and say, my Father, nor, give me my daily bread, nor, forgive me my trespasses, nor, lead me not into temptation, nor, deliver me from evil, but, our Father, give us our daily bread, forgive us our trespasses, lead us not into temptation, and so of others.

Qui es in cælis.

Which art in heaven. 1. The Priest in saying that God is in heaven doth not inclose or confine God within heaven, but endeavoureth to draw him which prayeth, up from earth to heaven.

2. In affirming our Father to be in heaven, we are put in mind that we are strangers here in earth, and far from our proper country and home which is in heaven.

Sanctificetur nomen tuum.

Hallowed be Thy name. The name of God hath in itself no need of sanctification, but because here in earth it is not worthily sanctified as it deserveth, and that by many, and even almost hourly, it is most sinfully profaned by execrable blasphemies, imprecations, detestations, cursings, swearings, forswearings, and the like, therefore we pray that the same may be honoured, praised, exalted, and sanctified of all in the world.

Adveniat regnum tuum.

Thy kingdom come. The kingdom of God in which He doth reign, is the Church Militant in earth and the Church Triumphant in heaven. Wherefore by, Thy kingdom come, is understood kingdom to kingdom, the militant to the triumphant, that these two may be united and made one kingdom. This likewise doth reprehend all those persons, who would prolong this worldly life, whereas the just do heartily pray that that kingdom of God would speedily come.

Fiat voluntas tua.

Thy Will be done. The Will of God is taken two manner of ways. The one His Will and decree as it is eternal, the other the signs of His Will which are temporal; and these are five, to wit, precept, prohibition, permission, counsel, and operation: these latter are not always fulfilled, for which cause we pray daily that they may be fulfilled, saying: *Fiat voluntas tua*, Thy Will be done, to wit, in all Thou commandest, in all Thou forbiddest, in all Thou permittest, in all Thou counsellest, in all Thou workest.

Sicut in cælo et in terra.

In earth as it is in heaven. By heaven is understood the heavenly spirits, to wit, the Saints and Angels. For the blessed Angels, so soon as they conceive the conception and mind of Almighty God, do incontinently, with inexplicable delight and readiness, transport themselves to accomplish the same. And therefore we pray that the Will of Almighty God may be fulfilled, *Sicut in cælo et in terra*, to wit, as by Angels in heaven, even so by men in earth.

Panem.

Bread. Four sorts of bread are necessary for us. Three whilst we are pilgrims in this life, and the fourth in the life and world to come, to wit, corporal, spiritual, Sacramental and Eternal. Of the first it is written, Man liveth not by bread only. Of the second, My meat is to do the Will of Him that sent Me. Of the third, He that eateth this Bread unworthily is guilty of the Body of our Lord. Of the fourth, I am the Bread of Life Which came down from heaven.

Nostrum quotidianum.

Our daily. Our, not mine, saith St. Chrysostom, because all whatsoever God giveth us, he giveth not to us alone but also to others by us; that of that which we have received of God, we also give part thereof unto the poor. Again our bread, to wit, got by our true labours, for all that which we eat, unjustly gotten or stolen, is not ours but other mens' bread. Again, our bread, to wit, the spiritual food of our souls, as, true Catholic doctrine, Sacraments, wholesome ceremonies, and the like; not others, that is, the doctrine and ceremonies of infidels or heretics. And this our bread is called daily, because we daily stand in need thereof.

Da nobis.

Give us. This doth Christ teach us, that we do not only pray that bread be given us, that we may have to eat, but, as St. Chrysostom saith, that what we eat we may receive from the hand of God. For to have to eat is common both to the good and to the bad, but to acknowledge it from the hand of God is proper or belongeth only unto the good.

Hodie.

This day. This day, to wit, in this present life, as St. Augustine expoundeth the same, which we ought to account but as one day, it is so frail and of so little lasting.

Et dimitte nobis.

And forgive us. Three manner of ways we offend and trespass, whereof we crave of God forgiveness. Against God, against ourselves, and against our neighbour. Because we have offended against God,

we say, *et dimitte*, and forgive, and because we have
offended against ourselves, we say, *nobis*, us, and
because we have likewise offended against our
neighbour, we say, *Sicut et nos dimittimus debitoribus
nostris*, As we forgive them that trespass against us.

Debita nostra.

Our trespasses. Our trespasses are called *debita*,
debts, because they make us debtors of pain, which
must of necessity be paid either in this life or in the
other. Again, sins or trespasses are called debts,
for that sin, being the wealth and substance of the
devil, a man which committeth sin is made a debtor
to the devil, even as he is made a debtor which
useth or holdeth another man's money.

Sicut et nos dimittimus debitoribus nostris.

As we forgive them that trespass against us. In this
request we ask to be forgiven upon condition, to
wit, as we forgive others; he, therefore, that asketh
to be forgiven, and doth not himself forgive, requireth of God not to be forgiven. By reason
whereof, whosoever is in hatred or malice, is more
hurt than holpen by this prayer, unless at the very
same present he have a purpose to forgive.

Et ne nos inducas in tentationem.

And lead us not into temptation. After we have
required forgiveness of sins past, we demand to be
preserved from those which we may commit for the
time to come, which we call by the name of tempta-

tion. Concerning which, we crave of Almighty God, not that we may not be led to temptation, but that we may not be led into it, that is, suffered to fall into it.

Sed libera nos a malo.

But deliver us from evil. Upon these last words Cardinal Bellarmine hath very learnedly noted, that our Lord with great wisdom teacheth us to demand to be delivered from all evil, and cometh not to particulars, as to poverty, sickness, and the like. For that oftentimes it seemeth that a thing is good for us, which God seeth is evil for us, and contrariwise evil for us, which He seeth to be good for us ; and that therefore, according to the instruction of our Lord, we demand that He vouchsafe to deliver us from that which He seeth and knoweth to be evil for us, be it prosperity or adversity, weal or woe. The Fathers of the Greek Church commonly understand by the name of evil the devil, as Chrysostom, Cyrillus, Euthymius, Germanus, Tertullian, and others. Yea, and some great Saints of God never would call the devil by any other name, as, amongst others, St. Catherine of Siena.

Amen.

After the answer of the assistants, the Priest saith *Amen*, which importeth a great confidence that God will give them their demand, even as if, having obtained, He sent them that by the Priest's means which they desired.

Or more briefly thus.

Our Father Which are in heaven, hallowed be Thy name, because Thou art our Father ; Thy kingdom come, because Thou art our King ; Thy Will be done in earth as it is in heaven, because Thou art our Spouse ; give us this day our daily bread, because Thou art our Pastor ; and forgive us our trespasses, as we forgive them that trespass against us, because Thou art our Judge ; and lead us not into temptation, because Thou art our Captain ; but deliver us from evil, because Thou art our Physician.   Amen.

Of the Priest's resuming the Paten.

By the roundness of the Paten, as before we said, is signified charity, and the hiding or covering thereof during the Sacrifice, wherein the mysteries of the Death and Passion of our Saviour are represented, signifieth the flight of the Apostles, who at the first, through the great affection and charity which they bore to their Lord and Master, promised to die at His feet, rather than they would ever forsake Him, yet, as soon as He was in the hands of His enemies, they all forsook Him and hid themselves.

Libera nos, quæsumus Domine, ab omnibus malis præteritis, præsentibus et futuris.

Deliver us, O Lord, we beseech Thee, from all evils, past, present, and to come. The Priest, in resuming the Paten, as aforesaid, repeateth the prayer made by the assistants at the conclusion of our Lord's

Prayer, which is neither in vain, nor superstitious, because it explicateth the same more particularly. Wherefore here there are named three sorts of evils, from the which we have great need to pray to be delivered, to wit, from all evils past, present, and to come, tempests, sudden and unprovided deaths, etc. All which because they are punishments due to our sins, we here pray to be delivered from them.

Et intercedente beata.

And the blessed Mary interceding. The Virgin Mary first is here called, blessed, for so the woman in the Gospel witnessed of her, saying: Blessed is the womb that bare thee, and the paps that gave thee suck. Or blessed, to wit, in the generations both of heaven and earth. Of heaven to whom she bare their Restorer, of earth to whom she brought forth their Redeemer.

Et gloriosa.

And glorious. Next she is said to be glorious, because she is the seat of the King of Glory, of whom He taking flesh, sat in her as in His seat. Or glorious, because she dwelleth on high, where she sitteth gloriously on the right hand of her Son. Or glorious, because she is most gloriously assumpted both in soul and body, and highly exalted far above all human and angelical virtues.

Semper Virgine.

Always Virgin. Always, to wit, before her delivery,

in her delivery, and after her delivery.   A virgin in body, in mind, in profession, in observation.

Dei Genitrice Maria.

Mary, Mother of God.   This blessed and glorious Virgin is said to be Mother of the Son of God, whereupon it followeth that she hath one Son common with God.   O wonderful mystery!   He hath not a Son, whereof Mary is not the mother, she hath not a Son whereof God is not the Father.

Cum beatis apostolis tuis, Petro.

With Thy blessed Apostles, Peter.   St. Peter is next named, because commandment was given to the holy women by the Angel, to carry the good tidings of our Lord's resurrection, which the Priest by-and-by goeth about to represent unto us, to the disciples, and in especial to St. Peter, he having need of particular consolation, because lately before he had denied his Master, and had now bitterly wept and done austere penance for the same.

Et Paulo, atque Andrea.

Paul and Andrew.   After our Lady and St. Peter, St. Paul and St. Andrew are next named for some special prerogatives. Gabriel Biel saith, that to obtain the gift of peace, these four, albeit recited before, are here introduced again, because these, above others, were most configurate to the Passion of Christ, in virtue whereof, peace is given unto us.

Et omnibus Sanctis.

And all Saints. By which words the intercession of other Saints is not omitted, but in the commemoration of these few, and those the most eminent, the suffrages of all are required. For so are all united to God, and so do all desire one thing, that in one all are in some sort included, and in one all are neglected.

Why the Priest signeth himself with the Paten.

That the Priest signeth himself with the Paten, it is done to signify that the chief of the Priests and the Pharisees signed and healed the stone of the sepulchre, setting soldiers and watchmen to keep the same.

Da propitius pacem.

Grant mercifully peace. Having prayed for our deliverance from evils, next we crave for perfect peace, to wit, in the remission of sin, perfect peace in the tranquillity of conscience, and perfect peace in amity with our neighbour, because this perfect peace is the holy and sacred band of all human society.

In diebus nostris.

In our days. To wit, in the time of this life, according as Titlemanus expoundeth the same. And this we crave after the example of King Ezechias, that we may live in the fear of God and observation of His holy commandments, without seeing the oppressions and incommodities, which the uncertain change of worldly things may unexpectedly bring upon us.

Ut ope misericordiæ tuæ adjuti.

That aided by the help of Thy mercy. That our petitions, which we offer and present to Almighty God, may take the better effect, it is most necessary that we have His merciful help and assistance hereunto, without the which we do confess that we cannot, as we ought, either begin, continue, or end, or ever obtain the thing which we desire.

Et a peccato simus semper liberi.

We may both be always free from sin. The thing, whereunto we principally require the aid of His mercy, is to be freed from our sins, because sin hath this property, that it always bringeth three evils with it.

The first is, it maketh us of free men, bondmen; for as our Saviour saith, he that committeth sin is the servant of sin. Secondly, it alienateth us from God's holy grace. Thirdly, it justly procureth His wrath against us.

And hence it is that St. Bernard saith, that so long as in any creature there is power to sin, it is secure in no place, neither in heaven, nor in paradise, nor in the world. For in heaven fell the Angels, even in God's presence. In paradise fell Adam from the place of pleasure, in the world fell Judas from the school of our Saviour.

Et ad omni perturbatione securi.

And secure from all perturbation. Next to be secure from the perturbations, tumult, and troubles of the world, because from thence proceedeth the matter of sin, and hindrance that when we approach to this most holy Communion, we come not in such purity as is fit and requisite.

Of sundry ceremonies performed by the Priest in this part of the Mass.

The first ceremony and its signification.

First he putteth the Paten under the Host, which, as we said before, by its roundness, representeth charity. The Host, therefore, laid upon the Paten to be broken and divided, signifieth that Christ of His love and charity exposed His Body to suffer death for our Redemption.

The second ceremony and its signification.

Next he uncovereth the Chalice. By the Chalice is signified the sepulchre. And the uncovering of the same is done, to signify how the Angel of our Lord removed away the stone from the door of the sepulchre.

The third ceremony and its signification.

After this he divideth or breaketh the Host into two parts, which signifieth the separation of the holy Soul of our Lord and Saviour from His blessed Body, the one descending into hell, and the other remaining in the sepulchre. Whereof Innocentius

tertius yieldeth another reason, saying that therefore
the Priest breaketh the Host, that in the breaking of
Bread we may know our Lord, as the two disciples
knew Him in breaking of Bread, to whom He
appeared the day of His Resurrection as they went
to Emmaus.

*Per eumdem Dominum nostrum Jesum Christum Filium
tuum.*

Through the same our Lord Jesus Christ Thy Son. In
dividing the Host he saith, *Per eumdem Dominum
nostrum.* To wit, unto Whom all power is given both
in heaven and earth. *Jesum,* Saviour, for He
cometh to save His people from their sins, *Christum,*
anointed above all His fellows with the oil of gladness,
Filium tuum, natural and only begotten. These words
ended, the part of the Host which he holdeth in His
right hand, he layeth upon the Paten, and from the
part in his left hand, he breaketh off another little
particle, and so the Host is divided into three parts.

The Host thus divided into three several parts,
representeth unto us the state of the Church in three
several places. The part held in the right hand,
which is no more divided but remaineth entire,
representeth the Church Triumphant, signified by the
right hand, which hath passed over all her troubles,
and hath now no more to suffer.

The other which is held in the left hand, and is
again divided, doth signify the estate of the Church
Militant, understood by the left hand, part whereof

remaineth in this life, and part in purgatory, both which are subject yet to suffer.

This part held in the left hand is next conjoined to that which lieth upon the Paten, and was before held in the right hand, to signify, that those which are in purgatory shall infallibly, after a while, have their part and fruition in glory, and be conjoined with the Church Triumphant.

The part sub-divided from the second, held in the right hand and put into the Chalice, signifieth those which yet remain in this present life, who, by doing penance for their sins, may obtain mercy and remission through the merits of Christ before their departure, and therefore the part which representeth them is not laid with the other, but is put into the sacred Blood contained in the Chalice. And let it here be noted, that this third part of the holy Host is held over the Chalice with two fingers, to wit, with the thumb, which is interpreted force and virtue, and with the second, named by the Latins *Index*, interpreted discretion of understanding, to declare that this divine mystery ought to be considered with force of faith and with discretion of understanding.

Qui tecum vivit et regnat in unitate Spiritus Sancti Deus.

Who liveth and reigneth with Thee in the unity of the Holy Ghost God. In the sub-division of the second

21

part as aforesaid, he saith, *Qui tecum vivit*, incessantly
in all eternity, *et regnat*, with all power and majesty,
in unitate, in essential identity of the Holy Ghost,
Spiritus Sancti Deus, the Third Person of the Holy
Trinity.

Per omnia sæcula sæculorum.

World without end. Having by sundry devout
ceremonies set before us the Death and Passion of our
blessed Saviour, he beginneth now not only by
signs, but also by words, to set before us the joy of
His Resurrection; for which cause he lifteth up his
voice saying: *Per omnia sæcula sæculorum.* And the
people answer: *Amen.* The Priest doth therefore
elevate his voice in this place, not only to have the
consent of the people, but also to represent the gladness which the Apostles and disciples had, when they
understood the joyful news of the Resurrection. For
as they were in great fear and sorrow to see their
Lord and Master in the hands of His enemies, and
afterwards to suffer His Death, so were they filled
with great joy when they saw Him restored again to
life. *Gavisi sunt discipuli, viso Domino,* The disciples
rejoiced, having seen our Lord.

Amen.

The people answer by this Hebrew word that they
do firmly and steadfastly so believe.

Pax + Domini sit + semper vobis + cum.

The peace of our Lord be always with you. To shew
this more evidently, the Priest saluteth the people
with the same words wherewith our Lord saluted
His Apostles at His Resurrection, saying : *Pax vobis.*
Now there are three sorts of peace right necessary
for us, to wit, spiritual, temporal, and eternal: and
according hereunto, the Priest maketh the sign of
the Cross three times in pronouncing the words
aforesaid. The spiritual peace is the repose and
tranquillity of conscience, which is obtained by the
means of a virtuous and innocent life. The temporal
peace is, that it would please Almighty God so to
bless us and our labours, that we may eat our bread
in peace and quietness : that is, to preserve us and all
ours from war, misfortunes, sicknesses, suits, wrong-
ful molestations, detractions, defamations, and all
other sorts of troubles and vexations. The peace
which is eternal is the chief and principal of all the
rest, which setteth us free from all the cares and
labours of this life, and bringeth us from mortality
to immortality, from corruption to incorruption, from
fear to felicity, from vexation to glorification, and
finally to the clear vision and everlasting fruition of
God Himself. He therefore, of His infinite mercy,
give unto us both the spiritual and the temporal
peace in this world, and peace everlasting in the
world to come. 21 *

Et cum spiritu tuo.

And with thy spirit. The assistants, for answer, desire to the Priest the same peace which he hath wished unto them, to the end, that being united by the bond of this celestial benediction, they may mutually receive the grace which they desire.

Of that part of the Host which is put into the Chalice.

This done, the Priest putteth one little part of the Host into the Chalice, to shew unto us hereby, that our Lord's Body is not without His Blood, nor His Blood without His Body, and neither Body and Blood without His holy and lively Soul. Secondly, to shew that but one Sacrament is made of the species, both of the bread and wine. Thirdly, to shew that as He joineth the Body to the Blood, so we, being conjoined to the same Body through the merits of the same Blood, are purged from our sins; and hereupon it is that he immediately asketh the remission of sins, saying: *Agnus Dei qui tollis peccata mundi,* Lamb of God Who takest away the sins of the world.

Hæc commixtio.

This commixtion. This commixtion of the Body and Blood of our Lord is not according to their true and real essences, in which sense they are never separated, but according to their exterior or Sacramental forms, under which the Body and Blood of Christ is truly contained. For many things which appertain to the only species, by the use of speaking, is attributed to that which is contained under the species.

Et consecratio Corporis et Sanguinis Domini nostri . Jesu Christi.

And consecration of the Body and Blood of our Lord Jesus Christ. Not that by this immission, the Body and Blood of our Lord Jesus Christ is either made holy or consecrated, but that the consecration first made, by virtue of the Sacramental forms, now taketh its effect in the mind of the receiver. And therefore it followeth,

Fiat accipientibus nobis.

Be to us receiving it. To wit, unto the Priests who receive it Sacramentally, and to all others who receive it really or spiritually by the means of the Priest, who is, as it were, the hand and mouth of the mystical Body of Christ, as by which, nourishment is drawn and imparted to all the several members of the Body.

In vitam æternam. Amen.

Into life eternal. Amen. To wit, by conservation of the spiritual life here in this world, which is done by daily augmentation of grace, wherewith our soul is sustained, lest through defect thereof, it decline and fall away by evil desires and hurtful deeds, and afterwards come utterly to lose the everlasting life in the world to come.

CHAPTER L.

OF THE "AGNUS DEI" AND COMMUNION.

Agnus Dei.

Lamb of God. The Priest having put the third part of the Host into the Chalice, as before we have declared, next he covereth the same, and knocking his breast, saith twice : Lamb of God, Which takest away the sins of the world, have mercy upon us. And once : Lamb of God, Which takest away the sins of the world, grant us Thy peace. And therefore *Agnus Dei* is said, the Chalice being covered, because Christ appeared to His Apostles, the doors being shut, and gave them power and authority to remit sins.

As touching the word itself, *Agnon* in Greek signifieth as much as gentle or meek in English. And Christ is here called a lamb, because a lamb hurteth nothing, neither man nor beast.

Again, *Agnus* is called *ab agnoscendo*, because amongst a great flock and multitude, by his only cry and bleating he is acknowledged by his mother. And even so, Christ the Lamb of God, hanging upon the Cross, by His voice and cry, was acknowledged by His Mother.

Qui tollis peccata mundi.

Who takest away the sins of the world. Upon which

words Theophylactus saith: *Non dixit qui tollet sed qui tollit: quasi semper hoc faciens*, He saith not, Who will take away, but Who doth take away, as daily and continually doing the same. For He did not only then take away our sins, as saith Ludolphus, when He suffered, but also from that time unto this present, He doth daily take them away, although He be not daily crucified for us.

Miserere nobis.

Have mercy on us. Have mercy on us, to wit, by taking away our sins, because St. John, whose words these are, hath assured us that He is the same Lamb, Who truly taketh away the sins of the world. And Algetus saith that with this faith we adore the Sacrament as a thing divine, and we both speak to It and pray to It as having life and reason, saying: Lamb of God, Who takest away the sins of the world, have mercy on us. Thus he.

Agnus Dei.

Lamb of God. Lamb of God, saith Biel, Which didst suck Thy Mother in the stable, didst follow her flying into Egypt, and didst hear her bleating, seeking Thee in the temple.

Qui tollis peccata mundi.

Which takest away the sins of the world. To wit, original by Baptism, mortal by Penance, and venial by the virtue of this holy Eucharist.

Miserere nobis.

Have mercy on us. Flying unto Thee for pardon for our sins past, for victory against temptation present, and for preservation from sins to come. Further, besides the former exposition, in these two words are plainly testified two notable verities of Christ our Saviour, the one of His Humanity, the other of His Divinity. Of His Humanity, in these words : *Agnus Dei*, Lamb of God, that is to say, sent of God as a most innocent Lamb to be offered up in sacrifice for our salvation. Of His Divinity, when he addeth, *Qui tollis peccata mundi*, Which takest away the sins of the world; because to take away sin is proper to God and to none other.

Agnus Dei, qui tollis peccata mundi.

Lamb of God, Which takest away the sins of the world. This *Agnus Dei* is said or recited the third time, because this Lamb of God not only was acknowledged of others, but also Himself acknowledged others, namely, His heavenly Father, His blessed Mother, and also us. He acknowledged His Father when He said : Father, into Thy hands I commend My spirit. He acknowledged His Mother when He said : Woman, behold thy Son. And He acknowledged us when He said : Father, forgive them, they know not what they do. So that *Agnus Dei* thrice repeated is as much to say as, Lamb of God, Which didst acknowledge Thy Father, have mercy on us. Lamb of God, Which didst acknowledge Thy Mother, have mercy on us. Lamb of God, Which didst acknowledge us, grant us Thy peace.

Dona nobis pacem.

Grant us Thy peace. The devil, that old perturber of peace, did ever labour to break and take away this triple peace, to wit, betwixt God and man, of man in himself, and betwixt man and man. For first he brake the peace betwixt God and man, when he seduced our first parents to transgress the commandment of Almighty God. Secondly, he brake the peace of man within himself, when leaving him confounded with the sight of his own shame, he sought for leaves to cover his nakedness. Thirdly, he brake the peace betwixt man and man, when through malice he incited one brother to murder the other. This triple peace, therefore, the Priest prayeth for, to wit, peace betwixt God and man, peace of man within himself, and peace betwixt neighbours, that is, betwixt man and man.

Why we ask mercy and peace for the living, and repose or rest for the departed.

The reason why we demand mercy and peace for the living, and repose or rest for the departed, is to signify the true and proper place of forgiveness to be in this world, as contrary, the other world is the place of justice and punishment. Again, in this world we are in continual war, as holy Job saith : *Militia est vita hominis super terram,* The life of man upon earth is a warfare. And for this cause we justly ask for ourselves peace, but as touching the departed, they are in peace although they are not in repose, for they are in peace with all their former enemies, the world, the flesh, and the devil, for otherwise they were not in a state of salvation ; but they are not yet in repose, but in pains and torments until they shall have fully satisfied for all their sins and offences, for which they remain indebted to Almighty God, and for this cause we do rather wish them repose than peace. And a petition for rest is therefore added thrice to the *Agnus Dei,* when we offer this holy Sacrifice for the dead, because there is wished to the souls departed a triple or threefold rest. One from the affliction of pain, another for the beatifying of the soul, and the third for the glorifying both of the soul and the body.

Domine Jesu Christe.

Lord Jesus Christ. To wit, most pitiful, merciful, loving, gentle and benign Lord Jesus.

Qui dixisti.

Who saidst. Being by Thy Passion to depart and leave this world.

Apostolis tuis.

To Thy Apostles. Called by Thee to the knowledge of the faith; sent by Thee to the preaching of the faith, and who suffered for Thee for the confession of the same faith.

Pacem relinquo vobis.

I leave you My peace. To the end, that they might firmly remain in peace, lest terrified and affrighted with miseries, they might fall from the faith.

Pacem meam do vobis.

I give you My peace. Giving us Thy peace, and taking to Thyself instead thereof all our evils. O change of incomparable charity !

Ne respicias peccata mea.

Behold not my sins. To wit, personal, wherewith, I, having offended Thy Majesty, am unworthy to obtain at Thy hands the peace of Thy Church, unworthy to offer up Thy sacred Body to Thy Father, and unworthy to take upon me to reconcile sinners unto Thee.

Sed fidem Ecclesiæ tuæ.

But the faith of Thy Church. Wherein Thou hast espoused her unto Thee as Thy spouse, wherein Thou hast sanctified her in the laver of the Word of life, wherein, lest she should fail, Thou hast for ever confirmed her.

Eamque secundum voluntatem tuam.

And according to Thy Will. To wit, Will most amorous, out of which Thou vouchsafedst to take frail flesh, Will most pitiful, out of which Thou vouchsafedst to die, Will most bountiful out of which Thou vouchsafedst to give Thyself in this holy Sacrament, in meat for her love, redemption and comfort.

Pacificare et coadunare digneris.

Vouchsafe to pacify and unite her together. That pacified in good, preserved from evil, co-united in charity, and governed within and without by Thee, she may be accounted worthy of the communion of so excellent a food.

Qui vivis et regnas Deus, per omnia sæcula sæculorum.

Who livest mightily and reignest wisely. God, consubstantially, world without end, sempiternally.

Of the Priest kissing the Pax, saying, Pax tecum.
Peace be with thee.

Innocentius tertius saith, that after our Lord had saluted His Apostles, He said again unto them: *Pax vobis*, Peace be unto you, and then breathed upon them, saying: Receive ye the Holy Ghost; which to signify unto us, the Priest in the Mass kisseth the Pax, which is reverently held unto him by him which serveth at the altar. And because the love of God is diffused in our heart by the Holy Ghost Which is given unto us, therefore, the kiss of peace is diffused in the Church amongst all the faithful.

The second reason.

By this ceremony we are admonished to have perfect love and concord with our neighbours; and that if we have any enemies, we endeavour to kiss them as we kiss the Pax, to wit, to reconcile ourselves unto them in such conjunction of perfect love, that we kiss them and embrace them as our dearest friends.

The third reason.

Again, this kiss of the Pax serveth us for three things. First, to shew that Jesus Christ hath appeased the wrath and anger of His Father towards us. Secondly, that we do all believe in one and the same God, and do swear to maintain one Christian doctrine. Thirdly, that we profess to love Christianly one another, purposing to reconcile us all to those who have any way offended us.

The fourth reason.

This custom certainly first came from our Lord Himself, for it is not probable that Judas would ever have been so hardy as to kiss his Master, were it not that this was the custom of the house of our

Lord, and a common thing amongst the Apostles, to use this sign of love when they returned from some journey, as well towards their Master, as one of them towards another. The which they have practised ever since, and exhorted other Christians to do the like, as we may see in the last chapter of the Epistle to the Romans, the first and second Epistle to the Corinthians, and the first of St. Peter, saying: Salute one another with a holy kiss. Neither is there any of our Doctors, who have expounded the mysteries of the Mass, that affirm not this ceremony to have come from the Apostles, and to be founded upon the places of Scripture before alleged. The which is evidently to be proved out of the liturgies of St. Basil, of St. James, and of St. Chrysostom. Out of the third chapter of the Ecclesiastical Hierarchy of St. Denis, out of the second and eighth book of the Apostolical Constitutions of St. Clement, out of the second Apology of St. Justin, martyr, and many others. Lastly, one principal reason of the institution of this ceremony was the dignity of this most holy Communion, to the which none ought to present himself with hatred and rancour, but first to be thoroughly reconciled to his brother.

Pax tecum.

The Priest, in kissing the Pax, saith: Peace be with thee, which, by this sign of a kiss, I represent unto thee.

Why the Pax is not given in the Mass for the dead.

In a Mass of *Requiem*, or for the repose of departed souls, the Pax is not given, because such a Mass is principally said for the souls in purgatory, amongst whom there is no discord nor dissension. But the same is given when Mass is said for the living, which oftentimes be at debate and discord, to the end to reconcile them to peace and concord.

Domine.

Lord. Here the Priest, having his eyes and intent fixed and bent towards the blessed Sacrament, speaketh unto our Lord Jesus Christ, really and truly present under the visible forms, saying: Lord.

Jesu Christe.

Jesus Christ. Saviour of all mankind, and anointed of the Father with the plenitude and abundance of the Holy Ghost.

Fili Dei vivi.

Son of the living God. Son of the living God, natural, consubstantial, and co-eternal.

Qui ex voluntate Patris.

Who by the Will of the Father. Who by the Will of the Father, most liberal, bountiful, and most merciful, sending Thee in the fulness of time unto us for our Redemption.

Cooperante Spiritu Sancto.

The Holy Ghost co-operating. The Holy Ghost co-operating, Who, as He hath with Thee and the Father one essence, so both in Will and work is inseparable and undivided.

Per mortem.

By the death. To wit, the most bitter, painful, and opprobrious death of the Cross, which Thou patiently enduring, didst thereby make Thyself obedient to the Will of Thy Father.

Tuam.

Thy. Thy, to wit, put in Thine own power, because Thou hadst power to lay down Thy life and power to take it again.

Mundum vivificasti.

Hast given life to the world. Hast given spiritual life to the world, for Thou art the true Bread Which camest down from heaven to give life to the world, all the whole world for one only sin being deprived of life.

Libera me.

Deliver me. Deliver me, offering this Sacrifice, as also all other faithful people for whom it is offered, that we may be in perfect liberty from all sin.

Per sacrosanctum Corpus et Sanguinem tuum.

By this Thy holy Body and Blood. Holy above all

holies, holy because It was made in the womb of the most holy Virgin by that high artificer the Holy Ghost, and holy because It was united to the holy Word.

Ab omnibus iniquitatibus meis.

From all mine iniquities. That is from all my sins, wherewith I have defiled and polluted my soul, made after the image of the holy Trinity.

Et universis malis.

And from all evils. To wit, either of soul or body, present or future, and to be endured either in this life or in the life to come.

Et fac me.

And make me. And make me who of myself am not able to do any good deed, nor yet so much as to think any one good thought, unless I be assisted and enabled by Thee.

Tuis semper inhærere mandatis.

Always to cleave to Thy commandments. Always, that is to say, that at no time I transgress Thy holy commandments. Or always, that is, that I obey and fulfil them all, lest offending in one, I be made, as the Apostle saith, guilty of all.

Et a te nunquam separari permittas.

And never suffer me to be separated from Thee. To wit, neither in this world by sin, neither in the world

22

to come by that horrible sentence to be pronounced against the reprobate: Depart ye cursed into everlasting fire.

Qui.

Who.   Who by Thy divine essence.

Cum eodem Deo Patre.

With the same God the Father.   Of Whom all paternity both in heaven and earth is denominated.

Et Spiritu Sancto.

And with the Holy Ghost.   The knot and bond of charity both of the Father and the Son.

Vivis.

Livest.   For as much as one is the life, divinity, and essence of the Father, the Son, and the Holy Ghost.

Et regnas.

And reignest.   Both in heaven and earth, as absolute Lord over all the inhabitants both in the one and in the other.

Deus.

God.   True, natural, and undivided.

In sæcula sæculorum.   Amen.

World without end.   Amen.   Infallibly, immutably, and eternally without all end.   Amen.

Perceptio Corporis tui.

The receiving of Thy Body.   The receiving of Thy

Body, which verily and truly lieth hid and veiled under this Divine and dreadful Sacrament.

Domine Jesu Christe.

O Lord Jesus Christ. O Lord Jesus Christ, O Lord Who hast created me, O Jesu Who hast redeemed me, O Christ Who shalt judge me.

Quod ego indignus.

Which I unworthy. Unworthy for my manifold and sundry sins committed. Unworthy for my great defect and want of fervour and devotion.

Sumere præsumo.

Presume to take. Not confiding in mine own justice, but in Thy great benignity, mercy, and bounty, which hast promised not to quench smoking flax, nor to break asunder a bruised reed.

Non mihi proveniat in judicium et condemnationem.

Be not to me to judgment and condemnation. Which the Apostle threateneth unto all those who approach unworthily to the same, because they discern not our Lord's Body, to the end that none which are dead do presume to take the meat of life.

Sed pro tua pietate.

But for Thy goodness. By the which through Thy only goodness Thou hast exalted me to the state of Priesthood, hitherto hast patiently borne with my offences, and mercifully expected my repentance.

22 *

Prosit mihi ad tutamentum mentis.

Let it profit me to the safeguard of soul. That so it preserve me for time to come, that I never consent in mind to sin, nor any way offend Thy gracious presence within my soul.

Et corporis.

And body. That neither by the way of my body or gates of my senses, I ever admit death into my soul, nor make the members of my body, consecrated unto Thee, weapons of sin to procure the death of soul and body.

Et ad medelam percipiendam. Qui vivis et regnas, etc.

And to the receiving of cure. Who livest and reignest, etc. To the receiving of medicine, to wit, of Thee Who art the true Physician both of soul and body, and only canst cure the diseases both of the one and the other.

Panem cælestem accipiam.

I will receive the celestial bread. Then having adored, he riseth up to take the healthsome Host, saying, I will receive, etc. To wit, I, a poor pilgrim in this world, will receive the Viaticum and Food of this frail life, in the strength whereof I will walk to the mount of God. I sick will receive the celestial Bread which fortifieth and corroborateth the heart of

man. I, hungry and starved, will receive the Bread,
Which whoso eateth, shall never hunger more. I, dis-
quieted and anxious, will receive the Bread Which
establisheth the heart, and calmeth the storms of a
troubled conscience. I, feeble and lame, will receive
the Bread, being invited of that great King unto the
supper, whereunto all the feeble and lame were
brought in. I, all sinful and unclean, will receive the
Bread, Which only can make clean that which was
conceived of unclean seed, and of stones can raise
up sons to Abraham. The celestial Bread, not made
of the grain of the earth, but of the Virgin's blood.
The celestial Bread, Which refresheth the Angels with
beatitude. The celestial Bread, Which descendeth
from above to nourish the hearts of His poor ones
aspiring and sighing after the celestial joys. The
celestial Bread Which changeth the receiver, though
a sinner, into a celestial creature and a saint.

Et nomen Domini invocabo.

And will call upon the Name of our Lord. That is,
will invoke or call the Name of the Lord upon myself,
and by the means of this celestial Bread will sup with
Christ, that He may shew mercy unto me now in-
habiting in heaven, as He did unto them that supped
with Him on earth. Or I will call upon the Name
of our Lord, that He may call me a sinner unto Him,

place me amongst the number of His elect, and for ever reconcile me unto His Father.

What the Priest doth before receiving of the Host.

This done, the Priest a little inclining his body, and uniting all his cogitations as much as possible, doth devoutly recollect himself, and directeth not only the corporal eyes of his body to the outward species and forms of the Sacrament, but much more the inward eyes of his faith to our Lord Jesus Christ, truly contained under those visible forms, Whom with all reverence, fear, devotion, charity, affection of mind and soul, he is to receive.

Domine.

Lord. The Priest, therefore, being ready to receive and harbour within his soul this sacred Host, first saith : *Domine*, Lord. Which word of itself doth clearly shew what manner of house it ought to be, and how it ought to be decked and adorned, wherein so sacred a Guest ought to be lodged, for a Lord ought to have a lordly lodging, and a noble personage a noble habitation. For, *talis hospes, tale hospitium*, such a Lord, such a lodging.

Non sum dignus.

I am not worthy. Next considering himself to be a miserable creature, and an earthly vessel of clay, he saith : I am not worthy. To wit, of mine own preparation, knowing that Thou hast said, that when we have done all that which is commanded us, we should still confess ourselves unprofitable servants. Yea which is more, although he should burn with seraphical charity, yet may he truly say he is not worthy.

Ut intres sub tectum meum.

That Thou shouldst enter under my roof. Darkened with the obscurity of sins, ruinous for defect of virtues, stirred to unlawful desires, subject to passions, replete with illusions, prone to evil, and proclive to vice, finally a wretched child of Adam, utterly unworthy of the Bread of Angels.

Sed tantum dic verbo, et sanabitur anima mea.

But say the word only, and my soul shall be healed. As Thou saidst the word to the sick of the palsy, willing him to take up his bed and walk, and he incontinently arose and walked. As Thou saidst the word to the woman sick of the issue of blood, who only touched the hem of Thy garment, and she was immediately healed. As Thou saidst the word to the faithful Centurion, and his servant was immediately cured.

Corpus Domini nostri Jesu Christi.

The Body of our Lord Jesus Christ. The Body of our Lord Jesus Christ, offered upon the altar of the Cross for the sins of all the world in expiation. The

Body of our Lord Jesus Christ, given unto us under this venerable Sacrament for our vivification.   The Body of our Lord Jesus Christ, to be received of me for the obtaining of future glorification.

Custodiat animam meam.

Keep my soul.   Preserve and keep my soul, to wit, from relapse into sin, lest I become contumelious against my Saviour Christ.   Keep my soul, to wit, by corroborating, fostering, and fortifying me daily more and more in the spiritual life.   Keep my soul, to wit, at the dreadful hour of my departure forth, from the claws and jaws of the fierce, devouring, and infernal lions.

In vitam æternam.   Amen.

To life eternal. Amen. That as the bread ministered by the Angel to the prophet Elias so fortified him, that in the force thereof he walked up to the mountain of God, Horeb.   And as the bread, which descended from heaven, brought the people of Israel through the desert into the land of promise, even so, O gracious Lord, I humbly beseech Thee, that this heavenly Bread may be my true viaticum, to lead me through the desert of this world, to that blessed and supernal country promised to all those that faithfully serve Thee.   Amen.

Of the Priest's receiving of the Chalice.

As before the receiving of the Body of our Lord,

the Priest, to acknowledge his own insufficiency, prepared himself thereunto by prayer and humility, even so, proceeding to the receiving of the Blood of our Lord, he doth again, by prayer and humiliation of himself, acknowledge his own indignity, saying:

Quid retribuam Domino.

What shall I render to our Lord. What shall I, dust and ashes, handiwork and workmanship of my Creator, frail, unworthy, and vile man, the lowest and least of all His servants, render unto our Lord, Who if I have but one good thought wherewith to render thanks unto Him, the selfsame thought is sent of Him, the selfsame thought proceedeth from Him.

Pro omnibus.

For all. For all things, whose number and immensity do far exceed all human sense and understanding. For, as Hugo saith, if thou shouldst look into the whole world, thou shalt find no kind of thing which doth not live to do Thee service.

Quæ retribuit mihi?

Which He hath given me? Not only to all in general, but to me in particular; to me, I say, His creature, His gift of mighty and marvellous creation, His gift of careful and Fatherly conservation, His gift of gentle and patient expectation, His gift of celestial and Divine inspiration, His gift of

all gifts, His precious Body and Blood, for my refection. Never am I able, O my Lord, to come out
of this debt, albeit I had as many lives to spend for
Thy sake, as I have several drops of blood within
my body.

Calicem salutaris accipiam.

I will take the Chalice of salvation. Accipiam, I will
take, being dry and thirsty for lack of the humour
of heavenly grace; I will take, being parched and
withered for want of the dew of Divine benediction;
I will take, being dead and unfruitful, for lack of
the fruits of good life; I will take, which am a
stranger and pilgrim in this world, and have as yet
a long and laboursome journey to my celestial
habitation.

Calicem, the Chalice, that is, the Blood of Jesus
Christ in the Chalice, the Blood which, in His last
supper, He gave to His disciples. The Blood which,
Longinus piercing His side, ran forth abundantly
out of His glorious breast. The Blood which, in
His glorious resurrection, to conserve the integrity
of His nature, He most miraculously reassumed.
The Blood which He commanded us to take in
memory of His Passion, saying: Drink ye all of
this; so often as you do this, do it in remembrance
of Me.

Salutaris, of salvation. So called, because it containeth in it Christ, the Author of our salvation. Or of salvation, as greatly wishing and desiring our salvation, which none may say so truly as our Saviour Christ, because never any so greatly desired and seriously sought the same as He. Or of salvation, by reason of the effects, because it effected our salvation when, shed on the Cross, it reconciled us to God.

Et nomen Domini invocabo.

And will call on the Name of our Lord. To the end that sacred Blood may come upon me to my benediction, which the wicked and perfidious Jews asked to come upon them, to their destruction and damnation, saying: *Sanguis ejus super nos, et super filios nostros,* His blood be upon us and upon our children.

Laudans invocabo Dominum.

Praising, I will invocate the Lord. Praising Him for the exhibition of so great a benefit, Who did not only shed the same His precious Blood for us, but also gave the same in drink unto us. And who but most ungrateful, will not laud our Lord for such a benefit?

Et ab inimicis meis salvus ero.

And I shall be safe from mine enemies. For this most precious Blood of Jesus Christ hath many singular effects and operations. It giveth grace, it giveth glory, it taketh away our sin, it fortifieth our frailty, it calleth Angels to us, and driveth the devils from us; and, as lions breathing forth fire, so depart we from this table, being made terrible unto them.

Sanguis Domini nostri Jesu Christi.

The Blood of our Lord Jesus Christ. The Blood of our Lord Jesus Christ, which is the foundation and laver of our emundation and sanctification. The Blood of our Lord Jesus Christ, which is the price of our Redemption and reparation. The Blood of our Lord Jesus Christ, which is to the worthy receiver the Chalice of all benediction.

Custodiat animam meam.

Keep my soul. Keep my soul in innocency of life and purity of heart, lest with Judas I cry, *Peccavi tradens sanguinem justum*, I have sinned, betraying the innocent Blood. Keep my soul from that smiting and plague of our Lord, which smote all the first-born of Egypt, whose posts of their houses were not sprinkled with the blood of the lamb. Keep my soul in spiritual force and vigour, that in virtue of this Blood, I may undertake to fight against devils and infernal furies, like as the elephant is encouraged to fight at the sight of blood.

In vitam æternam. Amen.

To life everlasting. Amen. According to the promise

of our Saviour Himself, saying : He that eateth My
Flesh and drinketh My Blood, hath life everlasting,
and I will raise him up at the last day, to wit, from
a temporal death to a perdurable, everlasting, and
eternal life.

Of the Priest's giving the holy Sacrament to the assist-
ants, when any be to communicate.

This done, the Priest, as Innocentius saith, communicateth to the people, insinuating that Christ,
after His Resurrection, did eat with His disciples, as
St. Luke testifieth, saying : Jesus took bread and
brake, and reached unto them.

And here let the Christian receiver understand,
that so much difference as there is betwixt heaven
and earth, betwixt the Creator and the creature, so
much difference is there betwixt this sacred viand
and all others which ever at any time God gave to
man. For in this divine Sacrament there is to
drink, there is to eat, there is wine, and there is
milk, there is bread and there is water. Drink for
hose that are dry, meat for those that are hungry,
wine for great ones, and milk for little ones, bread
to fortify and water to refresh. Finally, in this
divine Sacrament our Lord doth nourish us with
Himself, with His own true and proper substance, as
well divine as human. What could He do more for
us ? What banquet, what feast, could He provide
more exquisite or more noble for us ?

Quod ore sumpsimus Domine.

That which we have taken with our mouth, O Lord.
Where first let it be noted, that the Priest speaketh
in the plural number, saying : Which we have taken,
etc., signifying hereby, that he did not consecrate
this Sacrament only for himself, but for the whole
mystical Body of Christ, whereof he is a part, and,
as it were, the mouth of this Body.

Pura mente capiamus.

Let us receive with a pure mind. Free from all spot
and pollution of sin, from all spiritual drowsiness and
tepidity, with full faith, love, and fervent devotion,
to the strengthening of the soul, and to the spiritual
sustentation of all good actions. .

Et de munere temporali.

And of a gift temporal. To wit, as touching the
visible forms, which, of Thy gentle gift and bountiful
liberality, we have received.

Fiat nobis remedium sempiternum.

Let there be made unto us a remedy eternal. To wit,
against all diseases both of soul and body, that in
our last end, fortified with this viaticum, we may
be brought to the true beatifying and sempiternal
security, both of the one and the other.

Corpus tuum, Domine, quod sumpsi.

Thy Body, O Lord, which I have received. Under the

species of bread, Thy true Body, Thy natural Body, the same which was born of the Virgin Mary, laid in the manger, adored of the Sages, borne into Egypt, apprehended, whipped, crowned, and crucified of the Jews.

Et sanguis quem potavi.

And Blood which I have drunk. Which I have drunk under the species of wine, Thy very true and proper Blood, the same Blood which Thou didst shed being circumcised, the same which Thou didst sweat in the garden, the same which Thou didst shed being scourged, the same which ran out of Thy hands and feet being nailed, the same which gushed out of Thy most holy side being pierced.

Adhæreat visceribus meis.

Cleave unto my bowels. The bowels of our soul are her powers, such are our understanding, our will, our memory. And here we pray that to these powers of our soul, this precious food may so adhere, that it do not presently pass through our minds, as some liquid corporal meats pass through the stomach, leaving behind them no succour nor nourishment, but so to cleave to our bowels, that it make its abode and stay in our souls.

Et præsta, ut in me non remaneat scelerum macula.

And grant that there remain not in me spots of wickedness. By this spot of wickedness may be understood

the guilt of venial sin, or temporal pain remaining
in the soul, from the which he prayeth to be released,
for that existing and remaining in the soul, it cannot
be admitted to the joys of the blessed, although it be
adorned with grace and charity.

Quem pura et sancta.

Whom pure and holy. Pure, by reason that it
purifieth the mind from all impure cogitations. And
holy, because it is sanctification in itself, and also
sanctifieth the receiver, replenishing him with all
abundance of grace and sanctification.

Refecerunt Sacramenta. Qui vivis, etc.

Sacraments have refreshed. For this holy Sacrament refresheth the bowels of the soul of the worthy
receiver; it refresheth the understanding by the
illumination of knowledge ; it refresheth the will by
inflammation of love ; and it refresheth the memory
by exciting it to the rememoration of the Passion,
and by leaving a certain spiritual joy and sweetness
in the whole man.

Of the washing of the ends of the Priest's fingers after receiving.

After receiving of the holy Eucharist, the Priest
washeth the ends or tips of his fingers ; for it were
most unworthy, that the hands which have handled

that incorruptible Body, should touch a corruptible body, before they were first diligently washed and cleansed.

The second reason.

The triple washing of the Priest's hands, the first before he begin Mass, the second before the Offertory, and the third now after Communion, or as Innocentius saith, in the beginning, in the midst, and in the ending, doth insinuate the cleansing of thoughts, of words, and of works: or the purging of original, mortal, and venial sin. And this last ablution may properly be referred to the ablution of Baptism, the form whereof Christ instituted after His Resurrection, saying: Going, therefore, teach ye all nations, baptising them in the Name of the Father, and of the Son, and of the Holy Ghost. He that believeth and is baptised, shall be saved.*

Of the return of the Priest to the right hand of the altar.

Let us now come to the last point, which is of the return of the Priest to the right end of the altar, after the Communion. This is not done for superstition, as if the prayer were better at one end than at the other, as scoffing heretics do calumniate, but to signify some special mystery comprehended in the Holy Scripture, to wit, the final conversion of the

* St. Mark ch. 16, v. 16.

23

Jews. This, Hugo de Sancto Victore avoucheth most clearly, saying: *His completis*, etc., these things accomplished, the Priest returneth to the right end of the altar, signifying, that in the end of the world, Christ shall return to the Jews, whom now He hath rejected until the fulness of the Gentiles be entered in, for then the remainder of Israel, according to the Scriptures, shall be saved. This he.*

Of the anthem or Post-Communion.

It is more than manifest, that the custom and use of reciting a hymn or canticle in the end of the Mass is come unto us from Christ Himself and His Apostles: For after our Lord had communicated His Body and Blood to His Apostles, the Scripture presently addeth, *Et hymno dicto, exierunt in montem Oliveti*, And a hymn being said, they went forth unto Mount Olivet. This is most evidently to be seen in the Liturgy of St. James, wherein you shall find these four psalms following, to have been sung in this part of the Mass. *Dominus regit me. Benedicam Domino in omni tempore. Exaltabo te Deus meus rex. Laudate Dominum omnes gentes.*†

The second reason.

These psalms, canticles, and hymns aforesaid, were sung in the primitive Church during the time of the holy Communion, in which time the Chris-

* Lib. de special. Miss. Observ. cap. 4.
† Ps. 22, 33, 144, 116.

tians did communicate very often, yea every day, as divers histories do testify. For which cause the number of communicants being very great, the Church retained these long anthems, very agreeable to the fervent devotion of that time. But since the Christians ceasing to communicate every day, and the number of communicants much decreasing, so long canticles were not thought expedient, and therefore in place thereof, are said these short anthems after the Communion. Which is the reason and cause, that most, now at this day, do call them by the name of the Post-Communion.

The third reason.

Mystically, acccording to Innocentius, the anthem which is recited after the Communion doth signify the joy of the Apostles for Christ's Resurrection. According as it is written, saying : The disciples were glad when they saw the Lord. And therefore, in High Mass, the same is sung reciprocally, to insinuate that the disciples did mutually recite one to another the joy of the Resurrection. As St. Luke testifieth, that the two disciples, to whom our Lord appeared in the way to Emmaus, went back to Jerusalem, and they found the eleven gathered together, and those that were with them, saying : That the Lord is risen indeed, and hath appeared to Simon.*

* St. Luke ch. 24, v. 34.

23 *

Dominus vobiscum.

Our Lord be with you. According to some, these several salutations of the Priest to the people do represent unto us the several apparitions of our Saviour to His disciples. Or the promise of our Lord made unto them, touching the sending of the Holy Ghost.

Et cum spiritu tuo.

And with thy spirit. The property of Christian charity is, that every one should be careful, not only for himself, but also for his neighbour. For this cause the assistants answer the Priest, in recognisance of that which he hath done for them by his prayers, that God may be with his spirit to guide him by the inspiration of His Divine grace, wheresoever need is, for the execution of this his sacred function.

CHAPTER LI.

OF THE LAST COLLECTS AND END OF MASS.

The first reason.

THESE prayers are made after Communion in the end of Mass, to give us to understand that subsequent prayer is as necessary for us as precedent, because we are admonished to pray always without intermission.*

* St. Luke ch. 18.

The second reason.

Of these Collects or thanksgivings, we are admonished in sundry places of the Holy Scriptures to do the same, as in the third chapter of St. Paul's Epistle to the Colossians, saying : All whatsoever you do in word or in work, all things in the Name of our Lord Jesus Christ, giving thanks to God and the Father through Him. Besides, it is most conform to reason itself, that receiving so great a benefit from God, we should render due and convenient thanks unto Him for the same. And what greater benefit could we possibly receive at His hands, than the most precious Body and Blood of our Saviour Jesus, for the health and nourishment of our souls and bodies ?

The third reason.

Mystically, the Collects signify how the Apostles and disciples, after the Ascension of our Lord, persevered in prayer. As also the prayers of Jesus Christ our Head, Who maketh daily intercession unto His Father for us.

Dominus vobiscum.

Our Lord be with you. The Collects being ended, the Priest saluteth the people the second time, saying : Our Lord be with you. As if he should say : The time to let you depart is now at hand, but

albeit you depart from the temple of our Lord, yet
depart not away from our Lord, but so lead your
lives, that His holy grace never depart away from
your souls. And the people make answer saying :

Et cum spiritu tuo.

And with thy spirit. And with thy spirit, praying that in all ways wherein the Priest wisheth our
Lord to be with them, in the same sort our Lord
may also ever be and abide with him.

Of *Ite, missa est.*

Depart, Mass is ended. This was ordained to be
said to let the people know that the Mass was
ended, and so to give them leave to go away, because they are not to depart till Mass be ended, and
until they have received the Priest's benediction.
The word *missa* in this place is diversely expounded
by our learned Doctors. Some consider it adjec-
tively, and understand for the substantive, *Hostia aut
oblatio*, and so they interpret it thus : *Ite missa
est, scilicet, Hostia aut oblatio.* Go, or depart, the
Host or oblation is sent for you, that is to say,
is presented or offered up to God in your behalfs.
Others consider it substantively, sometimes referring
it to the Mystery which hath been celebrated, and
sometimes to the people which have assisted at the
same. When it is referred to the Mystery, the
sense is : *Ite, missa est dicta aut peracta*, Depart ye,

Mass is said or ended, which exposition in the opinion of many is the most proper, and most familiar. If one would refer it to the people, *missa* importeth as much as *missio*, and *missio* as much as *demissio*, that is to say, to let depart, to dismiss, or send away the people, and so the sense, according to this interpretation is: Go your ways, license or permission is given you to depart. For as by this word, *missa*, Mass, they understand commonly and properly the great and divine Mystery of all Christians, so when it is said unto them: *Ite, missa est*, they understand presently that Mass is ended, and that leave is granted them to withdraw themselves.

Innocentius the third saith, that this Sacrifice, that is, the holy Host, is called *Missa, quasi transmissa*, as sent betwixt. First from the Father to us, that it may be with us. And then to the Father from us, that it may intercede with the Father for us. By the Father to us, by the Incarnation of the Son, from us to the Father, by His Passion. In the Sacrament, by the Father to us by sanctification, and by us again to the Father by oblation.

Of the last benediction.

This done, the Priest kisseth the altar, and then with his hands elevated, giveth the last benediction unto the people, signifying that last benediction, which Christ, ascending, gave unto His disciples.

For as St. Luke saith : He brought them forth abroad into Bethany, and lifting up His hands He blessed them. And it came to pass, whilst He blessed them, He departed from them, and was carried into heaven. And for this cause, in a High or solemn Mass, after the last salutation which the priest maketh unto the people, the deacon with a high voice pronounceth, *Ite, missa est*, depart, it is sent or ascended for you. And the people presently with gratulation do answer, saying : *Deo gratias*, giving thanks to God, and imitating herein the Apostles of our Lord, who, as the same St. Luke saith, went back into Jerusalem with great joy, and they were always in the temple praising and blessing God.

It may likewise signify the mission of the Holy Ghost, Which our Lord sent down from heaven upon His Apostles, accordingly as He had promised them, saying : You shall receive the virtue of the Holy Ghost coming upon you.

St. Augustine maketh mention of this benediction, and holdeth that the Priest by the same offereth the people unto God, and leaveth them to Him in protection. In the Ecclesiastical History of Ruffinus is recited, that it was made with the hand, and he further saith, that himself was blessed in this manner by the hermits of Egypt.

Finally, *Ite, Missa est* is said upon solemn and

festival days, and that in sign of spiritual joy and jubilation.

Benedicamus Domino upon the week-days and days of fast, in which the songs of joy do cease in the Church, and is to admonish us that we ought to begin all our actions in Him, and to finish them through Him.

The Office ordained for those which are dead in the faith of Jesus Christ, endeth by this prayer, *Requiescant in pace*, May they rest in peace, to obtain unto them rest and repose.

To the two first the assistants answer, *Deo gratias*, in thanksgiving for the accomplishment of the holy mysteries of the Mass, to the end that they may not be blamed of ingratitude, as were the nine lepers mentioned in St. Luke, who returned not thanks, nor magnified Jesus Christ for the recovery of their health and healing.

To the prayer made by the Priest for the remedy of the souls departed, answer is made, *Amen*, which is as much as to say, be it so as hath been requested, and our Lord vouchsafe to give them everlasting repose, as He hath promised them, in Abraham's bosom.

Of the Gospel of St. John.

This Gospel, all Christian people have evermore held in wonderful reverence; for it hath been

accustomed to be read unto them, not only in the
end of Mass, but also after the sick have received
the Blessed Sacrament and the Extreme Unction,
when children are baptised, and when women are
churched; the which Gospel the very Paynims
themselves have much admired. For, as St. Augustine testifieth, a certain philosopher and Platonist
having read the same, was in so great admiration
thereof, that he said it was worthy to be written in
letters of gold, and to be placed by Christians in
all their churches in the most eminent places.
Finally, the praises of this Gospel can never be
sufficiently expressed, and especially where it is
said: *Et Verbum caro factum est et habitavit in nobis*,
And the Word was made Flesh and dwelt among us.
For reverence whereof, as we daily see, the Priest
falleth down on his knees at the pronunciation of
the said words.

I will briefly recite certain examples concerning
the efficacy of the same. In Aquitania there were
two possessed of the devil, both beggars; and the
one perceiving that more was given to his fellow
than to him, he said in secret to the Priest: If thou
wilt do what I shall tell thee, to wit, if thou wilt
read in my fellow's ear the Gospel, *In principio erat
Verbum*, but yet, so as I hear not the same, know
for certain the devil shall be driven out of him.

But the Priest understanding the craft of the devil, pronounced the said Gospel out aloud. And when he said, *Et Verbum caro factum est*, etc., presently the evil spirits flew from them, and both were dispossessed and delivered of the devil. It is also declared that the devil himself said unto a certain holy man, that there was a certain word of the Gospel very dreadful to the devils. Who asking what the word was, the devil would not tell. When the holy man had recited divers authorities, the devil answered to every one that it was not that. At the last, being asked if it were that, *Verbum caro factum est*, he answered not, but with fearful crying, forthwith vanished.

For conclusion, gentle reader, I will close up this discourse with the words of a godly writer, and not with mine own, saying: Let no man suppose, having heard this exposition, that this Sacrifice is sufficiently explicated, lest perhaps, in extolling the work of man, he do extenuate so divine a Sacrament. For in this Divine Office there are so many mysteries involved, that no man, unless divinely inspired, is able or sufficient to explicate the same. I, therefore, herein have done diligently what I could, not sufficiently what I would. The only recompense, which for this labour I look for from men, is that they would vouchsafe before the merciful

Judge, Who best knows with what intention of heart I wrote this treatise, to shed forth their devout prayers unto Him for my sins; beseeching Him, that if it profit not many, yet it may profit some, or at the least me alone, though never so little. Make this petition for me, and I shall hold myself abundantly paid for my pains.

FINIS.

R. WASHBOURNE, PRINTER, 18 PATERNOSTER ROW.

NEW BOOKS.

ALBERT THE GREAT: HIS LIFE AND SCHOLASTIC LABOURS. From original Documents. By Dr. Joachim Sighart, Professor of Philosophy in the Royal Lyceum of Freising. Translated by Rev. Father T. A. Dixon, O.P. With a Photographic Portrait. 8vo.

STORIES OF THE SAINTS. By M. F. S. 2 vols. 7s.

LEGENDS OF THE SAINTS. By M. F. S. 16mo, 3s. 6d.

STORIES OF MARTYR PRIESTS. By M. F. S. 3s. 6d.

LIFE OF GREGORY LOPEZ, THE HERMIT. By Canon Doyle, O.S.B. With a Photograph. 12mo, 3s. 6d.

CONFIDENCE IN THE MERCY OF GOD. By Mgr. Languet. Translated by Abbot Burder. 12mo, 3s.

LIVES OF THE FIRST RELIGIOUS OF THE VISITATION OF HOLY MARY. By Mother Frances Magdalen de Chaugy. With two Photographs. 2 vols. 12mo, 12s.

EASY WAY TO GOD. By Cardinal Bona. Translated by Father Collins, author of "Cistercian Legends." 3s.

LIVES OF THE SAINTS FOR EVERY DAY IN THE YEAR. Beautifully printed on thick toned paper, within borders from ancient sources. 4to, scarlet cloth gilt, gilt edges, 16s.

THE FIRST APOSTLES OF EUROPE. By Mrs. Hope, author of "Early Martyrs," &c. 2 vols. 12mo, 10s. [Originally puplished under the title of "Conversion of the Teutonic Race."]

CATECHISM OF CHRISTIAN DOCTRINE, illustrated with passages from the Holy Scriptures. By the Rev. J. B. Bagshawe. 12mo, 2s. 6d.

THRESHOLD OF THE CATHOLIC CHURCH. A Course of Plain Instructions for those entering her Communion. By the Rev. J. B. Bagshawe. 12mo, 4s.

ORATORIAN LIVES OF THE SAINTS. With Portrait, 12mo, 5s. a vol.

 I. S. BERNARDINE OF SIENA, MINOR OBSERVATINE.
 II. S. PHILIP BENIZI, FIFTH GENERAL OF THE SERVITES.
 III. S. VERONICA GIULIANI, AND B. BATTISTA VARANI.
 IV. S. JOHN OF GOD. By Canon Cianfogni.

LONDON: R. WASHBOURNE, 18 PATERNOSTER ROW.

GARDEN OF THE SOUL.

(WASHBOURNE'S EDITION.)

EDITED BY THE REV. R. G. DAVIS.

With Imprimatur of the Archbishop of Westminster.

THIRTEENTH THOUSAND.

This Edition retains all the Devotions that have made the GARDEN OF THE SOUL, now for many generations, the well-known Prayer-book for English Catholics. During many years various Devotions have been introduced, and, in the form of appendices, have been added to other editions. These have now been incorporated into the body of the work, and, together with the Devotions to the Sacred Heart, to Saint Joseph, to the Guardian Angels, the Itinerarium, and other important additions, render this addition pre-eminently the Manual of Prayer, for both public and private use. The version of the Psalms has been carefully revised, and strictly conformed to the Douay translation of the Bible, published with the approbation of the LATE CARDINAL WISEMAN. The Forms of administering the Sacraments have been carefully translated, *as also the rubrical directions*, from the Ordo Administrandi Sacramenta. To enable all present, either at baptisms or other public administrations of the Sacraments, to pay due attention to the sacred rites, the Forms are inserted without any curtailment, both in Latin and English. The Devotions at Mass have been carefully revised, and enriched by copious adaptations from the prayers of the Missal. The preparation for the Sacraments of Penance and the Holy Eucharist have been the objects of especial care, to adapt them to the wants those whose religious instruction may be deficient. Great attention has been paid to the quality of the paper and to the size of type used in the printing, to obviate that weariness so distressing to the eyes, caused by the use of books printed in small close type and on inferior paper.

Embossed, 1s. ; with rims and clasp, 1s. 6d. ; with Epistles and Gospels, 1s. 6d. ; with rims and clasp, 2s.

French morocco, 2s. ; with rims and clasp, 2s. 6d. ; with E. and G., 2s. 6d. ; with rims and clasp, 3s.

French morocco extra gilt, 2s. 6d. ; with rims and clasp, 3s. ; with E. and G., 3s. ; with rims and clasp, 3s. 6d.

Calf or morocco, 4s. ; with rims and clasp, 5s. 6d. ; with E. and G., 4s. 6d. ; with rims and clasp, 6s.

Calf or morocco extra gilt, 5s. ; with rims and clasp, 6s. 6d. ; with E. and G., 5s. 6d. ; with rims and clasp, 7s.

Morocco antique, 10s. ; with two patent clasps, 12s. ; with corners and clasps, 18s. ; with E. and G., 10s. 6d., 12s. 6d., and 18s. 6d.

Velvet, with rims and clasp, 7s. 6d., 10s. 6d., and 13s. ; with E. and G., 8s., 11s., and 13s. 6d.

Ivory, 14s., 16s., 20s., and 22s. 6d. ; with E. and G., 14s. 6d., 16s. 6d., 20s. 6d., and 23s.

Russia antique, with clasp, 10s., 12s. 6d. ; with corners and clasps, 20s. ; with E. and G., 10s. 6d., 13s., 20s. 6d.

The Epistles and Gospels, in cloth, 6d. ; roan, 1s. 6d.

" This is one of the best editions we have seen of one of the best of all our prayer-books. It is well printed in clear, large type, on good paper."—*Catholic Opinion.*

"A very complete arrangement of this which is emphatically the prayer-book of every Catholic household. It is as cheap as it is good, and we heartily recommend it."—*Universe.*

" Two striking features are the admirable order displayed throughout the book, and the insertion of the Indulgences in small type above Indulgenced Prayers. In the Devotions for Mass, the editor has, with great discrimination, drawn largely on the Church's Prayers, as given us in the Missal."—*Weekly Register.*

LONDON : R. WASHBOURNE, 18 PATERNOSTER ROW.

LITTLE GARDEN OF THE SOUL.

Edited by the Rev. R. G. DAVIS.

With Imprimatur of the Archbishop of Westminster.

This book, as its name imports, contains a selection from the "Garden of the Soul," of the Prayers and Devotions of most general use. Whilst it will serve as a *Pocket Prayer-Book* for all, it is, by its low price, *par excellence* the prayer-book for children, and for the very poor. In it are to be found the old familiar Devotions of the "Garden of the Soul," as well as many important additions, such as the Devotions to the Sacred Heart, to Saint Joseph, to the Guardian Angels, and others. The omissions are mainly the Forms of Administering the Sacraments, and Devotions that are not of very general use. It is printed in a clear type, on a good paper, both especially selected, for the purpose of obviating the disagreeableness of small type and inferior paper.

32mo, price, cloth, 6d.; with rims and clasp, 1s.

Embossed, red edges, 9d.; with rims and clasp, 1s. 3d.

Strong roan, 1s.; with rims and clasp, 1s. 6d.

French morocco, 1s. 6d.; with rims and clasp, 2s.

French morocco, extra gilt, 2s.; with rims and clasp, 2s. 6d.

Calf or morocco, 3s.; with rims and clasp, 4s.

Calf or morocco, extra gilt, 4s.; with rims and clasp, 5s.

Morocco, with patent clasp, 10s. 6d.

Velvet, rims and clasp, 5s.; superior ditto, 8s. 6d. and 10s. 6d.

Russia, 5s.; with clasp, &c., 8s.

Ivory, with rims and clasp, 10s. 6d., 13s., 15s., 17s. 6d.

Imitation ivory, with rims and clasp, 3s.

Antique bindings, morocco, 16s.; russia, 17s. 6d.

With oxydised silver or gilt mountings, in morocco case, 25s.

London : R. WASHBOURNE, 18 Paternoster Row

PATERNOSTER ROW No. 18, LONDON.

R. WASHBOURNE'S CATALOGUE.

FEBRUARY, 1876.

The Sufferings of our Lord Jesus Christ. Preached in London by Father Claude de la Colombière, S. J., in the Chapel Royal, St. James's, in the year 1677. 18mo. 1s. ; red edges, 1s. 6d.

Lenten Thoughts. Drawn from the Gospel for each day in Lent. By the Bishop of Northampton 1s. 6d.; stronger bound, 2s. ; red edges, 2s. 6d.

Devotions for Public and Private Use at the Way of the Cross. By Sister M. F. Clare (the Nun of Kenmare). Illustrated with the Pictures of the Stations. 16mo. 1s. ; red edges, 1s. 6d.

The Continental Fish Cook; or, a Few Hints on Maigre Dinners. By M. J. N. de Frederic. 18mo. 1s.

A Treatise on Confidence in the Mercy of God. By Mgr. Languet. Translated by Abbot Burder.

Sanctuary Meditations for Priests and Frequent Communicants. Translated from the Spanish.

Letters to my God-Child—Letter IV. On the Veneration of the Blessed Virgin. By Mrs. Stuart Laidlaw. 16mo. 4d.

Bessy; or the Fatal Consequence of Telling Lies. By the writer of " The Rat Pond, or the Effects of Disobedience." 1s. ; cloth gilt, 1s. 6d.

The Serving Boy's Manual and Book of Public Devotions, containing all those prayers and devotions for Sundays and Holidays, usually divided in their recitation between the Priest and the

⁎ *Though this Catalogue does not contain many of the books of other Publishers, R. W. can supply all of them, no matter by whom they are published.*

Congregation. Compiled from approved sources, and adapted to Churches, served either by the Secular or the Regular Clergy.

IN THE PRESS.

Stories for my Children.—The Angels and the Sacraments. Square 16mo. 1s. ; extra cloth, 2s. 6d.

Semi-Tropical Trifles. By Herbert Compton. Fcp. 8vo. Fancy boards, 1s.

Lives of the First Religious of the Visitation of Holy Mary. By Mother Frances Magdalen de Chaugy. With two Photographs. 2 vols., cr. 8vo. 12s.

Easy Way to God. By Cardinal Bona. Translated by Father Collins, author of "Cistercian Legends," "Spiritual Conferences." Fcap. 8vo. 3s.

Legends of the Saints. By M. F. S., author of "Stories of the Saints." Square 16mo.

Spiritual Conferences on the Mysteries of Faith and the Interior Life. By Father Collins, author of "Cistercian Legends," &c. Cr. 8vo. 4s.

Lives of the Saints for every Day in the Year. Translated from M. Didot's edition. Beautifully printed on thick toned paper, with borders from ancient sources, scarlet cloth gilt, gilt edges, 4to. 16s.

The Mass: and a devout method of assisting at it. From the French of M. Tronson. 4d.

Canon Schmid's Tales, selected from his works. New translation, with Original Illustrations, 3s. 6d. Separately: Canary Bird, 6d.; Dove, 6d.; Inundation, 6d. Rose Tree, 6d.; Water Jug, 6d.; Wooden Cross, 6d.

The Elements of Gregorian or Plain Chant and Modern Music. By the Professor of Music and Organist in All Hallows' College, Dublin. 2s. 6d.

The English Religion. Letters addressed to an Irish Gentleman. By A. M. 1s.

Confraternity of the Holy Family. By Henry Edward, Cardinal-Archbishop of Westminster. 8vo. 3d.

Elevations to the Heart of Jesus. By Rev. Father Doyotte, S. J. Fcap. 8vo. 3s.

S. Vincent Ferrer, of the Order of Friar Preachers: his Life, Spiritual Teaching, and practical Devotion. By the Rev. Fr. Andrew Pradel, of the same Order. Translated from the French by the Rev. Fr. T. A. Dixon, O.P. With a Photograph. Crown 8vo. 5s.

The History of the Italian Revolution. The Revolution of the Barricades. (1796—1849.) By the Chevalier O'Clery, M.P., K.S.G. 8vo. 7s. 6d.

Stories of Holy Lives. By M. F. S., author of "Stories of the Saints," "Catherine Hamilton," "Catherine grown Older," "Tom's Crucifix and other Tales." Fcp. 8vo. 3s.

The Rule of our most holy Father St. Benedict, Patriarch of Monks. From the old English edition of 1638. Edited by one of the Benedictine Fathers of St. Michael's, near Hereford. Fcap. 8vo. 4s. 6d.

First Communion Picture. Tastefully printed in gold and colours. Price 1s., or 10s. a dozen, *net.*

"Just what has long been wanted, a really good picture, with Tablet for First Communion and Confirmation."—*Tablet.*

Book of Family Crests and Mottos. Upwards of four thousand engravings. Eleventh edition. 2 vols., cr. 8vo., 24s.

New Testament, Catholic Vers., Notes and References, 19 large Illustrations. Large 4to., cloth gilt, 12s. 6d.

Road to Heaven. A game for family parties. By Miss M. A. Macdaniel. 3s. 6d.

Balmes' Letters to a Sceptic on Matters of Religion. 6s.

The Dove of the Tabernacle. By Fr. Kinane. 1s. 6d.

Munster Firesides ; or, the Barrys of Beigh. By E. Hall. 3s. 6d.

The Mirror of Faith : your Likeness in it. By Father Cuthbert. 3s.

The Christian Instructed in the Nature and Use of Indulgences. By Rev. F. A. Maurel. 3s.

New Model for Youth ; or, Life of Richard Aloysius Pennefather. 3s. 6d.

The Blessed Sacrament of the Miracle. 10 Photographs. Price 2s. 6d.

Recollections of Cardinal Wiseman, &c. By M. J. Arnold. 2s. 6d.

The Child. By Mgr. Dupanloup. Translated, 3s. 6d.

The Christian Instructed in the nature and use of Indulgences. By Rev. F. A. Maurel, S.J. 3s.

Protestantism and Liberty. By Professor Ozanam. Translated by W. C. Robinson. 8vo. 1s.

Düsseldorf Society for the Distribution of Good, Religious Pictures. R. Washbourne is now Sole Agent for Great Britain and Ireland. Yearly Subscription is 8s. 6d. *Catalogue post free.*

Düsseldorf Gallery. 8vo. half morocco, 31s. 6d. This volume contains 127 Engravings handsomely bound in half morocco, full gilt. Cash 25s.

Düsseldorf Gallery. 4to. half morocco, £5 5s. This superb work contains 331 Pictures. Handsomely bound in half morocco, full gilt.

"We confidently believe that no wealthy Catholic could possibly see this volume without ordering it for the adornment of his drawing-room table."—*Tablet.* "The most beautiful Catholic gift-book that was ever sent forth from the house of a Catholic publisher."—*Register.*

Catholicism, Liberalism, and Socialism. Translated from the Spanish of Donoso Cortes, by Rev. W. M'Donald. 6s.

The Pope of Rome and the Popes of the Oriental Orthodox Church. By the Rev. Cæsarius Tondini, Barnabite. Second edition. 3s. 6d.

Dramas, Comedies, Farces.

He would be a Lord. From the French of "Le Bourgeois Gentilhomme." Three Acts. (Boys.) 2s.

St. Louis in Chains. Drama in Five Acts, for boys. 2s.

"Well suited for acting in Catholic schools and colleges."—*Tablet.*

The Expiation. A Drama in Three Acts, for boys. 2s.

"Has its scenes laid in the days of the Crusades."—*Register.*

Shandy Maguire. A Farce for boys in Two Acts. 1s.

The Reverse of the Medal. A Drama in Four Acts, for young ladies. 6d.

Ernscliff Hall: or, Two Days Spent with a Great-Aunt. A Drama in Three Acts, for young ladies. 6d.

Filiola. A Drama in Four Acts, for young ladies. 6d.

The Convent Martyr, or Callista. By Dr. Newman. Dramatized by Dr. Husenbeth. 1s.

Garden of the Soul. (WASHBOURNE'S EDITION.) *With Imprimatur of the Archbishop of Westminster.* This edition has over all others the following advantages :—1. Complete order in its arrangements. 2. Introduction of Devotions to Saint Joseph, Patron of the Church. 3. Introduction into the English Devotions for Mass to a very great extent of the Prayers from the Missal. 4. The Full Form of Administration of all the Sacraments publicly administered in Church. 5. The insertion of Indulgences above Indulgenced Prayers. 6. Its large size of type. Embossed, 1s. ; with rims, 1s. 6d. ; with Epistles and Gospels, 1s. 6d. ; with rims, 2s. French morocco, 2s. ; with rims, 2s. 6d. ; with E. and G., 2s. 6d. ; with rims, 3s. French morocco extra gilt, 2s. 6d. ; with rims, 3s. ; with E. and G., 3s. ; with rims, 3s. 6d. Calf or morocco, 4s. ; with rims, 5s. 6d. ; with E. and G., 4s. 6d. ; with rims, 6s. Calf or morocco extra, 5s. ; with rims, 6s. 6d. ; with E. and G., 5s. 6d.; with rims, 7s. Velvet, with rims, 8s., 10s. 6d., and 13s.; with E. and G., 8s. 6d., 11s., and 13s. 6d. Russia, antique, with clasp, 10s. 6d., 12s. 6d.; with E. and G., 11s., 13s. Ivory, 12s. 6d., 16s., 20s., 22s. 6d., and 30s. ; with E. and G., 13s., 16s. 6d., 20s. 6d., 23s. and 30s. 6d. Morocco, with two patent clasps, 12s. Antique bindings, with corners and clasps : morocco, 18s., with E. and G., 18s. 6d. ; russia, 20s., with E. and G., 20s. 6d.

"This is one of the best editions we have seen of one of the best of all our Prayer-books. It is well printed in clear large type, on good paper."—*Catholic Opinion.* "A very complete arrangement of this, which is emphatically the Prayer-book of every Catholic household. It is as cheap as it is good, and we heartily recommend it."—*Universe.* "Two striking features are the admirable order displayed throughout the book, and the insertion of the Indulgences, in small type, above Indulgenced Prayers."—*Weekly Register.*

Some Documents concerning the Association of Prayers, in Honour of Mary Immaculate, for the Return of the Greek-Russian Church to Catholic Unity. By the Rev. C. Tondini. 3d.

The Epistles and Gospels in cloth, 6d., roan, 1s. 6d.

The Little Garden. Cloth, 6d., with rims, 1s.; embossed, 9d., with rims, 1s. 3d.; roan, 1s., with rims, 1s. 6d.; french morocco, 1s. 6d., with rims, 2s.; french morocco, extra gilt, 2s., with rims, 2s. 6d.; imitation ivory, with rims, 3s.; calf or morocco, 3s., with rims, 4s.; calf or morocco, extra gilt, 4s., with rims, 5s.; velvet, with rims, 5s., 8s. 6d., 1cs. 6d.; russia, with clasp, 8s.; ivory, with rims, 10s. 6d., 13s., 15s., 17s. 6d.; antique binding, with clasps: morocco, 16s.; russia, 17s. 6d; morocco, with a patent clasp, 10s. 6d.; with oxydized silver or gilt mountings, in morocco case, 25s.

A Few Words from Lady Mildred's Housekeeper. 2d.

"If any of our lady readers wish to give to their servants some hints as to the necessity of laying up some part of their wages instead of spending their money in dressing above their station, let them get 'A Few Words from Lady Mildred's Housekeeper,' and present it for the use of the servants' hall or downstairs departments. The good advice of an experienced upper servant on such subjects ought not to fall on unwilling ears."—*Register.*

Religious Reading.

"Vitis Mystica;" or, the True Vine. A Treatise on the Passion of Our Lord. Translated, with Preface, by the Rev. W. R. Bernard Brownlow. With Frontispiece. 18mo. 4s., red edges, 4s. 6d.

"It is a pity that such a beautiful treatise should for so many centuries have remained untranslated into our tongue."—*Tablet.* "It will be found very acceptable spiritual food."—*Church Herald.* "We heartily recommend it for its unction and deep sense of the beauties of nature."—*The Month.* "Full of deep spiritual lore." —*Register.* "Every chapter of this little volume affords abundant matter for meditation."—*Universe.* "An excellent translation of a beautiful treatise."—*Dublin Review.*

Ebba; or, the Supernatural Power of the Blessed Sacrament. In French. 12mo. 1s. 6d.; cloth gilt, 2s. 6d.

"There are thoughts in the work which we value highly."—*Dublin Review.* "Will do good to all who read it."—*Universe.*

Apostleship of Prayer. By Rev. H. Ramière. 6s.

The Happiness of Heaven. By a Father of the Society of Jesus. Fcap. 8vo. 4s.

God our Father. By the same Author. Fcap. 8vo. 4s,

Holy Places ; their Sanctity and Authenticity. By the Rev. Fr. Philpin. With Maps. Crown 8vo. 6s.

"It displays an amount of patient research not often to be met with." —*Universe.* " Dean Stanley and other sinners in controversy are treated with great gentleness. They are indeed thoroughly exposed and refuted."—*Register.* " Fr. Philpin has a particularly nervous and fresh style of handling his subject, with an occasional picturesqueness of epithet or simile."—*Tablet.* " We do not question his learning and industry, and yet we cannot think them to have been uselessly expended on this work."—*Spectator.* ". . . Fr. Philpin there weighs the comparative value of extraordinary, ordinary, and natural evidence, and gives an admirable summary of the witness of the early centuries regarding the holy places of Jerusalem, with archæological and architectural proofs. It is a complete treatise of the subject."—*The Month.* "The author treats his subject with a thorough system, and a competent knowledge. It is a book of singular attractiveness and considerable merit."—*Church Herald.* " Fr. Philpin's very interesting book appears most opportunely, and at a time when pilgrimages have been revived."—*Dublin Review.*

The Consoler ; or, Pious Readings addressed to the Sick and to all who are afflicted. By the Rev. P. J. Lambilotte, S.J. Translated by the Right Rev. Abbot Burder, O. Cist. Fcp. 8vo. 4s. 6d., red edges, 5s.

"As 'The Consoler' has the merit of being written in plain and simple language, and while deeply spiritual contains no higher flights into the regions of mysticism where poor and ignorant readers would be unable to follow, it is very specially adapted for one of the subjects which its writer had in view, namely, its introduction into hospitals."—*Tablet.* "A work replete with wise comfort for every affliction."—*Universe.* "A spiritual treatise of great beauty and value."—*Church Herald.*

The Selva, or a Collection of Matter for Sermons. By St. Liguori. 5s.

The Souls in Purgatory. Translated from the French, by the Right Rev. Abbot Burder, O. Cist. 32mo. 3d.

" It will be found most useful as an aid to the cultivation of this especial devotion."—*Register.*

Flowers of Christian Wisdom. By Lucien Henry. With a Preface by the Right Hon. Lady Herbert of Lea. 18mo. 2s. ; red edges, 2s. 6d.

"A compilation of some of the most beautiful thoughts and passages in the works of the Fathers, the great schoolmen, and eminent modern Churchmen, and will probably secure a good circulation."—*Church Times.* "It is a compilation of gems of thought, carefully selected."—*Tablet.* "It is a small but exquisite bouquet, like that which S. Francis of Sales has prepared for *Philothea.*"—*Universe.*

A General History of the Catholic Church : from the
commencement of the Christian Era until the
present time. By the Abbé Darras. 4 vols.,
large 8vo. cloth, 48s.

The Book of Perpetual Adoration ; or, the Love of
Jesus in the most Holy Sacrament of the Altar.
By Mgr. Boudon. Edited by the Rev. J. Red-
man, D.D. Fcap. 8vo. 3s. ; red edges, 3s. 6d.

" This new translation is one of Boudon's most beautiful works,
. . . and merits that welcome in no ordinary degree."—*Tablet.* "The
devotions at the end will be very acceptable aids in visiting the
Blessed Sacrament, and there are two excellent methods for assisting
at Mass."—*The Month.* "It has been pronounced by a learned
and pious French priest to be 'the most beautiful of all books
written in honour of the Blessed Sacrament." -*The Nation.*

Spiritual Works of Louis of Blois, Abbot of Liesse.
Edited by the Rev. John Edward Bowden, of the
Oratory. Fcap. 8vo. 3s. 6d ; red edges, 4s.

" No more important or welcome addition could have been made
to our English ascetical literature than this little book. It is a model
of good translation."—*Dublin Review.* " This handy little volume
will certainly become a favourite."—*Tablet.* " Elegant and flowing."—*Register.* " Most useful of meditations."—*Catholic Opinion.*

Heaven Opened by the Practice of Frequent Confession and Communion. By the Abbé Favre.
Translated from the French, carefully revised by
a Father of the Society of Jesus. Third Edition.
Fcap. 8vo. 3s. 6d. ; red edges, 4s. Cheap edit. 2s.

"This beautiful little book of devotion. We may recommend it to
the clergy as well as to the laity."—*Tablet.* "It is filled with quota-
tions from the Holy Scriptures, the Fathers, and the Councils of the
Church, and thus will be found of material assistance to the clergy,
as a storehouse of doctrinal and ascetical authorities on the two great
sacraments of Holy Eucharist and Penance."—*Register.*

The Spiritual Life.—Conferences delivered to the *En-
fants de Marie* by Père Ravignan. Cr. 8vo. 5s.

" Père Ravignan's words are as applicable to the ladies of London
as to those of Paris. They could not have a better book for their
spiritual reading."—*Tablet.* " A depth of eloquence and power of
exhortation which few living preachers can rival."—*Church Review.*

The Supernatural Life. Translated from the French
of Mgr. Mermillod, with a Preface by Lady Herbert. Cr. 8vo. 5s.

Holy Communion : it is my Life. By H. Lebon. 4s.

The Eucharist and the Christian Life. By Mgr. de la
Bouillerie. Translated. Fcap. 8vo. 3s. 6d.

The Jesuits, and other Essays. By Willis Nevin.
Fcap. 8vo. 2s. 6d.

On Contemporary Prophecies. . By Mgr. Dupanloup.
Translated by Rev. Dr. Redmond. 8vo. 1s.

Good Thoughts for Priests and People; or Short
Meditations for Every Day in the Year. By Rev.
T. Noethen. 12mo. 8s.

One Hundred Pious Reflections. Extracted from
Alban Butler's "Lives of the Saints." 18mo,
cloth, red edges, 2s. ; cheap edition, 1s.

"A happy idea. The author of 'The Lives of the Saints' had a
way of breathing into his language the unction and force which
carries the truth of the Gospel into the heart."—*Letter to the Editor
from* THE RIGHT REV. DR. ULLATHORNE, BISHOP OF BIRMING-
HAM. "Well selected, sufficiently short, and printed in good bold
type."—*Tablet.* "Good, sound, practical."—*Church Herald.*

The Imitation of Christ. With reflections. 32mo.
1s. . Persian calf, 3s. 6d. Also an Edition with
ornamental borders. Fcap. cloth, red edges, 3s. 6d.

Following of Christ. Small pocket edition, 1s. cloth ;
1s. 6d. embossed ; roan, 2s. ; French morocco, 2s.
6d. ; calf or morocco, 4s. 6d. ; calf or morocco
extra gilt, 5s. 6d. ; ivory, 15s. and 16s. ; morocco,
antique, 17s. 6d. ; russia antique, 20s.

Conversion of the Teutonic Race. By Mrs. Hope,
author of " Early Martyrs." Edited by the Rev.
Father Dalgairns. 2 vols. crown 8vo. 12s.

I. Conversion of the Franks and the English, 6s.

II. S. Boniface and the Conversion of Germany, 6s.

"It is good in itself, possessing considerable literary merit ; it
forms one of the few Catholic books brought out in this country
which are not translations or adaptations."—*Dublin Review.* "It
is a great thing to find a writer of a book of this class so clearly
grasping, and so boldly setting forth, truths which, familiar as they
are to scholars, are still utterly unknown by most of the writers of
our smaller literature."—*Saturday Review.* "A very valuable
work . . . . Mrs. Hope has compiled an original history, which
gives constant evidence of great erudition, and sound historical judgment."—*Month.* "This is a most taking book : it is solid history
and romance in one."—*Catholic Opinion.* "It is carefully, and
in many parts beautifully written."—*Universe.*

Contemplations on the Most Holy Sacrament of the Altar, drawn from the Sacred Scriptures. 18mo. cloth, 2s. ; cloth extra, red edges, 2s. 6d.

" This is a welcome addition to our books of Scriptural devotion. It contains thirty-four excellent subjects of reflection before the Blessed Sacrament, or for making a spiritual visit to the Blessed Sacrament at home ; for the use of the sick."—*Dublin Review.*

Cistercian Order: its Mission and Spirit. Comprising the Life of S. Robert of Newminster, and the Life of S. Robert of Knaresborough. By the author of " Cistercian Legends." Crown 8vo. 3s. 6d.

Cistercian Legends of the 13th Century. Translated from the Latin by the Rev. Henry Collins. 3s.

" Interesting records of Cistercian sanctity and cloistral experience."—*Dublin Review.* " A casquet of jewels."—*Weekly Register.* " Most beautiful legends, full of deep spiritual reading."—*Tablet.* " Well translated, and beautifully got up."—*Month.* " A compilation of anecdotes, full of heavenly wisdom."—*Catholic Opinion.*

The Directorium Asceticum; or Guide to the Spiritual Life. By Scaramelli. Translated and edited at St. Beuno's College. 4 vols. crown 8vo. 24s.

Maxims of the Kingdom of Heaven. New and enlarged Edition. 5s. ; red edges, 5s. 6d. ; calf or morocco, 10s. 6d.

"The selections on every subject are numerous, and the order and arrangement of the chapters will greatly facilitate meditation and reference."—*Freeman's Journal.* " We are glad to see that this admirable devotional work, of which we have before spoken in warm praise, has reached a second issue."—*Weekly Register.* " It has an Introduction by J. H. N., and bears the Imprimatur of the Archbishop of Westminster. We need say no more in its praise."—*Tablet.* " A most beautiful little book."—*Catholic Opinion.* "This priceless volume."—*Universe.* " Most suitable for meditation and reference."—*Dublin Review.*

The Oxford Undergraduate of Twenty Years Ago: his Religion, his Studies, his Antics. By a Bachelor of Arts. [Author of "The Comedy of Convocation."] 2s. 6d. ; cloth, 3s. 6d.

" The writing is full of brilliancy and point."—*Tablet.* " Time has not dimmed the author's recollection, and has no doubt served to sharpen his sense of undergraduate humour and his reading of undergraduate character."—*Examiner.* " It will deservedly attract attention, not only by the briskness and liveliness of its style, but also by the accuracy of the picture which it probably gives of an individual experience."—*The Month.*

The Infallibility of the Pope. A Lecture. By the Author of "The Oxford Undergraduate." 8vo. 1s.

"A splendid lecture, by one who thoroughly understands his subject, and in addition is possessed of a rare power of language in which to put before others what he himself knows so well."—*Universe.* "There are few writers so well able to make things plain and intelligible as the author of 'The Comedy of Convocation.'. . . The lecture is a model of argument and style."—*Register.*

Comedy of Convocation in the English Church. Edited by Archdeacon Chasuble, D.D. 2s, 6d.

Reply to the Bishop of Ripon's Attack on the Catholic Church. By the same Author. 6d.

The Harmony of Anglicanism. Report of a Conference on Church Defence. [By T. W. M. Marshall, Esq.] 8vo. 2s. 6d.

" 'Church Defence' is characterized by the same caustic irony, the same good-natured satire, the same logical acuteness which distinguished its predecessor, the 'Comedy of Convocation.' . . . A more scathing bit of irony we have seldom met with."—*Tablet.* "Clever, humorous, witty, learned, written by a keen but sarcastic observer of the Establishment, it is calculated to make defenders wince as much as it is to make all others smile."—*Nonconformist.*

Thy Gods, O Israel. A Picture in Verse of the Religious Anomalies of our Time. Cr. 8vo. 2s.

The Roman Question. By Dr. Husenbeth. 6d.

Consoling Thoughts of St. Francis de Sales. By Père Huguet. 18mo., 2s.

Holy Readings. Short Selections from well-known Authors. By J. R. Digby Beste, Esq. 32mo. cloth, 2s.; cloth, red edges, 2s. 6d.; roan, 3s.; morocco, 6s. [See "Catholic Hours," p. 23.]

St. Peter; his Name and his Office as set forth in Holy Scripture. By T. W. Allies. *Second Edition.* Revised. Crown 8vo. 5s.

" A standard work. There is no single book in English, on the Catholic side, which contains the Scriptural argument about St. Peter and the Papacy so clearly or conclusively put."—*Month.* "An admirable volume."—*The Universe.* "This valuable work." —*Weekly Register.* "A second edition, with a new and very touching preface."—*Dublin Review.*

Sancti Alphonsi Doctoris Officium Parvum—Novena and Little Office in honour of St. Alphonsus. Fcap. 8vo. 1s.; cloth, 2s.; cloth extra, 3s.

The Life of Pleasure.   Translated from the French
of Mgr. Dechamps.   Fcap. 8vo. 1s. 6d.

Sure Way to Heaven : a little Manual for Confession
and Holy Communion. 32mo. cloth, 6d. Persian
2s. 6d.   Calf or morocco, 3s. 6d.

Compendium of the History of the Catholic Church,
By Rev. T. Noethen.   12mo. 8s.

History of the Catholic Church, for schools.   By
Rev. T. Noethen.   12mo. 5s. 6d.

Benedictine Almanack.   Price 2d.

Catholic Calendar and Church Guide. ~ Price 6d. ;
interleaved, 8d.

Catholic Directory for Scotland.   1s.

Dr. Pusey's Eirenicon considered in Relation to
Catholic Unity.   By H. N. Oxenham.   2s. 6d.

Familiar Instructions on Christian Truths. By a Priest.
No. 1, Detraction. 4d. No. 2, The Dignity of the
Priesthood.   3d.   No. 3, Necessity of hearing
the Word of God.   Why it produces no fruit, and
how to be heard. ⸢On the necessity of Faith. 3d.

Sweetness of Holy Living ; or Honey culled from the
Flower Garden of S. Francis of Sales.   1s.
French morocco, 3s.

" In it will be found some excellent aids to devotion and meditation."—*Weekly Register.*

The Tradition of the Syriac Church of Antioch, concerning the Primacy and Prerogatives of S. Peter,
and of his successors, the Roman Pontiffs.   By
the Most Rev. C. B. Benni. 8vo. 21s., for 7s. 6d.

Père Lacordaire's Conferences. God, 6s. Jesus Christ,
6s.   God and Man, 6s.   Life, 6s.

Commonitory of S. Vincent of Lerins.   12mo. 1s. 3d.

Men and Women of the English Reformation, from
the days of Wolsey to the death of Cranmer.   By
S. H. Burke, M.A.   Vol. i. is out of print. Vol.
ii., 6s. 6d.

The chief topics of importance in the second volume are : Archbishop Cranmer's opinions upon Confession ; The Religious Houses
of Olden England ; Burnet as a Historian ; What were Lord Crom-
well's Religious Sentiments? Effects of the Confiscation on the

People ; The Church and the Holy Scriptures ; Death-bed Horrors of Henry VIII. ; Scenes upon the Scaffold—Lady Jane Grey's heroic Death ; The Rack and the Stake ; The Archbishop condemned to be Burnt Alive—Awful Scene ; A General View of Cranmer's Life.

" It contains a great amount of curious and useful information."—*Dublin Review.* " Interesting and valuable."—*Tablet.* " The only dispassionate record of a much contested epoch we have ever read."—*Cosmopolitan.* "So forcibly, but truthfully written, that it should be in the hands of every seeker after truth."—*Catholic Opinion.*—"On all hands admitted to be one of the most valuable historical works ever published."—*Nation.* " Full of interest."—*Church Review.* " Replete with information."—*Church Times.*

A Devout Paraphrase on the Seven Penitential Psalms ; or, a Practical Guide to Repentance. By the Rev. Fr. Blyth. To which is added :—Necessity of Purifying the Soul, by St. Francis of Sales. 18mo., 1s. 6d. ; red edges, 2s. ; cheap edition, 1s.
" A new edition of a book well known to our grandfathers. The work is full of devotion and of the spirit of prayer."—*Universe.* " A very excellent work, and ought to be in the hands of every Catholic." —*Waterford News.*

A New Miracle at Rome ; through the Intercession of Blessed John Berchmans. 2d.

Cure of Blindness ; through the Intercession of Our Lady and St. Ignatius. 2d.

BY THE POOR CLARES OF KENMARE.

Woman's Work in Modern Society. 7s. 6d.

A Nun's Advice to her Girls. 2s. 6d.

Daily Steps to Heaven. Fcap. 8vo. 4s. 6d.

Book of the Blessed Ones. 4s. 6d.

Jesus and Jerusalem ; or, the Way Home. 4s. 6d.

A Homely Discourse ; Mary Magdalen. Cr. 8vo. 6d.

Extemporaneous Speaking. By Rev. T. J. Potter. 5s.

Pastor and People. By Rev. T. J. Potter. 6s.

Eight Short Sermon Essays. By Dr. Redmond. 1s.

One Hundred Short Sermons. By Rev. H. T. Thomas. 8vo. 12s.

Catholic Sermons. By Father Burke, and others. 2s.

The Light of the Holy Spirit in the World. Five Sermons by the Rt. Rev. Bishop Hedley, O.S.B. 1s. ; cloth, 1s. 6d.

R. Washbourne, 18 *Paternoster Row, London.*

The Church of England and its Defenders. By the
Rev. W. R. Bernard Brownlow. 8vo. 1s. 6d.

Lectures on the Life, Writings, and Times of Edmund
Burke. By Professor Robertson. 3s. 6d.

Professor Robertson's Lectures on Modern History
and Biography. Crown 8vo. cloth, 6s.

The Knight of the Faith. By the Rev. Dr. Laing.

1. A Favourite Fallacy about Private Judgment. 1d.
2. Catholic not Roman Catholic. 4d.
3. Rationale of the Mass. 1s.
4. Challenge to the Churches of England, Scotland,
and all Protestant Denominations. 1d.
5. Absurd Protestant Opinions concerning *Intention*,
and Spelling Book of Christian Philosophy. 4d.
6. Whence the Monarch's right to rule. 2s. 6d.
7. Protestantism against the Natural Moral Law. 1d.
8. What is Christianity? 6d.

Abridged Explanation of the Medal or Cross of S.
Benedict. 1d.

Diary of a Confessor of the Faith. 12mo. 1s.

Sursum, 1s. Homeward, 2s. Both by Rev. Fr. Rawes.

Sermon at the Month's Mind of the Most Rev. Dr.
Spalding, Archbishop of Baltimore. 1s.

Exposition of the Epistles of St. Paul. By the Right
Rev. Dr. MacEvilly. 2 vols. 18s.

Commentary on the Psalms. By Bellarmin. 4to. 6s.

Monastic Legends. By E. G. K. Browne. 8vo. 6d.

BY DR. MANNING, ARCHBISHOP OF WESTMINSTER.

The Convocation in Crown and Council. 6d. net.

Confidence in God. Reprinting.

Temporal Sovereignty of the Popes. 1s. ; cloth, 1s. 6d.

The Church, the Spirit, and the Word. 6d.

BY THE PASSIONIST FATHERS.

The School of Jesus Crucified. Reprinting.

The Manual of the Cross and Passion. 32mo. 2s. 6d.

The Manual of the Seven Dolours. 32mo. 1s. 6d.

The Christian Armed. 32mo. 1s. 6d. ; mor. 3s. 6d.

Guide to Sacred Eloquence. 2s.

Religious Instruction.

The Catechism, Illustrated with Passages from the Holy Scriptures. Arranged by the Rev. J. B. Bagshawe, with Imprimatur. Crown 8vo. 2s. 6d.

"I believe the Catechism to be one of the best possible books of controversy, to those, at least, who are inquiring with a real desire to find the truth."—*Extract from the Preface.*

"An excellent idea. The very thing of all others that is needed by many under instruction."—*Tablet.* "It is a book which will do incalculable good. Our priests will hail with pleasure so valuable a help to their weekly instructions in the Catechism, while in schools its value will be equally recognized."—*Weekly Register.* "A work of great merit."—*Church Herald.* "We can hardly wish for anything better, either in intention or in performance."—*The Month.* "Very valuable."—*Dublin Review.*

The Threshold of the Catholic Church. A course of Plain Instructions for those entering her Communion. By Rev. J. B. Bagshawe. Cr. 8vo. 4s.

"A scholarly, well-written book, full of information."—*Church Herald.* "An admirable book, which will be of infinite service to thousands."—*Universe.* "Plain, practical, and unpretentious, it exhausts so entirely the various subjects of instruction necessary for our converts, that few missionary priests will care to dispense with its assistance."—*Register.* "It has very special merits of its own. . It is the work, not only of a thoughtful writer and good theologian, but of a wise and experienced priest."—*Dublin Review.* "Its characteristic is the singular simplicity and clearness with which everything is explained. . . It will save priests hours and days of time."—*Tablet.* "There is much in it with which we thoroughly agree."—*Church Times.* "There was a great want of a manual of instruction for convents, and the want has now been supplied, and in the most satisfactory manner."—*The Month.*

The Catechism of Christian Doctrine. Approved for the use of the Faithful in all the Dioceses of England and Wales. Price 1d. ; cloth, 2d.

A First Sequel to the Catechism. By the Rev. J. Nary. 32mo. 1d.

"It will recommend itself to teachers in Catholic schools as one peculiarly adapted to the use of such children as have mastered the Catechism, and yet have nothing else to fall back upon for higher religious instruction."—*Weekly Register.*

Catechism made Easy. A Familiar Explanation of "The Catechism of Christian Doctrine." By Rev. H. Gibson. Vol. I., 4s. Vol. II., 4s.

A General Catechism of the Christian Doctrine. By the Right Rev. Dr. Poirier. 18mo. 9d.

A Dogmatic Catechism. By Frassinetti. Translated from the original Italian by the Oblate Fathers of St. Charles. Fcap. 8vo. 3s.

"We give a few extracts from Frassinetti's work, as samples of its excellent execution."—*Dublin Review.* "Needs no commendation."—*Month.* "It will be found useful, not only to catechists, but also for the instruction of converts from the middle class of society."—*Tablet.*

Mgr. de Ségur's Books for Little Children. Translated. Confession ; Holy Communion ; Child Jesus ; Piety ; Prayer ; Temptation. 3d. each.

The Seven Sacraments explained and defended. Edited by a Catholic Clergyman. 1s. 6d.

Burton's Ecclesiastical History. 1s.

Protestant Principles Examined by the Written Word. Originally entitled, "The Protestant's Trial by the Written Word." *New edition.* 18mo. 1s.

"An excellent book."—*Church News.* "A good specimen of the concise controversial writing of English Catholics in the early part of the seventeenth century."—*Catholic Opinion.* "A little book which might be consulted profitably by any Catholic."—*Church Times.* "A clever little manual."—*Westminster Gazette.* "A useful little volume."—*The Month.* "An excellent little book."—*Weekly Register.* "A well-written and well-argued treatise."—*Tablet.*

Descriptive Guide to the Mass. By the Rev. Dr. Laing. 1s. ; extra cloth, 1s. 6d.

"An attempt to exhibit the structure of the Mass. The logical relation of parts is ingeniously effected by an elaborate employment of differences of type, so that the classification, down to the minutest subdivision, may at once be caught by the eye."—*Tablet.*

The Necessity of Enquiry as to Religion. By Henry John Pye, M.A. 4d. ; cloth, 6d.

"Mr. Pye is particularly plain and straightforward."—*Tablet.* "It is calculated to do much good. We recommend it to the clergy, and think it a most useful work to place in the hands of all who are under instruction."—*Westminster Gazette.* "A thoroughly searching little pamphlet."—*Universe.* "A clever little pamphlet. Each point is treated briefly and clearly."—*Catholic Opinion.*

The Grounds of Catholic Doctrine. By Dr. Challoner. Large type edition. 18mo. cloth, 4d.

Dr. Butler's *First* Catechism, ½d. *Second* Catechism, 1d. ; *Third* Catechism, 1½d.

Dr. Doyle's Catechism, 1½d.

Lessons on the Christian Doctrine, 1½d.

Fleury's Historical Catechism. Large edition, 1½d.

Bible History for the use of Catholic Schools and Families. By the Rev. R. Gilmour. 2s.

Origin and Progress of Religious Orders, and Happiness of a Religious State. By Fr. Jerome Platus, S.J. ; translated by Patrick Mannock. 2s. 6d.
" The whole work is evidently calculated to impress any reader with the great advantages attached to a religious life."—*Register.*

Children of Mary in the World. 32mo. 1d.

The Christian Teacher. By Ven. de la Salle. 1s. 8d.

Christian Politeness. By the Ven. de la Salle. 1s.

Duties of a Christian. By the Ven. de la Salle. 2s.

The Young Catholic's Guide to Confession and Holy Communion. By Dr. Kenny. *Third edition.* Paper, 4d. ; cloth, 6d. ; cloth, red edges, 9d.

Instructions for the Sacrament of Confirmation. 6d.

Auricular Confession. By Rev. Dr. Melia. 1s. 6d.

Explanation of the Epistles and Gospels, &c. By the Rev. Fr. Goffine. Illustrated. 7s.

Rules for a Christian Life. By S. Charles Borromeo. 2d.

Anglican Orders. By the Very Rev. Canon Williams. *Second Edition.* Crown 8vo. 3s. 6d.

Little by Little ; or, the Penny Bank. By the Rev. Fr. Richardson. 1d.

The Crusade, or Catholic Association for the Suppression of Drunkenness. By the same. 1d.

Catholic Sick and Benefit Club ; or, the Guild of our Lady, and St. Joseph's Burial Society. By the Rev. Fr. Richardson. 32mo. 4d. Burial Society by itself, 2d.

Home Rule. By Rev. Fr. Richardson. 1d.

The Monks of Iona and the Duke of Argyll. By the Rev. J. Stewart M'Corry, D.D. 8vo. 3s. 6d.

Lives of Saints, &c.

Life of the Ven. Anna Maria Taigi. Translated from the French of Calixte, by A. V. Smith Sligo. 8vo. 5s.

Butler's Lives of the Saints. 2 vols., 8vo., cloth, 28s.; or in cloth gilt, 34s. ; or in 4 vols., 8vo., cloth, 32s. ; or in cloth gilt, 48s. ; or in leather gilt, 64s.

Life, Passion, Death, and Resurrection of Our Blessed
  Lord. Translated from Ribadeneira. 1s.
Oratorian Lives of the Saints. Second Series. Post 8vo.
  Vol. I.—S. Bernardine of Siena. 5s.
  Vol. II.—S. Philip Benizi. 5s.
  Vol. III.—S. Veronica Giuliani, and Blessed
    Battista Varani. 5s.
  Vol. IV.—S. John of God. 5s.

The works translated from will be in most cases the Lives
drawn up *for* or *from* the processes of canonization or beatification,
as being more full, more authentic, and more replete with anecdote,
thus enabling the reader to become better acquainted with the
Saint's disposition and spirit ; while the simple matter-of-fact style
of the narrative is, from its unobtrusive character, more adapted
for spiritual reading than the views and generalizations, and pro-
logetic extenuations of more recent biographers. The work is published with the permission and approval of superiors. Every volume
containing the Life of a person not yet canonized or beatified by the
Church will be prefaced by a protest in conformity with the decree
of Urban VIII., and in all Lives which introduce questions of
mystical theology great care will be taken to publish nothing which
has not had adequate sanction, or without the reader being informed
of the nature and amount of the sanction. Each volume is em-
bellished with a Portrait of the Saint.

Life of Sister Mary Cherubina Clare of S. Francis,
  Translated from the Italian, with Preface by Lady
  Herbert. Cr. 8vo. with Photograph, 3s. 6d.
Stories of the Saints. By M. F. S., author of " Tom's
  Crucifix, and other Tales," " Catherine Ham-
  ilton," &c. 2 vols., each 3s. 6d., gilt, 4s. 6d.
Life of B. Giovanni Colombini. By Feo Belcari.
  Translated from the editions of 1541 and 1832.
  with a Photograph. Cr. 8vo. 3s. 6d.
Sketch of the Life and Letters of the Countess Adel-
  stan. By E. A. M., author of " Rosalie, or the
  Memoirs of a French Child," " Life of Paul
  Seigneret, &c." 2s. 6d.
Life and Prophecies of S. Columbkille, 3s. 6d.

LIVES OF THE ENGLISH SAINTS.
Life of St. Augustine of Canterbury. 12mo. 3s. 6d.
Life of St. German. 12mo. cloth, 3s. 6d.
Life of Stephen Langton. 12mo. cloth, 2s. 6d.

Prince and Saviour. A Life of Christ for the Young.
By Rosa Mulholland. 6d. Enlarged edition
with extra matter. With 12 beautiful illustrations
in gold and colours. Fcap. 8vo. 2s. 6d.

S. Paul of the Cross. By the Passionist Fathers. 2s. 6d.

Nano Nagle. By Rev. W. Hutch, D.D. 7s. 6d.

Life of St. Boniface, and the Conversion of Germany.
By Mrs. Hope. Edited, with a Preface, by the
Rev. Father Dalgairns. Cr. 8vo. 6s.
"Every one knows the story of S. Boniface's martyrdom, but
every one has not heard it so stirringly set forth as in her 22nd
chapter by Mrs. Hope."—*Dublin Review.*

Louise Lateau: her Life, Stigmata, and Ecstasies. By
Dr. Lefebvre. Translated from the French by T. S.
Shepard. Fcap. 8vo. 2s.

Venerable Mary Christina of Savoy. 6d.

Memoirs of a Guardian Angel. Fcap. 8vo. 4s.

Life of St. Patrick. 12mo. 1s.

Life of St. Bridget, and of other Saints of Ireland. 1s.

Insula Sanctorum : the Island of Saints. 1s.; cloth, 2s.

Life of Paul Seigneret, Seminarist of Saint-Sulpice.
Fcap. 8vo., 1s. ; cloth extra, 1s. 6d. ; gilt, 2s.
"An affecting and well-told narrative. . . It will be a great favourite, especially with our pure-minded, high-spirited young people."
—*Universe.* "Paul Seigneret was remarkable for the simplicity and
the heroism of both his natural and his religious character."—*Tablet.*
"We commend it to parents with sons under their care, and especially do we recommend it to those who are charged with the education and training of our Catholic youth."—*Register.*

A Daughter of St. Dominic. By Grace Ramsay.
Fcap. 8vo. 1s. 6d. ; cloth extra, 2s.
"A beautiful little work. The narrative is highly interesting."—
Dublin Review. "It is full of courage and faith and Catholic
heroism."—*Universe.* "One who has lived and died in our own
day, who led the common life of every one else, but yet who learned
how to supernaturalize this life in so extraordinary a way that we
forget 'the doctor's daughter in a provincial town,' while reading
Grace Ramsay's beautiful picture of the wonders effected by her
ubiquitous charity, and still more by her fervent prayer."—*Tablet.*

The Glory of St. Vincent de Paul. By the Most Rev.
Dr. Manning, Archbishop of Westminster. 1s.

Life of S. Edmund of Canterbury. From the French
of the Rev. Father Massé, S. J. 1s. and 1s. 6d.

The Life of St. Francis of Assisi. Translated from
the Italian of St. Bonaventure by Miss Lockhart.
With a Preface by His Grace the Archbishop of
Westminster. Fcap. 8vo; 4s. gilt.
Life of Fr. de Ravignan. Crown 8vo. 9s.
The Pilgrimage to Paray le Monial, with a brief notice
of the Blessed Margaret Mary. 6d.
Patron Saints. By Eliza Allen Starr. Cr. 8vo. 10s.
His Eminence Cardinal Wiseman; with full account
of his Obsequies; Funeral Oration by Archbishop
Manning, &c. 1s.; cloth, red edges, 1s. 6d.
Count de Montalembert. By George White. 6d.
Life of Mgr. Weedall. By Dr. Husenbeth. 7s. 6d.,
for 1s.
Life of Pope Pius IX. 6d. Cheap edition, 1d.
Challoner's Memoirs of Missionary Priests. 8vo. 6s.

BY THE POOR CLARES OF KENMARE.

O'Connell: his Life and Times. 2 vols., 24s.
The Liberator: his Public Speeches and Letters. 2
vols., 24s.
Life of Father Matthew. 2s. 6d.
Life of St. Aloysius. 6d.; St. Joseph, 6d., cloth, 9d.;
St. Patrick, 6d., cloth, 9d.
Life of St. Patrick. Illustrated by Doyle. 4to. 20s.

Our Lady.

Regina Sæculorum, or, Mary venerated in all Ages.
Devotions to the Blessed Virgin from ancient
sources. Fcap. 8vo. 3s.
Readings for the Feasts of Our Lady, and especially
for the Month of May. By the Rev. A. P. Bethell.
18mo. 1s. 6d.; cheap edition, 1s.
The History of the Blessed Virgin. By the Abbé
Orsini. Translated from the French by the Very
Rev. F. C. Husenbeth, D.D. With eight Illus-
trations. Crown 8vo. 3s. 6d.
Manual of Devotions in Honour of Our Lady of Sor-
rows. Compiled by the Clergy at St. Patrick's
Soho. 18mo. 1s.; cloth, red edges, 1s. 6d.

Our Blessed Lady of Lourdes: a Faithful Narrative of
the Apparitions of the Blessed Virgin. By F. C.
Husenbeth, D.D. 18mo. 6d.; cloth, 1s.; with
Novena, 1s.; cloth, 1s. 6d. Novena, separately,
4d.; Litany, 1d., or 6s. per 100.

Devotion to Our Lady in North America. By the
Rev. Xavier Donald Macleod. 8vo. 7s. 6d.

"The work of an author than whom few more gifted writers have
ever appeared among us. It is not merely a religious work, but it has
all the charms of an entertaining book of travels. We can hardly
find words to express our high admiration of it."—*Weekly Register.*

Life of the Ever-Blessed Virgin. Proposed as a Model
to Christian Women. 1s.

The Blessed Virgin's Root traced in the Tribe of
Ephraim. By the Rev. Dr. Laing. 8vo. 10s. 6d.

Litany of the Seven Dolours. 1d. each, or 6s. per 100.

Month of Mary for all the Faithful. By Rev. P.
Comerford. 1s.

Month of Mary for Interior Souls. By M. A. Macdaniel. 18mo. 2s.

Month of Mary, principally for the use of religious
communities. 18mo. 1s. 6d.

A Devout Exercise in Honour of the Blessed Virgin
Mary. From the Psalter and Prayers of S.
Bonaventure. In Latin and English, with Indul-
gences applicable to the Holy Souls. 32mo. 1s.

The Definition of the Immaculate Conception. 6d.

The Little Office of the Immaculate Conception. In
Latin and English. By the Very Rev. Dr. Husenbeth. 32mo. 4d.; cloth, 6d.; roan, 1s.; calf or
morocco, 2s. 6d.

Life of Our Lady in Verse. Edited by C. E. Tame. 2s.

Our Lady's Lament, and the Lamentation of St.
Mary Magdalene. Edited by C. E. Tame. 2s.

The Virgin Mary. By Dr. Melia. 8vo. 11s. 3d. cash.

Archconfraternity of Our Lady of Angels. 1s. per 100.

Litany of Our Lady of Angels. 1s. per 100.

Concise Portrait of the Blessed Virgin. 1s. per 100.

Origin of the Blue Scapular. 1d.

Miraculous Prayer—August Queen of Angels. 1s. 100.

Prayer-Books.

Washbourne's Edition of the "Garden of the Soul," in medium-sized type (small type as a rule being avoided). For prices see page 5.

The Little Garden. 6d., and upwards. *See page* 6.

The Lily of St. Joseph; a little Manual of Prayers and Hymns for Mass. Price 2d.; cloth, 3d.; or with gilt lettering, 4d.; more strongly bound, 6d.; or with gilt edges, 8d.; roan, 1s.; French morocco, 1s. 6d.; calf, or morocco, 2s,; gilt, 2s. 6d.

"It supplies a want which has long been felt; a prayer-book for children, which is not a childish book, a handy book for boys and girls, and for men and women too, if they wish for a short, easy-to-read, and devotional prayer-book."—*Catholic Opinion.* "A very complete prayer-book. It will be found very useful for children and for travellers."—*Weekly Register.* "A neat little compilation, which will be specially useful to our Catholic School-children. The hymns it contains are some of Fr. Faber's best."—*Universe.*

Devotions for Public and Private Use at the Way of the Cross. By Sister M. F. Clare. Illustrated, 1s.; red edges, 1s. 6d.

Path to Paradise. 36 full page Illustrations. Cloth, 3d. With 50 Illustrations, cloth, 4d.

Manual of Catholic Devotion. 6d.; roan, 1s. 6d.; calf or morocco, 2s, 6d.

S. Patrick's Manual. By the Poor Clares. 4s. 6d.

S. Angela's Manual; a book of devout Prayers and Exercises for Female Youth. *Second edition.* 16mo., cloth, red edges, 2s.; Persian, 3s. 6d.; calf, 4s. 6d.

Crown of Jesus. Persian calf, 6s.; morocco, 7s. 6d. and 8s. 6d., with rims, 10s. 6d.; morocco, extra gilt, 10s. 6d., with rims, 12s. 6d.; ivory, with rims, 21s., 25s., 27s. 6d. and 30s.

Burial of the Dead (Adults and Infants) in Latin and English. Royal 32mo. cloth, 6d.; roan, 1s. 6d.

"Being in a portable form, will be found useful by those who are called upon to assist at that solemn rite."—*Tablet.*

In Suffragiis Sanctorum. Commem S. Josephi. Commem S. Georgii. Set of five for 4d.

Paradise of God; or Virtues of the Sacred Heart. 4s.

Devotions to the Sacred Heart. By the Rev. S.
Franco. 4s., paper covers, 2s.

Devotions to the Sacred Heart. By the Rev. J. Joy
Dean. Fcap. 8vo. 3s.

Devotions to Sacred Heart of Jesus. By the Rt. Rev.
Dr. Milner. *New Edition.* To which is added
Devotions to the Immaculate Heart of Mary.
3d.; cloth, 6d.; gilt, 1s.

Sacred Heart of Jesus offered to the Piety of the Young
engaged in Study. By Rev. A. Deham, S.J. 6d.

Pleadings of the Sacred Heart. By Rev. P. Comerford.
18mo. 1s.; gilt, 2s.; with the Handbook of the
Confraternity, 1s. 6d.; Handbook, separately, 3d.

Treasury of the Sacred Heart. With Epistles and
Gospels. 18mo. cloth, 3s. 6d.; roan, 4s. 6d.

Little Treasury of Sacred Heart. 32mo. 2s., roan 2s. 6d.
calf or morocco, 5s.

Manual of Devotion to the Sacred Heart, from the
Writings of Bl. Margaret Mary Alacoque. By
Denys Casassayas. · Translated. 3d.

Act of Consecration to the Sacred Heart. 1d.

Act of Reparation to the Sacred Heart. 1s. per 100.

The Little Prayer-Book for Ordinary Catholic Devotions. Cloth, 3d.

Missal (complete). Persian calf, 8s. 6d.; morocco,
10s. 6d., with rims, 13s. 6d.; morocco, extra gilt,
12s. 6d., with rims, 15s. 6d.; morocco, with turn-
over edges, 13s. 6d.; morocco antique, 15s.; russia
antique, 20s.; ivory, with rims, 31s. 6d.

Catholic Hours: a Manual of Prayer, including Mass
and Vespers. By J. R. Digby Beste, Esq. 32mo.
cloth, 2s; red edges, 2s. 6d.; roan, 3s.; morocco, 6s.

A Prayer to be said for three days before Holy Communion, and another for three days after. 1d.,
or 6s. 100.

Ursuline Manual. Persian calf, 7s. 6d.; morocco, 10s.

A New Year's Gift to our Heavenly Father. 4d.

Manual of Catholic Piety. Edition with green border. French mor., 2s. 6d. ; mor., 4s.

Occasional Prayers for Festivals. By Rev. T. Barge. 32mo. 4d. and 6d. ; gilt, 1s.

Illustrated Manual of Prayers. 32mo. 3d. ; cloth, 4d.

Key of Heaven. Very large type, 1s. Leather 2s. 6d. gilt, 3s.

Catholic Piety. 32mo. 6d. ; roan, 1s. ; with Epistles and Gospels, roan, 1s. ; French morocco, 1s. 6d., with rims and clasp, 2s.; imitation ivory, rims and clasp, 2s. 6d. ; velvet rims and clasps, 3s. 6d.

Key of Heaven. Same size and prices.

Catholic Piety, or Key of Heaven, with Epistles and Gospels. Large 32mo. roan 2s. ; French morocco, with rims, 3s. ; extra gilt, 3s. ; with rims, 3s. 6d.

Novena of Meditations in Honour of S. Joseph, according to the method of S. Ignatius; preceded by a new exercise for hearing Mass according to the intentions of the souls in Purgatory. 18mo. 1s. 6d.

Novena to St. Joseph. Translated by M. A. Macdaniel. To which is added a Pastoral of the late Right Rev. Dr. Grant. 32mo. 4d. ; cloth, 6d.

Devotions for Mass. Very large type, 2d.

Memorare Mass. By the Poor Clares of Kenmare, 2d.

Fourteen Stations of the Holy Way of the Cross. By St. Liguori. Large type edition, 1d.

Indulgences attached to Medals, Crosses, Statues, &c., by the Blessing of His Holiness and of those privileged to give his Blessing. 1s. 2d. per 100, post free.

A Union of our life with the Passion of our Lord by a daily offering. 1s. 2d. per 100, post free.

Prayer for one's Confessor. 1s. 2d. per 100, post free.

Prayer to S. Philip Neri. 1d. each, or 6d. a dozen.

Litany of Resignation. 1s. 2d. per 100, post free.

A Christmas Offering. 1s. a 100, or 7s. 6d. a 1000.

Intentions for Indulgences. 7d. per 100, post free.

Devotions to St. Joseph. 1s. 2d. per 100, post free.

Litany of S. Joseph, &c. 1s. 2d. per 100, post free.

Devotion to St. Joseph as Patron of the Church. 1d.

Catholic Psalmist: or, Manual of Sacred Music, with the Gregorian Chants for High Mass, Holy Week, &c. Compiled by C. B. Lyons, 4s.

The Complete Hymn Book, 136 Hymns. Price 1d.

Douai Bible. 2s. 6d.; Persian calf, 5s.; calf or morocco, 7s.; gilt, 8s. 6d.

Church Hymns. By J. R. Digby Beste, Esq. 6d.

Catholic Choir Manual: Vespers, Hymns and Litanies, &c. Compiled by C. B. Lyons. 1s.

Prayers for the Dying. 1s. 2d. per 100, post free.

Indulgenced Prayer before a Crucifix. 1d. ea., or 6s. 100.

Indulgenced Prayers for Souls in Purgatory. 1s. per 100.

Indulgenced Prayers for the Rosary for the Holy Souls. 1d. each, 6d. a dozen, 3s. per 100.

The Rosary for the Souls in Purgatory, *with Indulgenced Prayer.* 6d., 8d. and 9d. each. Medals separately, 1d. each, 9s. gross.

Rome, &c.

Two Years in the Pontifical Zouaves. By Joseph Powell, Z.P. With 4 Engravings. 8vo. 3s. 6d.

"It affords us much pleasure, and deserves the notice of the Catholic public."—*Tablet.* "Familiar names meet the eye on every page, and as few Catholic circles in either country have not had a friend or relative at one time or another serving in the Pontifical Zouaves, the history of the formation of the corps, of the gallant youths, their sufferings, and their troubles, will be valued as something more than a contribution to modern Roman history."—*Freeman's Journal.*

The Victories of Rome. By Rev. Fr. Beste. 1s.

Rome and her Captors. Letters collected and edited by Count Henri d'Ideville, and translated by F. R. Wegg-Prosser. Cr. 8vo. 4s.

Defence of the Roman Church against Fr. Gratry. By Dom Gueranger. 1s. 6d.

Personal Recollections of Rome. By W. J. Jacob, Esq., late of the Pontifical Zouaves. 8vo. 1s. 6d.

Supremacy of the Roman See. By C. E. Tame. 6d.

The Roman Question. By F. C. Husenbeth, D.D. 6d.

Henri V. (Comte de Chambord), September 29, 1873. By W. H. Walsh. With a Portrait. 8vo. 1s. 6d.

The Rule of the Pope-King. By Rev. Fr. Martin. 6d.

The Years of Peter. By an Ex-Papal Zouave. 1d.

The Catechism of the Council. By a D.C.L. 2d.

Civilization and the See of Rome. By Lord Robert Montagu, M.P. 6d.

Rome, semper eadem. By Denis Patrick Michael O'Mahony. 1s. 6d.

A Few Remarks on a pamphlet entitled the "Divine Decrees." 6d.

Tales, or Books for the Library.

Tom's Crucifix, and other Tales. By M. F. S. 3s.

"Eight simple stories for the use of teachers of Christian doctrine."—*Universe.* "This is a volume of short, plain, and simple stories, written with the view of illustrating the Catholic religion practically by putting Catholic practices in an interesting light before the mental eyes of children....The whole of the tales in the volume before us are exceedingly well written."—*Register.*

Simple Tales. Square 16mo. cloth antique, 2s. 6d.

"Contains five pretty stories of a true Catholic tone, interspersed with some short pieces of poetry. . . Are very affecting, and told in such a way as to engage the attention of any child."—*Register.* "This is a little book which we can recommend with great confidence. The tales are simple, beautiful, and pathetic."—*Catholic Opinion.* "It belongs to a class of books of which the want is generally much felt by Catholic parents."—*Dublin Review.* "Beautifully written. 'Little Terence' is a gem of a Tale."—*Tablet.*

Terry O'Flinn's Examination of Conscience. By the Very Rev. Dr. Tandy. Fcap. 8vo. 1s. 6d. ; extra gilt, 2s. ; cheap edition, 1s.

"The writer possesses considerable literary power."—*Register.*

The Adventures of a Protestant in Search of a Religion : being the Story of a late Student of Divinity at Bunyan Baptist College ; a Nonconformist Minister, who seceded to the Catholic Church. By Iota. 5s. ; cheap edition, 3s.

"Will well repay its perusal."—*Universe.* "This precious volume."—*Baptist.* "No one will deny 'Iota' the merit of entire originality."—*Civilian.* "A valuable addition to every Catholic library.' *Tablet.* "There is much cleverness in it."—*Nonconformist.* "Malicious and wicked."—*English Independent.*

The People's Martyr, a Legend of Canterbury. 4s.

Rupert Aubray. By the Rev. T. J. Potter. 3s.

Farleyes of Farleye. By the same author. 2s. 6d.

Sir Humphrey's Trial. By the same author. 2s. 6d.

A Wasted Life. By Rosa Baughan. 8vo. 3s. 6d.

The Village Lily. Fcap. 8vo. 1s.; gilt, 1s. 6d.

Fairy Tales for Little Children. By Madeleine Howley
    Meehan. Fcap. 1s.; cloth extra, 1s. 6d.; gilt, 2s.

"Full of imagination and dreams, and at the same time with excellent point and practical aim, within the reach of the intelligence of infants."—*Universe.* "Pleasing, simple stories, combining instruction with amusement."—*Register.*

Rosalie; or, the Memoirs of a French Child. Written by
    herself. Fcap. 8vo., 1s. and 1s. 6d.; extra gilt, 2s.

"It is prettily told, and in a natural manner. The account of Rosalie's illness and First Communion is very well related. We can recommend the book for the reading of children."—*Tablet.* "The tenth chapter is beautiful."—*Universe.*

The Story of Marie and other Tales. Fcap. 8vo., 2s.;
    cloth extra, 2s. 6d.; gilt, 3s.; or separately:—The
    Story of Marie, 2d.; Nelly Blane, and A Contrast,
    2d.; A Conversion and a Death-Bed, 2d.; Herbert
    Montagu, 2d.; Jane Murphy, The Dying Gipsy,
    and The Nameless Grave, 2d.; The Beggars, and
    True and False Riches, 2d.; Pat and his Friend, 2d.

"A very nice little collection of stories, thoroughly Catholic in their teaching."—*Tablet.* "A series of short pretty stories, told with much simplicity."—*Universe.* "A number of short pretty stories, replete with religious teaching, told in simple language."—*Weekly Register.*

The Last of the Catholic O'Malleys. A Tale. By
    M. Taunton. 18mo. cloth, 1s. 6d.; extra, 2s.

"A sad and stirring tale, simply written, and sure to secure for itself readers."—*Tablet.* "Deeply interesting. It is well adapted for parochial and school libraries."—*Weekly Register.* "A very pleasing tale."—*The Month.*

Eagle and Dove. From the French of Mademoiselle
    Zénaïde Fleuriot. By Emily Bowles. Cr. 8vo., 5s.

"We recommend our readers to peruse this well-written story."—*Register.* "One of the very best stories we have ever dipped into."—*Church Times.* "Admirable in tone and purpose."—*Church Herald.* "A real gain. It possesses merits far above the pretty fictions got up by English writers."—*Dublin Review.* "There is an air of truth and sobriety about this little volume, nor is there any attempt at sensation."—*Tablet.*

Cistercian Legends of the 13th Century. Translated
    from the Latin by the Rev. Henry Collins. 3s.

Cloister Legends: or, Convents and Monasteries in
    the Olden Time. *Second Edition.* Cr. 8vo. 4s.

Chats about the Rosary; or, Aunt Margaret's Little Neighbours. Fcap. 8vo. 3s.

"There is scarcely any devotion so calculated as the Rosary to keep up a taste for piety in little children, and we must be grateful for any help in applying its lessons to the daily life of those who already love it in their unconscious tribute to its value and beauty."—*Month.* "We do not know of a better book for reading aloud to children, it will teach them to understand and to love the Rosary."—*Tablet.* "A graceful little book, in fifteen chapters, on the Rosary, illustrative of each of the mysteries, and connecting each with the practice of some particular virtue."—*Catholic Opinion.*

Margarethe Verflassen. Translated from the German by Mrs. Smith Sligo. Fcap. 8vo. 3s.; gilt, 3s. 6d.

"A portrait of a very holy and noble soul, whose life was passed in constant practical acts of the love of God."—*Weekly Register.* "It is the picture of a true woman's life, well fitted up with the practice of ascetic devotion and loving unwearied activity about all the works of mercy."—*Tablet..*

Keighley Hall and other Tales. By Elizabeth King. 18mo. 6d.; cloth, 1s.; gilt, 1s. 6d.; or, separately, Keighley Hall, Clouds and Sunshine, The Maltese Cross, 3d. each.

Sir Ælfric and other Tales. By the Rev. G. Bampfield. 18mo. 6d.; cloth, 1s.; gilt, 1s. 6d.

Ned Rusheen. By the Poor Clares. Crown 8vo. 6s.

The Prussian Spy. A Novel. By V. Valmont. 4s.

Adolphus; or, the Good Son. 18mo. gilt, 6d.

Nicholas; or, the Reward of a Good Action. 6d.

The Lost Children of Mount St. Bernard. 18mo. gilt, 6d.

The Baker's Boy; or, the Results of Industry. 6d.

A Broken Chain. 18mo. gilt, 6d.

"All prettily got up, artistically illustrated, and pleasantly-written. Better books for gifts and rewards we do not know."—*Weekly Register.* "We can thoroughly recommend them."—*Tablet.*

The Truce of God: a Tale of the Eleventh Century. By G. H. Miles. 4s.

Tales and Sketches. By Charles Fleet. 8vo. cloth, 2s. and 2s. 6d.; cloth, gilt, 3s. 6d.

The Artist of Collingwood. By Baron Na Carriag. 3s. 6d.

The Convent Prize Book. By the author of "Geraldine." Fcap. 8vo. 2s. 6d.; gilt, 3s. 6d.

Catherine Hamilton. By the author of " Tom's Crucifix," &c. Fcap. 8vo. 2s. 6d. ; gilt, 3s.

Sir Thomas Maxwell and his Ward. By Miss Bridges.
Fcap. 8vo. 2s.

Forty Years of American Life. By T. L. Nichols,
M.D. 5s.

Catherine grown Older : a sequel to " Catherine
Hamilton." Fcap. 8vo. 2s. 6d. ; gilt 3s.

Canon Schmid's Tales, selected from his works. A
new translation, with 6 original Illustrations.
Fcap. 8vo. 3s. 6d.

The Journey of Sophia and Eulalie to the Palace of
True Happiness. Translated by the Rev. Father
Bradbury, Mount St. Bernard's. Fcap. 8vo.
3s. 6d. ; cheap edition, 2s. 6d.

The Fisherman's Daughter. By Conscience. 4s.

The Amulet. By Hendrick Conscience. 4s.

Count Hugo of Graenhove. By Conscience. 4s.

The Village Innkeeper. By Conscience. 4s.

Happiness of being Rich. By Conscience. 4s.

Margaret Roper. By A. M. Stewart. 6s., gilt, 7s.

Florence O'Neill. By A. M. Stewart. 5s. and 6s.

Limerick Veteran. By the same. 5s. and 6s.

The Three Elizabeths. By the same. 5s. and 6s.

Alone in the World. By the same. 3s. 6d. and 4s. 6d.

Festival Tales. By J. F. Waller. 5s.

Shakespeare's Plays and Tragedies. Abridged and
Revised for the use of Schools. 8vo. 7s. 6d.

Poems. By H. N. Oxenham. *Third Edition.* 3s. 6d.

Culpepper. An entirely New Edition of Brook's Family
Herbal. Cr. 8vo., 150 engravings, 3s. 6d. ; drawn
and coloured from living specimens. 5s. 6d.

The Catholic Alphabet of Scripture Subjects. Price,
on a sheet, plain, 1s. ; coloured, 2s. ; mounted
on linen, to fold in a case, 3s. 6d. ; varnished, on
linen, on rollers, 4s.

Bell's Modern Reader and Speaker. Cloth, 3s. 6d.

Cogery's Third French Course, with Vocabulary. 2s.

Educational and Miscellaneous.

Horace. Literally translated by Smart. 2s.

Virgil. Literally translated by Davidson. 2s. 6d.

History of Modern Europe. With a Preface by the Right Rev. Dr. Weathers. 12mo. cloth, 5s. ; gilt, 6s. ; roan, 5s. 6d.

"A work of special importance for the way in which it deals with the early part of the present Pontificate."—*Weekly Register.*

Biographical Readings. By A. M. Stewart. 4s. 6d.

General Questions in History, Chronology, Geography, the Arts, &c. By A. M. Stewart. 4s. 6d.

University Education, under the Guidance of the Church ; or, Monastic Studies. By a Monk of St. Augustine's, Ramsgate. 8vo. 2s. 6d.

Elements of Philosophy, comprising Logic, and General Principles of Metaphysics. By Rev. W. H. Hill, S.J. Second edition, 8vo. 6s.

History of England. By W. Mylius. 12mo. 3s. 6d.

Catechism of the History of England. Cloth, 1s.

History of Ireland. By T. Young. 18mo. cloth, 2s. 6d.

The Illustrated History of Ireland. By the Nun of Kenmare. Illustrated by Doyle. 8vo. 11s.

The Patriots' History of Ireland. By the Poor Clares of Kenmare. 18mo. cloth, 2s. ; cloth gilt, 2s. 6d.

A Chronological Sketch of the Kings of England and France. With Anecdotes for the use of Children. By H. Murray Lane. 2s. 6d. ; or separately, England, 1s. 6d., France, 1s. 6d.

"Admirably adapted for teaching young children the elements of English and French history."—*Tablet.* "A very useful little publication."—*Weekly Register.* "An admirably arranged little work for the use of children."—*Universe.*

Extracts from the Fathers and other Writers of the Church. 12mo. cloth, 4s. 6d.

Brickley's Standard Table Book, ½d.

Washbourne's Multiplication Table on a sheet, 3s. per 100. Specimen sent for 1d. stamp.

Music (*Net*).

BY HERR WILHELM SCHULTHES.

Veni Domine. Motett for Four Voices. 2s.; vocal arrangement, 6d.

Cor Jesu, Salus in Te Sperantium. 2s.; with harp accompaniment, 2s. 6d.; abridged edition, 3d.

Mass of the Holy Child Jesus, and Ave Maria for unison and congregational singing, with organ accompaniment. 3s.

The Vocal Part. 4d.; or in cloth, 6d.

The Ave Maria of this Mass can be had for Four Voices, with the Ingressus Angelus. 1s. 3d.

Recordare. Oratio Jeremiæ Prophetæ. 1s.

Ne projicias me a facie Tua. Motett for Four Voices. (T.B.) 1s. 3d.

Benediction Service, with 36 Litanies. 6s.

Oratory Hymns. 2 vols., 8s.

Regina Cœli. Motett for Four Voices. 3s.; vocal arrangement, 1s.

Twelve Latin Hymns, for Vespers, &c. 2s.

Litanies. By Rev. J. McCarthy. 1s. 3d.

Six Litany Chants. By F. Leslie. 6d.

Ave Maria. By T. Haydn Waud. 1s. 6d.

Fr. Faber's Hymns. Various, 9d. each.

Portfolio. With a patent metallic back. 3s.

A separate Catalogue of FOREIGN Books, Educational Books, Books for the Library or for Prizes, supplied; also a Catalogue of School and General Stationery, a Catalogue of Second-hand Books, and a Catalogue of Crucifixes and other Religious Articles.

INDEX TO AUTHORS.

CONTENTS.

R. WASHBOURNE, 18 PATERNOSTER ROW.